Caterina Bonan and Adam Ledgeway (Eds.)
***It*-Clefts**

Trends in Linguistics
Studies and Monographs

Editors
Chiara Gianollo
Daniël Van Olmen

Editorial Board
Walter Bisang
Tine Breban
Volker Gast
Hans Henrich Hock
Karen Lahousse
Natalia Levshina
Caterina Mauri
Heiko Narrog
Salvador Pons
Niina Ning Zhang
Amir Zeldes

Editor responsible for this volume
Chiara Gianollo

Volume 362

It-Clefts

Empirical and Theoretical Surveys and Advances

Edited by
Caterina Bonan and Adam Ledgeway

DE GRUYTER
MOUTON

ISBN 978-3-11-221381-0
e-ISBN (PDF) 978-3-11-073414-0
e-ISBN (EPUB) 978-3-11-073424-9
ISSN 1861-4302

Library of Congress Control Number: 2023943397

Bibliographic information published by the Deutsche Nationalbibliothek
The Deutsche Nationalbibliothek lists this publication in the Deutsche Nationalbibliografie; detailed bibliographic data are available on the internet at http://dnb.dnb.de.

© 2025 Walter de Gruyter GmbH, Berlin/Boston
This volume is text- and page-identical with the hardback published in 2024.
Typesetting: Integra Software Services Pvt. Ltd.
Printing and binding: CPI books GmbH, Leck

www.degruyter.com

Contents

Caterina Bonan and Adam Ledgeway
It-clefts: State-of-the-art, and some empirical challenges —— 1

Anna Cardinaletti
1   Cleft wh-questions as biclausal structures —— 11

Sabrina Bertollo
2   What is it that requires or constrains clefts? (Dis)Favouring factors for clefting in Germanic and Romance —— 35

Adriana Belletti and Giuliano Bocci
3   Subject versus object clefts: A fresh perspective on a robust asymmetry —— 81

Charlotte Bourgoin and Kristin Davidse
4   Making the case for distinguishing information structure from specification in English *it*-clefts —— 105

Karen Lahousse and Morgane Jourdain
5   The emergence and early development of *c'est* 'it is' clefts in French L1 —— 135

Giuseppe Samo and Paola Merlo
6   Distributed computational models of intervention effects: A study on cleft structures in French —— 157

Alina McLellan
7   *It*-cleft constructions in Réunion Creole —— 181

Mara Marsella and Laura Tramutoli
8   (*It*-)clefts in Palenquero Creole and the specificational copula —— 217

Wenli Tang
9   A cartographic approach to Chinese V *de* O clefts —— 235

Index —— 257

Caterina Bonan and Adam Ledgeway
It-clefts: State-of-the-art, and some empirical challenges

Abstract: This chapter provides a brief overview of recent research into clefts with a particular focus on *it*-clefts. In addition to dealing with many of the traditional and ongoing challenges that cleft structures pose for formal description and theoretical analysis, the chapter reviews some new problems of analysis and suggests some future directions of research. This general overview is integrated with a consideration and comparison of a number of the insights that emerge from the analyses of the chapters contained in this volume.

Keywords: clefts, it-clefts, monoclausality, biclausality, Trevisan, French, wh-questions, focus

1 Introduction

Clefts are intricate syntactic objects which, starting with Jespersen (1927), have motivated much work in descriptive and formal linguistics. Nonetheless, almost a century later their exact internal structure and status are still widely debated, which is why we believe that a multi-disciplinary volume on this theoretically complex structure across different languages of the world is greatly needed.

This cooperative work brings together scholars from all over Europe, and aims at providing new insights into these complex structures to help the linguistic community answer some questions that we raise in this introduction and which our contributors outline and discuss throughout the rest of the volume. While we are not able here to answer all possible questions on the distribution and internal structure of clefts in all natural languages, we present new cross-linguistic data, experimental results, and theoretical insights that will hopefully help shape the future of the theory of clefts and, more generally, that of nominal focalisations.

Given the wide array of cleft types attested cross-linguistically (cf. Lambrecht 2001 for a thorough review), the scope of this volume is restricted to the investigation of so-called *it*-clefts, a variety that has already been widely discussed in

---

Caterina Bonan, University of Cambridge, e-mail: caterina.bonan@outlook.com
Adam Ledgeway, University of Cambridge, e-mail: anl21@cam.ac.uk

Romance but is still remarkably understudied compared to more well-known structures such as non-cleft wh-interrogatives. Conversely, in an attempt to provide as complete a picture as possible, the number of languages and language families covered in the volume is broad and ranges from languages that are well-known in the formal linguistics literature such as English and other Germanic languages, Italian and French, to less studied varieties such as Palanquero and Réunion creoles and Mandarin Chinese. In the interest of completeness, this volume has been conceived as a multi-disciplinary work and includes contributions featuring traditional field-work techniques, corpus-based and experimental studies, computational investigations, as well as studies on L1 acquisition or L2 performance, and much more.

Our hope is that this volume will help the advancement of the theory of clefts and focus, and promote the importance of multi-disciplinary and cross-linguistic investigations in the study of these and many other complex structures.

1.1 *It*-clefts

It-clefts are widely understood to consist of a higher and an embedded clause. In most attested cases, the higher clause contains a quasi-argumental pronoun (in the sense of Bolinger 1977, Chomsky 1981, a.o.), a copula, and a focused element. Conversely, the lower clause displays a relative-like structure and is composed of a relativizer that links the lower clause to the focused element, followed by a proposition that contains the trace of the displaced constituent. This is illustrated in (1) using Spoken French examples.

(1) Spoken French
    a. C'est [$_{focus}$ JEAN$_i$] qui ___$_i$ me l'a raconté.
        it=is   Jean   who   me= it=has told
        '(It's) JEAN (who) told me.'
    b. C'est [$_{focus}$ QUI$_i$] qui ___$_i$ te l'a raconté?
        it=is   who   that   you= it=has told
        'WHO (is it that) told you?'

The relativizer, as will become clear from many of the contributions in this volume, is not compulsory or available in all varieties and when it is, it does not have a specialised form for subjects such as the French *qui* ('who', as opposed to *que*, for non-subjects) seen in (1).

Clefts can be declarative, as in (1a), or interrogative, as in (1b). The quasi-argumental pronoun, *c(e)* in the French examples above, does not have a phonological form in all languages. Eastern Trevisan (Veneto)[1] as described in Bonan (2021) is an example of language with phonologically silent quasi-argumental pronouns, as illustrated in (2).

(2) Eastern Trevisan
 Zé Giani ke me-o gà contà.
 (it) is Gianni that me=it.$_M$= has told
 '(It's) GIANNI (who) told me.'

Surprisingly, some languages such as Portuguese, spoken French and Eastern Trevisan also display inverse clefts of the type in (3), where the copula exceptionally follows the focused element (Kato & Ribeiro 2009, Kato 2014, Mioto & Lobo 2016, Bonan 2017, a.o.).

(3) Spoken French
 [$_{focus}$ QUI] c'est qui te l'a raconté]?
 who it=is who you= it=has told
 'WHO (is it that) told you?'

In some varieties, inverse structures are limited to declaratives or interrogatives, but in other cases they are attested in both types of structure. Eastern Trevisan, for instance, allows both structures (Bonan 2021). An example of an inverse declarative is provided in (4).

(4) Trevisan
 Giani zé ke me-o gà contà!
 (it) Giani is that me=it.$_M$ has told
 '(It's) GIANNI (who) told me (as opposed to someone else)!'

The reasons behind the inconsistent distribution of declarative and interrogative regular/inverse clefts cross-linguistically are yet to be determined and constitute, in our opinion, an interesting topic of investigation for the future. In this volume, Bertollo (Chapter 2) offers a first study of the distribution of clefts in languages in which these structures are very productive such as the Venetan dialects (Poletto and Vanelli 1997), compared to Germanic languages where their use is severely constrained (Durrell 2002, Fischer 2009). What the author demonstrates is that, regardless of the language under consideration, there exist factors that favour

---

[1] See Bonan (2021) for an overview of the main morpho-syntactic properties of this dialect of northern Italy.

clefting and factors that inhibit it. On the basis of a thorough analysis of linguistic microvariation in several Venetan varieties, Bertollo curiously shows that even in the domain of mandatory clefting some restrictions apply, which enable her to draw a scale for the obligatoriness of clefting that is based on the nature of the subject and its relationship with the lexical verb.

Regardless of the relative order between copula and the quasi-argumental pronoun, it is widely accepted that the relative portion of the cleft systematically contains a syntactic gap that is co-indexed with the focalised element. Scholars indeed agree that at least one long-distance dependency is established within clefts, as illustrated in the spoken French examples in (5):

(5) Spoken French
    a. C'est [MON PÈRE]$_i$ qui ___$_i$ est allé à la messe.
       it=is   my father   who   is gone to the mass
       'It's MY FATHER that attended mass'
    b. C'est [MON PÈRE]$_i$ que tu as vu ___$_i$.
       it=is   my father   that you have seen
       'It's MY FATHER that you saw'

This property is fundamental for these structures, and is observed in all varieties described and analysed throughout this volume.

One reason that makes *it*-clefts worthy of study is that interrogative clefts are remarkably understudied compared to their declarative counterparts, and relatively little has been said about the different distributional properties of cleft vs non-cleft truth-semantically equivalent sentences. In this volume, Cardinaletti (Chapter 1) makes a remarkable contribution in this respect by investigating the differences between cleft and non-cleft wh-questions in Italian. By investigating the syntactic, pragmatic, and prosodic properties of cleft wh-questions and comparing these to simple wh-questions, cleft declaratives, and focalisations, the author outlines and explains the similarities and differences between cleft and non-cleft wh-questions in the language, while providing additional evidence in favour of a derivation à la Belletti (2015) for Italian clefts (see §1.2 for a brief introduction). In so doing, Cardinaletti provides the first systematic comparison of otherwise identical cleft and non-cleft structures which, we hope, will inspire many colleagues to do the same for other languages and varieties.

1.2 On focus and biclausality

To date, most scholars agree that clefts involve a biclausal syntax while expressing a single proposition. Monoclausal sentences and their clefted counterparts, although not interchangeable in all discourse contexts, have been argued to share the same truth-values (Lambrecht 1988, Karssenberg & Lahousse 2018, a.o.).

Moreover, clefts come in many shapes and sizes but, according to the existing literature, all of them constitute a form of focalisation. In this volume however, Bourgoin & Davidse (Ch 4) revisit the notion of 'focus' in English *it*-clefts, and challenge the received view according to which the syntax of clefts codes focus-presupposition semantics. The authors argue that, at least in English, *it*-clefts are specificational constructions whose relative clause and antecedent represent an open proposition and its filler. Accordingly, the variable and value are related to each other by the identifying matrix, which triggers an implicature of exhaustiveness. Grounding their case in the close contextual study of the prosody of text examples of full and reduced *it*-clefts in English, Bourgoin & Davidse demonstrate that for most full *it*-clefts, the interpretation of the relative part as intrinsically presupposed cannot be maintained. Additionally, the authors insist that the occurrence of selective focus on only a part of the antecedent NP argues against assigning focal meaning to the whole clefted constituent. This work, we believe, constitutes a pioneering piece of research that has the potential of radically challenging what we (think we) know about clefts and focus.

In recent generative work on clefts, Haegeman, Meinunger & Vercauteren (2015) have claimed that 'embedded' cartographic analyses of clefts à la Belletti (2009; 2015) are to be preferred to 'matrix' accounts à la Meinunger (1997) and Frascarelli & Ramaglia (2013). The main difference between the two analyses is that, while the latter take clefts to be monoclausal, in embedded analyses clefts are biclausal throughout the derivation. In this volume, Belletti & Bocci (Chapter 3) and Samo & Merlo (Chapter 6) revisit a well-known asymmetry between subject and non-subject clefts first introduced and widely discussed in Belletti (2009, 2015). Accordingly, only subject clefts can be used to answer a question, which in a biclausal derivation à la Belletti (2015) can be explained in terms of intervention and (feature) Relativized Minimality (Rizzi 1990, Villata, Rizzi & Franck 2016). Working on standard Italian and French with experimental and computational techniques, these authors lend further support to the robustness of the asymmetry, to which Belletti's (2015) analysis of clefts is anchored, but also to the validity of Belletti's proposed biclausal derivation of clefts for these languages.

Another interesting account that investigates *it*-clefts using feature relativised minimality and the study of their Information Structure is offered by Lahousse & Jourdain (Chapter 5). The authors study the development of French *it*-clefts in L1 learners to better understand the formal development of the main and embedded clauses of clefts, and to determine whether clefts produced by children and by adults have the same Information Structure. The work, which is the only contribution solely focused on language acquisition in this volume, provides additional original insights into the distribution and interpretation of *it*-clefts.

1.3 Future challenges

We believe that the need for a strictly biclausal derivation defended in Haegeman Meinunger & Vercauteren (2015) and in this volume could potentially be challenged by the many dialectal and spoken varieties that present an invariant copula, although this prediction requires further empirical and theoretical work to be appropriately assessed. It thus remains to be determined whether both structural analyses are actually possible (or necessary), inasmuch as we believe that they may characterise related but distinct stages of the grammaticalization of clefts as exemplified in different diachronic, diatopic and diastratic varieties of the same language (or language family). Consider, for instance, the variation in the realisation of the copula in formal French, as in (6a), as opposed to spoken French, as in (6b).

(6) Spoken French
    a. Ce **sont** eux qui étudient la syntaxe.
        Ce= are them who study the syntax
    b. C'est eux qui étudient la syntaxe.
        Ce=is them who study the syntax
        'It's them that are studying syntax.'

The presence/absence of person features on the copula could be an indicator of different stages in the evolution of clefts and therefore, possibly, of the existence of different underlying structures. In this volume, for instance, Tang (Chapter 9) argues against the existence of a subject/non-subject asymmetry in Mandarin Chinese 'V *de* O' clefts, i.e., the Chinese equivalent of English *it*-clefts, and outlines several empirical and theoretical reasons against the adoption of a one-fits-all derivation cross-linguistically. In a similar way, McLellan (Chapter 7) utilises corpus techniques and grammaticality judgements to demonstrate that French-lexified Reunion Creole *sé*-clefts are structurally similar to the *it*-clefts of English and French yet display unique characteristics that are excluded in the other two languages, such as the possible omission of the relative marker in subject clefts. Additionally, Tramutoli & Marsella (Chapter 8) present a first account of *it*-clefts in Palenquero

Creole, insisting on the description of the different uses of copulas across age groups in the language, and the possibility to omit the matrix subject under certain circumstances, in an otherwise non-*pro*-drop language. These works thus provide novel insights into the structure of *it*-clefts in three understudied languages while, incidentally, also supporting the hypothesis that clefts are complex and variegated structures which allow higher degrees of variation than we thought possible, both across languages and across different varieties of the same language.

Another interesting phenomenon that we believe deserves attention, and will have to be assessed in future work, is the systematic correlation between the availability of focus fronting and the non-availability of clefting, as observed in Lambrecht (2001). Indeed, some Romance languages such as Romanian and southern Italian dialects do not have clefts, but they all have focus fronting. By contrast, modern French and most northern Italian dialects do not show informational focus fronting, but they do have clefts (Zafiu 2013, Cruschina 2015, Ledgeway 2020). We believe that this correlation, which is unfortunately not investigated in this volume, should be tested not only within and beyond Romance, but also diachronically: all documented medieval Romance varieties allowed focus fronting as a part of their V2 syntax, but an open question is whether they also allowed clefting and when the latter first emerged. It seems also important to establish whether declarative and interrogative clefts always go hand-in-hand in all languages, not only synchronically but also diachronically and, if not, in which order they emerge. Even a broad examination of the cross-linguistic variation in the availability, form and distribution of clefts as reviewed above and throughout this volume raises numerous theoretical questions. What makes inverse structures possible? Are these pragmatically different from their regular counterparts? Why do some languages have both structures? Should *it*-clefts in all varieties really be explained as biclausal? Are there exceptions? Are there languages in which only declarative clefts are possible, or vice-versa? If so, what does this tell us about the architecture of focal projections? If not, which sentence type is acquired or lost first? Is the moved constituent of clefts necessarily focalised? These are only a few of the many questions that we believe still deserve investigating to better understand the intricate structure of *it*-clefts and their interpretational properties with respect to their non-cleft counterparts.

Our belief is that the synchrony of clefts will only be appropriately understood once diachronic, typological, historical, experimental, and dialectological aspects are all brought together. We offer with this volume a first attempt at providing such a variegated picture of the cross-linguistic morphosyntax of *it*-clefts, exploring empirical and theoretical insights that, hopefully, will help the linguistic community to answer these questions, and many more.

References

Belletti, Adriana. 2009. *Structures and strategies*. (Routledge Leading Linguists 16). New York: Routledge.
Belletti, Adriana. 2015. The focus map of clefts: Extraposition and predication. In Ur Shlonsky (ed.), *Beyond functional sequence*, 42–59. (The Cartography of Syntactic Structures 10). Oxford: Oxford University Press.
Bolinger, Dwight. 1977. *Meaning and form*. (English Language Series 11). London: Longman.
Bonan, Caterina. 2017. Sé or c'est? On the Cartography of Clefts. *GG@G (Generative Grammar in Geneva)* X. 131–151. https://doi.org/10.13097/cjg3-tfud.
Bonan, Caterina. 2021. Romance interrogative syntax. Formal and typological dimensions of variation. (Linguistik Aktuell/Linguistics Today 266). Amsterdam: Benjamins. https://doi.org/10.1075/la.266
Chomsky, Noam. 1981. *Lectures on Government and Binding*. Dordrecht: Foris.
Cruschina, Silvio. 2015. Some notes on clefting and fronting. In Elisa Di Domenico, Cornelia Hamann & Simona Matteini (eds.), *Structures, strategies and beyond. Studies in honour of Adriana Belletti*, 181–208. (Linguistik Aktuell/Linguistics Today 223). Amsterdam: John Benjamins.
Durrell, Martin. 2002. *Hammer's German grammar and usage*. 4th edn. London: Arnold.
Fischer, Kerstin. 2009. Cleft sentences: Form, function, and translation. *Journal of Germanic Linguistics* 21(2). 167–191. doi:10.1017/S1470542709000257.
Frascarelli, Mara & Francesca Ramaglia. 2013. (Pseudo) Clefts at the syntax-prosody-discourse interface. In Katharina Hartmann & Tonjes Veenstra (eds.), *Cleft Structures*, 97–128. (Linguistik Aktuell/Linguistics Today 208). John Benjamins.
Haegeman, Liliane, André Meinunger & Aleksandra Vercauteren. 2015. The syntax of *it*-clefts and the Left periphery of the clause. In Ur Shlonsky (ed.), *Beyond functional sequence*, 73–90. (The Cartography of Syntactic Structures 10). Oxford: Oxford University Press.
Jespersen, Otto. 1927. *A Modern English grammar on historical principles. Part II: Syntax*. Heidelberg: C. Winters.
Karssenberg, Lena & Karen Lahousse. 2018. The information structure of French *il y a* & *c'est* clefts: A corpus-based analysis. *Linguistics* 56(3). 463–516.
Kato, Mary Aizawa & Ilza Ribeiro. 2009. Cleft sentences from old Portuguese to modern Portuguese. In Andreas Dufter & Daniel Jacob (eds.), *Focus and background in Romance languages*, 123–154. (Studies in Language Companion 112). Amsterdam: John Benjamins.
Kato, Mary Aizawa. 2014. The role of the copula in the diachronic development of focus constructions in Portuguese. In Marie-Hélène Côté & Éric Mathieu (eds.), *Variation within and across Romance languages*, 297–314. (Current Issues in Linguistic Theory 333). Place: John Benjamins.
Lambrecht, Knud. 1988. Presentational cleft constructions in spoken French. In John Haiman & Sandra A. Thompson (eds.), *Clause combining in grammar and discourse*, 135–179. Place: John Benjamins.
Lambrecht, Knud. 2001. A framework for the analysis of cleft constructions. *Linguistics* 39. 463–516.
Ledgeway, Adam. 2020. The north-south divide: Parameters of variation in the clausal domain. *L'Italia Dialettale* 81. 29–77.
Meinunger, André. 1997. The structure of clefts and pseudo-cleft sentences. In Michelle Moosally & Ralph Blight (eds.), *The Syntax and Semantics of Predication*, 235–246. (*Texas Linguistic Forum* 38). University of Texas at Austin: Department of Linguistics.
Mioto, Carlos & Maria Lobo. 2016. Wh-movement: Interrogatives, relatives and clefts. In W. Leo Wetzels, Sergio Menuzzi & João Costa (eds.), *The Handbook of Portuguese Linguistics*, 275–294. Oxford: Wiley.

Poletto, Cecilia & Laura Vanelli. 1997. Gli introduttori delle frasi interrogative nei dialetti italiani settentrionali. In Paola Benincà & Cecilia Poletto (eds.), *Strutture interrogative dell'Italia settentrionale*. Padova: Quaderni di lavoro ASIt. http://asit.maldura.unipd.it/papers.html

Rizzi, Luigi. 1990. *Relativized minimality*. Cambridge Mass.: The MIT Press.

Villata, Sandra, Rizzi, Luigi & Julie Franck. 2016. Intervention effects and Relativized Minimality: New experimental evidence from graded judgments. *Lingua* 179. 76–96.

Zafiu, Rodica. 2013. Information structure. In Gabriela Pană Dindelegan (ed.), *The Grammar of Romanian*, 568–575. Oxford: Oxford University Press.

Anna Cardinaletti
1 Cleft wh-questions as biclausal structures
A comparison with simple wh-questions, cleft declaratives, and focalizations

Abstract: The aim of the paper is to contribute to the debate on the internal structure of cleft sentences by (i) analysing the distribution of the subjunctive mood, lexical subjects, and *perché* 'why' in Italian declarative and interrogative cleft sentences and (ii) discussing a difference between simple and cleft wh-questions. While simple wh-questions with marginalized DPs (in the sense of Antinucci and Cinque 1977 and Cardinaletti 2001, 2002) are ambiguous between a subject and an object reading of those DPs, cleft wh-questions are not ambiguous: The marginalized material can only be the subject. The paper investigates the syntactic, pragmatic, and prosodic properties of cleft wh-questions and compares them to simple wh-questions, cleft declaratives, and focalizations.

Keywords: clefts, wh-questions, Italian, Marginalization, syntax, prosody

1 Introduction: On cleft wh-questions

Cleft wh-questions as in (1a) and (2a) are frequent in informal Italian (Belletti 2015) and can be used in free variation with simple wh-questions like (1b) and (2b), respectively:

(1) a. *Chi è che ha telefonato?*
   who is that has called
   'Who is it that called?'
  b. *Chi ha telefonato?*
   who has called
   'Who called?'

Note: Previous versions of this paper were presented at the Workshop on Subject, Topic and Clausal Architecture, Florianópolis, November 11–14, 2019, and at an online seminar in the framework of the Igra Lectures, Leipzig, July 9, 2021. I kindly thank the audiences for their questions and comments. I am also indebted to an anonymous reviewer for very helpful comments. All remaining errors are my own.

Anna Cardinaletti, Università Ca' Foscari Venezia, e-mail: cardin@unive.it

(2) a. Chi è che hai salutato?
    who is that have.2SG greeted
    'Who is it that you greeted?'
  b. Chi hai salutato?
    who have.2SG greeted
    'Who did you greet?'

The answer to both types of questions in (1) and (2) can be *nessuno* 'no one'. This means that cleft wh-questions do not have the existential presupposition typical of cleft declaratives. In the context in (3), in which such presupposition is not met, cleft declaratives cannot be used (3a). Focalization, either in situ or left peripheral, is instead allowed (3b-c):[1]

(3) *Hai fatto qualcosa?*
    have.2SG done something
    'Did you do anything?'
  a. **È NIENTE che ho fatto.*
    is nothing that have.1SG done
  b. *Non ho fatto niente.*
    not have.1SG done nothing
    'I didn't do anything.'
  c. *NIENTE ho fatto.*
    nothing have.1SG done
    'I did nothing.'

In a comparative perspective, note that this property also characterizes French cleft wh-questions with sentence-initial wh-phrases (4a), while wh-clefts with post-copula wh-phrases display the restriction found in cleft declaratives (4b): an answer like *rien* 'nothing' is not acceptable (Shlonsky 2012: 248):

(4) a. *Qu' est-ce que tu fais dans la vie? Rien.*
    what is-it that you do in the life nothing
    'What is it that you do in life?' 'Nothing.'
  b. *C'est quoi que tu fais dans la vie? #Rien.*
    it is what that you do in the life nothing
    'What is it that you do in life?' 'Nothing.'

---

[1] In (3a), (3c), and throughout, small caps indicate prosodically prominent constituents like cleft and focalized constituents.

Shlonsky (2012: 249) also observes that an exhaustive/uniqueness presupposition is associated with French cleft wh-questions with post-copula wh-phrases (5a), as in declarative clefts (see Frascarelli and Ramaglia 2013: 113 for Italian declarative clefts). The same presupposition is not found in Italian cleft wh-questions, where the wh-phrase always occurs sentence-initially (5b):

(5) a. *C'est à   qui   que   tu   as   parlé   à   la   soirée   de*
        it is   to   whom   that   you   have   talked   at   the   party   of
        Bertrand? (J'ai   parlé)   à   Marie,   entre   autres.
        Bertrand   I have   talked   to   Marie,   among   others
    b. *A   chi   è   che   hai   parlato   alla   festa   di   Gianni?*
        to   whom   is   that   have.2SG   talked   at.the   party   of   Gianni
        'To whom is it that you talked at Gianni's party?'
        Ho   parlato   a   Maria,   tra   gli   altri/   e   anche
        have.1SG   talked   to   Maria   among   the   others/   and   also
        a   Sandra.
        to   Sandra
        'I talked to Maria, among others / and to Sandra, too.'

In what follows, we focus on wh-clefts like (1a) and (2a), parallel to (4a), while we disregard structures like (4b) and (5a), which are not possible in Italian.[2]

2 The analysis of clefts

The internal structure of declarative clefts with a corrective reading, as in (6a), has been subject to debate. Two types of analyses are reported here. Both capture the similarity between clefting (6a) and focalization (6b). Following Haegeman, Meinunger and Vercauteren (2015), I refer to the two analyses with the terms "embedded" and "matrix", respectively. The "embedded" analysis, schematized in (7a), takes clefts to be complex sentences (Belletti 2009, 2015; Cruschina 2015). The copula heads the matrix VP and selects a reduced clausal complement, FocusP. The cleft constituent moves to the left-peripheral focus position of the embedded clause, while the complementizer *che* occurs in the embedded Fin head. The "matrix" anal-

---

[2] In Italian, cleft sentences with post-copula wh-phrases are only possible as echo questions, similarly to simple wh-questions with in situ wh-phrases. They are instead possible as real questions in Northern Italian dialects like that spoken in Treviso, which also allows in situ wh-phrases in simple wh-questions (Bonan 2017).

ysis (Frascarelli and Ramaglia 2013), schematized in (7b), instead claims that the cleft constituent is merged as the predicate of a small clause and targets the same position as focalized constituents, namely specFocusP of the root clause, while the presupposed *che*-clause is merged as the specifier of a left-peripheral Familiar-TopicP. In this analysis, the copula occurs higher than FocP, in GroundP (irrelevant details are omitted):[3]

(6) a. *È GIANNI che ho salutato.*
    is Gianni that have.1SG greeted
    'It's Gianni that I greeted.'
  b. *GIANNI ho salutato.*
    Gianni have.1SG greeted
    'Gianni I greeted.'

(7) a. [$_{TP}$ è [$_{VP}$ è [$_{FocP}$ Gianni [$_{FinP}$ che ho salutato ~~Gianni~~]]]]
  b. [$_{GP}$ è [$_{FocP}$ Gianni [$_{FamTopP}$ [che ho salutato] [$_{IP}$ è [$_{sc}$ ~~Gianni~~]]]]

Haegeman, Meinunger, and Vercauteren (2015) discuss many arguments against the "matrix" analysis of clefts. I concentrate here on their observation on pp. 80–81, which concerns cleft wh-questions. They observe that the analysis in (7b) cannot account for cleft interrogatives like the ones in (1a) and (2a), where the clause-initial wh-phrase occurs in a position higher than the copula. A further position to the left of the copula would be needed to host the wh-phrase. No such ad hoc solution is instead necessary in the "embedded" analysis of clefts. If the cleft element is a wh-phrase, as in (1a) and (2a), it can be taken to raise from the embedded clause to the matrix clause similar to long wh-movement, as in (8) (without however violating Freezing, cf. Rizzi 2010 and Belletti 2015 for proposals to this purpose based on the extraposition of FinP and further remnant movement of embedded FocP to the matrix specFocP; the details of the analysis are omitted here):

---

3 In this paper, we disregard subject clefts such as French (ii), whose subject DP may be a new-information focus in the answer to the question in (i) and which have a different structure from clefts with a corrective reading (cf. Belletti 2009, 2012, 2015):

(i) *Qui a parlé?*
    who has spoken
    'Who spoke?'
(ii) *C'est Jean.*
    it is Jean
    'Jean did.'

(8) a. [_FocP chi [_TP è [_VP è [_FocP __ [_FinP che [_TP ha [_VP chi telefonato]]]]]]
    b. [_FocP chi [_TP è [_VP è [_FocP __ [_FinP che [_TP hai [_VP salutato chi]]]]]]

Like simple wh-questions (Cardinaletti 2007, 2021), I take cleft wh-questions to not display any I-to-C movement and the copula to occur in matrix T.

In what follows, I provide further arguments in favour of the "embedded" analysis of clefts. They are based on the distribution of the subjunctive mood (section 3), subject DPs (section 4), and the wh-word *perché* 'why' (section 5). I then compare simple and cleft wh-questions with respect to the distribution of marginalized constituents (sections 6 and 7). Marginalized constituents are sentence-final, deaccented elements which typically occur in wh-questions as in other constructions derived by A'-movement and are not necessarily informationally given (Antinucci and Cinque 1977; Cardinaletti 2001, 2002).

3 On the distribution of the subjunctive mood

In both declarative and interrogative clefts, the copula can embed a complex sentence. Depending on the lexical verb of the cleft clause, the embedded verb is either indicative or subjunctive. *Dire* 'say' in (9) selects the indicative, *pensare* 'think' in (10) selects the subjunctive:

(9) a. *È   a ROMA che ha   detto che andava.*
        is to Rome that has said that went.IND.3SG
        'It is to Rome that he said that he would go.'
     b. *Dov' è   che ha   detto che andava?*
        where is that has said that went. IND.3SG
        'Where is it that he said that he would go?'

(10) a. *È   a ROMA che penso   che sia   andato.*
        is to Rome that think.1SG that is.SUBJ gone
        'It is to Rome that I think he went.'
     b. *Dov' è   che pensi   che sia   andato?*
        where is that think.2SG that is.SUBJ gone
        'Where is it that you think he went?'

Clefts themselves can be embedded. In (11), the matrix verb *dire* 'say' embeds a cleft clause containing indicative verbs:

(11) *Maria ha detto che è GIANNI che ha scritto una cosa*
Maria has said that is Gianni that has written a thing
del genere
of.the sort
'Maria said that it is Gianni that wrote such a thing.'

With matrix verbs selecting the subjunctive mood such as *pensare* 'think' in (12), either the copula (12a) or the finite verb of the clause embedded under the copula (here, the modal *potere* 'can') (12b) or, marginally, both (12c) can be in the subjunctive. Those in (13) are real examples taken from the web. (13a) instantiates the option in (12a), (13b) the option in (12c):

(12) a. *Penso che sia LUI che può scrivere una*
think.1SG that is.SUBJ him that can.IND write a
cosa del genere.
thing of.the sort
b. *Penso che è LUI che possa scrivere una*
think.1SG that is.IND him that can.SUBJ write a
cosa del genere.
thing of.the sort
c. ?*Penso che sia LUI che possa scrivere una*
think.1SG that is.SUBJ him that can.SUBJ write a
cosa del genere.
thing of.the sort
'I think that it is him that can write such a thing.'

(13) a. *Penso che sia LUI che ha fatto sparire*
think.1SG that is.SUBJ him that has.IND made disappear
la Statua della Libertà.
the Statue of.the liberty
'I think that it is him that made the Statue of Liberty disappear.'
b. *E penso che sia QUI che il neoconservatorismo*
and think.1SG that is.SUBJ here that the neoconservatism
abbia agito al contrario.
has.SUBJ acted in reverse
'And I think that it is here that neoconservatism has acted in reverse.'

The occurrence of the subjunctive mood in the clause embedded under the copula is problematic for the "matrix" analysis of clefts. If the cleft *che*-clause occurs in the specifier of FamTopP, as in (7b), it should not be possible for the matrix verb to select a subjunctive inside that clause because it is not its complement. In the "embedded" analysis, this is instead expected since the *che*-clause is embedded under the matrix verb and c-commanded by it. Given the absence of the Force projection in the clause embedded under the copula, as in the analysis sketched in (7a) and (8) above, the copula and the subordinate verb may be taken to share the Mood feature. This explains why the verb embedded under the copula may also be subjunctive. The fact that the copula itself can be indicative as in (12b) may be due to the reduced inflection displayed by the copula in clefts. The copula is usually uninflected for Tense. A present indicative copula as in (12b) may be taken to be a default form.

A similar distribution of the subjunctive mood is found with embedded cleft wh-questions. Either the copula (14a) or the finite verb of the clause embedded under the copula (here, the modal *potere* 'can') (14b) or, marginally, both (14c) can be subjunctive in subject clefts. Those in (15) are real examples taken from the web. (15a-b) instantiate the option in (14a), (15c) the option in (14b):[4]

(14) a. *Non so   chi   sia   che può   scrivere una cosa*
           not know.1SG who is.SUBJ that can.IND write   a   thing
           del   genere.
           of.the sort
      b. *Non so   chi   è   che possa   scrivere una cosa*
           not know.1SG who is.IND that can.SUBJ write   a   thing
           del   genere.
           of.the sort
      c. ?*Non so   chi   sia   che possa   scrivere una cosa*
           not know.1SG who is.SUBJ that can.SUBJ write   a   thing
           del   genere.
           of.the sort
           'I do not know who it is that can write such a thing.'

---

4 Both verbs can be indicative. In colloquial Italian, many speakers including myself may use the indicative in embedded questions. (i) is a real example taken from the web:

(i)   *Non so   chi   è   che gestisce   questa pagina.*
       not know.1SG who is.IND that manages.IND this   page
       'I do not know who it is that is managing this page.'

(15) a. *Non so   chi   sia   che   commissiona   i   tweet*
       not know.1SG who   is.SUBJ that commissions.IND the   tweet
       contro di me.
       against of me
       'I don't know who commissions the tweets against me.'
   b. *Non so   chi   sia   che   gestisce   le   nuove*
       not know.1SG who   is.SUBJ that manages.IND the   new
       offerte.
       offers
       'I do not know who it is that is managing the new offers.'
   c. *Non so   chi   è   che   possa   aver   fatto tutto*
       not know.1SG who   is.IND   that can.SUBJ   have   done   all
       questo.
       this
       'I do not know who it is that could have done all this.'

Embedded non-subject clefts, by contrast, only display indicative copulas and subjunctive embedded verbs, (16b) and (17b). The sentence in (18) is a real example from the web, parallel to (17a), which I judge ungrammatical:

(16) a. **Non so   chi   sia   che   Maria   ha   invitato.*
       not know.1SG who   is.SUBJ that Maria   has.IND   invited
   b. *Non so   chi   è   che   Maria   abbia   invitato.*
       not know.1SG who   is.IND   that Maria   has.SUBJ invited
       'I do not know who it is that Maria invited.'
   c. **Non so   chi   sia   che   Maria   abbia   invitato.*
       not know.1SG who   is.SUBJ that Maria   has.SUBJ invited

(17) a. **Non so   quando   sia   che   Maria   ha   telefonato.*
       not know.1SG when   is.SUBJ that Maria   has.IND   called
   b. *Non so   quand'   è   che   Maria   abbia   telefonato.*
       not know.1SG when   is.IND   that Maria   has.SUBJ called
       'I do not know when it is that Maria called.'
   c. **Non so   quando   sia   che   Maria   abbia   telefonato.*
       not know.1SG when   is.SUBJ that Maria   has.SUBJ called

(18) *Non so   dove   sia   che   stanno   ballando.*
     not know.1SG where is.SUBJ that are.IND   dancing
     'I do not know where it is that they are dancing.'

As noted above, the occurrence of the subjunctive mood in the clause embedded under the copula is problematic for the "matrix" analysis of clefts but can be explained under the "embedded" analysis of clefts. The reason why the copula can be subjunctive mainly in subject wh-clefts remains to be established (cf. the ungrammaticality of (16a,c), (17a,c), and (18)).

4 On the distribution of subject DPs

The distribution of subject DPs is different in simple and cleft wh-questions. While preverbal subjects are ungrammatical in simple wh-questions (19), they are grammatical in cleft wh-questions (20a), as they are in cleft declaratives (20b). As for focalizations (21), judgments may vary among speakers, something I signal with # (Cardinaletti 2009):

(19) *Chi Maria ha   salutato?
     who Maria has greeted
     Intended meaning: 'Who did Maria greet?'

(20) a. Chi è   che   Maria ha   salutato?
        who is that Maria has greeted
        'Who is it that Maria greeted?'
     b. È   GIANNI che   Maria ha   salutato, non me.
        Is Gianni that Maria has greeted   not me
        'It is Gianni that Maria greeted, not me.'

(21) #GIANNI Maria ha   salutato, non me.
     Gianni   Maria has greeted   not me
     'Maria greeted Gianni, not me.'

The restriction shown in (19) has been discussed in many studies since Rizzi (1996), but there is still disagreement on why preverbal subjects are ungrammatical in simple wh-questions (see Cardinaletti 2021 for an overview). Two observations are relevant for our discussion here. First, the co-occurrence of preverbal subjects and A'-moved constituents is only banned in main clauses, while embedded wh-questions allow preverbal subjects (Rizzi 1996; Cardinaletti 2021). Compare (19) with (22):

(22) *Mi   chiedo   chi   Maria   ha   salutato.*
     myself ask.1SG who   Maria   has   greeted
     'I wonder who Maria greeted.'

The grammaticality of (20) is thus compatible with the hypothesis that cleft sentences include a subordinate clause, as assumed in the "embedded" cartographic analysis of clefts.

Second, cleft wh-questions allow the subject to be marginalized at the end of the clause (23b), on a par with simple wh-questions (23a). Marginalization of the subject is also possible with declarative clefts (23c) and left-peripheral focalizations (23d):

(23) a. *Chi ha salutato, Maria?*
        'Who did Maria greet?'
     b. *Chi è che ha salutato, Maria?*
        'Who is it that Maria greeted?'
     c. *È GIANNI che ha salutato, Maria, non me.*
        'It is Gianni that Maria greeted, not me.'
     d. *GIANNI ha salutato, Maria, non me.*
        'Maria greeted Gianni, not me.'

As I said above, marginalized constituents are sentence-final, deaccented elements (Antinucci and Cinque 1977). In (23) and all examples below, the comma signals the change in intonation which occurs between the element which gets sentential stress (here, the past participle verb form *salutato* 'greeted') and the deaccented sentence-final constituent (here, *Maria*).

I take the marginalized constituents in (23) to occur clause-internally in their first-merge position (Cardinaletti 2001, 2002, 2018). Evidence is based on the fact that (i) *ne*-extraction is possible from marginalized objects (24a) and marginalized subjects of unaccusative verbs (24b), and (ii) the marginalized subject can be quantified (25):

(24) a. *Quando ne   hai   visti, due?*
        when   of.them   have.2SG   seen   two
        'When did you see two of them?'
     b. *Quando ne   sono   arrivati, due?*
        when   of.them   are   arrived   two
        'When did two of them arrive?'

(25) a. *Chi ha   incontrato, ogni   studente?*
        who has met   every   student
        'Who did every student meet?'

b. *Dove non è andato, nessuno?*
   where not is gone nobody
   'Where did nobody go?'
c. *Che cosa non ha fatto, nessuno?*
   what not has done nobody
   'What did nobody do?'

The marginalization of the subject, which is similar across the A'-constructions in (23), is expected under the "embedded" analysis of clefts, but not under the "matrix" analysis. If the embedded CP occurring in SpecFamTopP is background information, it is not clear why it should be organized internally in such a way that a marginalized constituent appears. It is also not clear why cleft sentences should share the intonation of the other A'-constructions in (23).

5 On the interpretation of post-verbal subjects and the peculiar behaviour of *perché*

Bocci and Pozzan (2014) point out an important difference among wh-questions. When the pre-verbal position is unavailable, as in a wh-question like (19), repeated here as (26a), a post-verbal marginalized subject as in (23a), repeated here as (26b), is the unmarked option. The subject is licensed in post-verbal position independently of its discourse-related properties. It is neither a topic nor a focus. The marginalized subject indeed does not bear sentential stress and does not have the narrow focus interpretation typical of post-verbal subjects in Italian, (26c) vs. (26d) (cf. Belletti 2001, 2004). When the preverbal position is available, as with *perché* 'why' (27a), the post-verbal subject can bear sentential stress and be interpreted as a narrow focus (27b):[5]

(26) a. **Chi Maria ha salutato?*
    b. *Chi ha salutato, Maria$_{subj}$?*
       who has greeted Maria
       'Who did Maria greet?'

---

[5] With *perché*, the subject may also be marginalized, in which case it is the verb that is narrowly focused:

(i) *Perché telefona, Gianni (e non manda un messaggio?)*
    why calls Gianni and not sends a message
    'Why does Gianni call (and not send a message)?'

c. *Chi$_{obj}$ ha salutato Maria$_{subj}$?
d. L' ha salutato Maria$_{subj}$ (e non Luisa).
   him has greeted Maria (and not Luisa)
   'Maria greeted him, not Luisa.'

(27) a. Perché Gianni telefona?
        Why   Gianni calls
        'Why is Gianni calling?'
   b. Perché telefona Gianni (e non Mario)?
      Why   calls   Gianni (and not Mario)
      'Why is Gianni calling, and not Mario?'

This is an important contrast, which adds another property to the peculiar behavior of *perché* with respect to the other wh-phrases (cf. Rizzi 2001).

The analysis of cleft sentences reveals that the constraint against a narrow-focus post-verbal subject as in (26c) is independent of the availability of a preverbal subject. This constraint also applies in cleft wh-questions (28a) and cleft declaratives (28b), which, as we have seen in (20a) and (20b), respectively, do allow preverbal subjects:

(28) a. *Chi$_{obj}$ è che ha salutato Maria$_{subj}$?
        who   is that has greeted Maria
        Intended meaning: 'Who is it that Maria greeted?'
   b. *È GIANNI$_{obj}$ che ha salutato Maria$_{subj}$.
      is Gianni   that has greeted Maria
      Intended meaning: 'It is Gianni that Maria greeted.'

The ungrammaticality of (26c) and (28) can be attributed to the constraint against two foci in one and the same sentence. Differently from topics, which may be reiterated, only one focus per sentence is allowed (Rizzi 1997; Belletti 2004: 40; Bocci 2013: Ch.3). The sentences (26c) and (28) contain two foci, namely the wh- or cleft constituent and the post-verbal subject. For the same reason, a narrow-focus post-verbal subject is ungrammatical with left-peripheral focalizations:[6]

---

[6] As expected, no such restriction is found with left-peripheral topics, which may co-occur with narrow-focus post-verbal subjects:

(i) Quelle bambine$_{obj}$ le   pettina la mamma$_{subj}$ (non la zia).
    those girls   them combs   the mum   not the aunt
    'The mum is combing those girls' hair (not their aunt).'

(29) *GIANNI_obj ha salutato Maria_subj.
Gianni has greeted Maria
Intended meaning: 'Maria greeted Gianni.'

Note that the restriction does not apply in embedded wh-questions, in which the wh-phrase can co-occur with both a fronted focus as in (30a) (Rizzi 2001: 291; Bocci, Saito, and Rizzi 2018) and a post-verbal subject, as in (30b):

(30) a. *Mi domando a GIANNI che cosa abbiano detto*
myself ask.1SG to Gianni what have.SUBJ.3PL said
(non a Piero).
not a Piero
'I wonder what they said to Gianni (not to Piero).'
b. *Mi domando che cosa abbia detto Gianni (non Piero).*
myself ask.1SG what has. SUBJ said Gianni not Piero
'I wonder what Gianni said, not Piero.'

The contrast between main wh-phrases as in (26c) and embedded wh-phrases as in (30b) can be accounted for by suggesting that only the former include a [focus] feature (Bocci, Bianchi, and Cruschina 2020).

The grammaticality of (27b) confirms the special status and distribution of *perché* with respect to the other wh-phrases. *Perché* is merged in left-peripheral IntP (located above FocusP, Rizzi 2001), which is not a position for focalized elements. Thus, *perché* does not interact with the rest of the sentence in this respect. It can co-occur with an in-situ focus as in (27b), as well as with a fronted, left-peripheral focus as in (31), taken from Rizzi (2018: 351):

(31) *Perché le CHIAVI hai messo nel cassetto, non le*
why the keys have.2SG put in.the drawer not the
sigarette?
cigarettes
'Why did you put in the drawer THE KEYS, not the cigarettes?'

The special first-merge position of *perché* allows us to explain another peculiarity of its distribution. *Perché* cannot occur in cleft wh-questions, with the subject in either position:

(32) a. **Perché è che Gianni telefona?*
why is that Gianni calls

b. *Perché   è   che   telefona Gianni?
   why   is   that calls   Gianni
   Intended meaning: 'Why is it that Gianni is calling?'

This piece of data can be accommodated under the hypothesis that in cleft sentences, the copula selects a reduced complement, FocP, as shown in the structures (7a) and (8) above, to the exclusion of higher projections such as IntP which hosts *perché*. This means that *perché* cannot first-merge in the clause embedded under the copula and can thus never occur in cleft wh-questions. *Perché* is expectedly also ungrammatical in embedded clefts, with the subject in either position:

(33) a. *Non so   perché è   che Gianni   telefona.
        not know.1SG   why   is   that Gianni   calls
     b. *Non so   perché è   che telefona Gianni.
        not know.1SG   why   is   that calls   Gianni
        Intended meaning: 'I do not know why it is that Gianni is calling.'

Note that the ungrammaticality of (32) and (33) (vs. the grammaticality of wh-clefts with other wh-elements) can be taken as an additional argument for the "embedded" analysis of cleft sentences, formulated in cartographic terms as in (7a) and (8) above. The "matrix" analysis of clefts would be unable to distinguish among different wh-elements in wh-clefts (unless only the position for wh-elements different from *perché* is assumed to occur above GroundP in the structure in (7b), a move which I take to be an ad-hoc stipulation. No such stipulation is needed in the "embedded" analysis of clefts).

5.1 D-linked wh-phrases

Like *perché*, D-linked wh-phrases are ungrammatical in wh-clefts:

(34) a. *Quale   bambina è   che   ha   visto   Maria?
        which   girl   is   that has   seen   Maria
        Intended meaning: 'Which girl is it that saw Maria?'
     b. *Quale   bambina è   che   Maria ha   visto?
        which   girl   is   that Maria has   seen
        Intended meaning: 'Which girl is it that Maria saw?'

D-linked wh-phrases also occur in positions higher than specFocP, which by hypothesis are absent in the clause embedded under the copula (as shown in the structures (7a) and (8) above).

Note that like *perché*, D-linked wh-phrases are compatible with preverbal subject DPs (Rizzi 1996: 87, note 16; Cardinaletti 2021):

(35) Quale bambina Maria ha   visto?
      which girl   Maria has seen
      'Which girl did Maria see?'

Differently from *perché*, however, a D-linked wh-phrase cannot occur with a narrow-focus post-verbal subject because of the constraint against two foci (see section 6 below).

6 On prosodic properties

In the case of simple wh-questions on the subject, two different intonations are possible. The intonation we have discussed so far is the one in (36a) and (37a): the wh-word and the verb build a prosodic constituent, the verb receives main sentence stress (Nuclear Pitch Accent, cf. Calabrese 1982; Marotta 2001; Bianchi, Bocci, and Cruschina 2018; Bocci, Bianchi, and Cruschina 2020), and the object is marginalized at the end of the sentence. The other intonation is as in (36b) and (37b): the subject builds a phonological phrase by itself, and the verb and the object build another phonological phrase, with phrasal stress falling on the object. This intonation is possible because in Italian, postfocal material is not destressed; it builds a phonological phrase whose head is the rightmost element and is stressed (Bocci and Avesani 2015). The prosodic change after the wh-phrase is signalled here by #. In (36)–(37) and the other examples below, we use number mismatch to facilitate the interpretation of the sentences. Since *chi* 'who' is only singular, in (37) we use a *which*-phrase to exemplify the case of a plural verb:[7]

---

[7] In my central Italian variety, *raddoppiamento sintattico* (initial consonantal fortition) applies in (36a), but not in (36b), confirming the different prosodic phrasing:
(i)   Chi [pp]ettina, le mamme?
(ii) Chi # [p]ettina le mamme?

Experimental data show that the intonation in the a. sentences of (36)–(37) is by far more frequent than the one in the b. sentences (Bocci, Bianchi, and Cruschina 2020).

(36) a. *Chi$_{subj}$ pettina, le mamme$_{obj}$?*
 b. *Chi$_{subj}$ # pettina le mamme$_{obj}$?*
   who combs the mums
   'Who is combing the mums' hair?'

(37) a. *Quali bambine$_{subj}$ pettinano, le mamme$_{obj}$?*
 b. *Quali bambine$_{subj}$ # pettinano le mamme$_{obj}$?*
   which girls comb the mums
   'Which girls are combing the mums' hair?'

The two intonations are not in free variation and seem to correlate with different interpretations. Let us consider (37). The question in (37a) can be uttered in a context in which there are two groups of children, one is combing their mother, the other is hugging their mother. Thus, the marginalized object *le mamme* can be given and part of the background. The question in (37b) is uttered in a different context: there are two groups of children, one is combing their mother, the other one is doing something else.

Note that the possibility in (36)–(37) is only open to subject wh-questions. If the wh-phrase is the object and the post-verbal DP is the subject, the sentence is ungrammatical:

(38) a. **Chi$_{obj}$ # pettinano le mamme$_{subj}$?*
   who comb the mums
   Intended meaning: 'Who are the mums combing?'
 b. **Quale bambina$_{obj}$ # pettinano le mamme$_{subj}$?*
   which girl comb the mums
   Intended meaning: 'Which girl are the mums combing?'
 c. **Quali bambine$_{obj}$ # pettina la mamma$_{subj}$?*
   which girls combs the mum
   Intended meaning: 'Which girls is the mum combing?'

(Non-marginalized, non-right-dislocated) post-verbal subjects of transitive verbs necessarily have a narrow-focus interpretation (Belletti 2001). As we saw in section 5 above, a narrow-focus post-verbal subject is incompatible with a wh-phrase because of the constraint against two foci. I claim that the constraint against two foci applies in (38) as well.[8] The data show that the constraint applies independently of the intonation which is chosen for the wh-question.

The same restriction operates in both interrogative and declarative cleft sentences. In (39a) and (40a), respectively, the cleft subject can be separated from the phonological phrase formed by the *che*-clause (which contains the lexical verb and the object). This intonation is not possible in object clefts. In (39b) and (40b), the narrow-focus post-verbal subject *le mamme* is incompatible with the preverbal focused object. The constraint against two foci applies. The same restriction expectedly holds with left-peripheral focalizations, as shown in (41).[9] Note that the copula in (39a) does not trigger *raddoppiamento sintattico* on the complementizer (**chi è # [kk]e pettina le mamme?*, which confirms the proposed prosodic phrasing, cf. fn. 7):

(39) a. Chi$_{subj}$ è # che pettina le mamme$_{obj}$?
        who   is   that combs the mums
        'Who is it that is combing the mums' hair?'
   b. *Chi$_{obj}$ è # che pettinano le mamme$_{subj}$?
        Who   is   that comb   the mums
        Intended meaning: 'Who is it that the mums are combing?'

(40) a. È la BAMBINA$_{subj}$ # che pettina le mamme$_{obj}$.
        is the girl   that combs the mums
        'It is the girl that is combing the mums' hair.'
   b. *È la BAMBINA$_{obj}$ # che pettinano le mamme$_{subj}$.
        is the girl   that comb the mums
        Intended meaning: 'It is the girl that the mums are combing.'

(41) a. La BAMBINA$_{subj}$ # pettina le mamme$_{obj}$.
        the girl   combs the mums
        'The girl is combing the mums' hair.'

---

8 The constraint against two foci is independent of the syntactic function of the focalized constituent and may also apply to objects. If in (37b), the object *le mamme* is a narrow focus, the sentence is ungrammatical. This is also true of (39a)–(41a) below. The difference between subjects and objects is that objects are not necessarily narrow foci.

9 To express the meaning of the ungrammatical sentences in (39b)–(41b), the intonation seen in (23b–d) should be used, where the lexical verb gets main stress and the post-verbal subject is marginalized:

(i) a. Chi$_{obj}$ è che pettinano, le mamme$_{subj}$?
   b. È la BAMBINA$_{obj}$ che pettinano, le mamme$_{subj}$.
   c. La BAMBINA$_{obj}$ pettinano, le mamme$_{subj}$.

b. *La BAMBINA$_{obj}$ # pettinano le mamme$_{subj}$.
    the girl   comb   the mums
    Intended meaning: 'The mums are combing the girl's hair.'

These data can also be taken to support the "embedded" analysis of clefts. If the embedded clause were background information sitting in specFamTopP, it should be insensitive to the prosodic articulation of the rest of the sentence and should not interact with its information structure. An anonymous reviewer asks whether the data can be accounted for under the "matrix" analysis of clefts by observing that the *che*-clause, being background information, should not contain any focal material. While this analysis might be on the right track, it would only apply to cleft sentences. We have however seen that one and the same behaviour is displayed by the different A'-constructions. Adopting the "matrix" analysis of clefts, an important generalization would be lost.

7 A difference between simple and cleft wh-questions

As we said in section 4, wh-questions may contain marginalized constituents, i.e., sentence-final, deaccented elements (Antinucci and Cinque 1977; Cardinaletti 2001, 2002). Marginalized constituents may be of any category and bear any theta role. The sentence in (23a) contained a marginalized subject; in (36a)–(37a), we saw marginalized objects. A simple wh-question such as (42) containing the marginalized constituent *Maria* is thus judged as ambiguous by native speakers of Italian. *Maria* can either be the subject (42a) or the object (42b) of the sentence. Cleft wh-questions are different. A sentence such as (43) is judged as non-ambiguous: the marginalized constituent *Maria* can only be the subject (43a), while the opposite interpretation is ungrammatical (43b):[10]

---

[10] In (43a), we have taken the subject to be marginalized. Note that it may also be right-dislocated, i.e., anticipated by a (null) subject pronoun, on a par with the object in (47). This analysis is shown in (i):

(i)   Chi$_{obj}$ è   che   pro   ha   salutato, Maria$_{subj}$?
     who   is   that   she has   greeted   Maria
    'Who is it that Maria greeted?'

Since the anticipatory pronoun is null in Italian, it is not easy to distinguish between the two analyses. It can however be shown that the subject is not necessarily right-dislocated, and can indeed be

(42) Chi   ha   salutato, Maria?
      who   has greeted   Maria
   a. Chi$_{obj}$ ha salutato, Maria$_{subj}$?
      'Who did Maria greet?'
   b. Chi$_{subj}$ ha salutato, Maria$_{obj}$?
      'Who greeted Maria?'

(43) Chi   è   che   ha salutato, Maria?
      who   is that has greeted   Maria
   a. Chi$_{obj}$ è che ha salutato, Maria$_{subj}$?
      'Who is it that Maria greeted?'
   b. *Chi$_{subj}$ è che ha salutato, Maria$_{obj}$?
      Intended meaning: 'Who is it that greeted Maria?'

Ambiguity in simple wh-questions only occurs when the two DPs share the number feature, as in (42). If the marginalized DP is plural, the sentences are not ambiguous (44). The same holds true if the wh-question contains a plural *which*-phrase and a singular marginalized DP, as in (45):

(44) a. Chi$_{obj}$ hanno salutato, le signore$_{subj}$?
        who   have greeted   the ladies
        'Who did the ladies greet?'

---

taken to be marginalized. First, *ne*-extraction is possible, as in (iia); second, a quantified subject can occur in a cleft wh-question, as in (iib-c). In both cases, the post-verbal subject can be said to occur in a clause-internal position similarly to what happens with Marginalization in simple wh-questions (see (24) and (25) above):

(ii) a. Quand' è   che   ne   sono arrivati, due?
        when   is that of.them are arrived   two
        'When is it that two of them arrived?'
   b. Chi è che ha incontrato, ogni studente?
      who is that has met   each student
      'Who is it that every student met?'
   c. Dov' è che non è andato, nessuno?
      where is that not is gone nobody
      'Where is it that nobody went?'
   d. Cos' è che non ha fatto, nessuno?
      what is that not has done nobody
      'What is it that nobody did?'

b. *Chi$_{subj}$ ha salutato, le signore$_{obj}$?*
   who has greeted the ladies
   'Who greeted the ladies?'

(45) a. *Quali bambine$_{obj}$ ha salutato, Maria$_{subj}$?*
       which girls has greeted Maria
       'Which girls did Maria greet?'
   b. *Quali bambine$_{subj}$ hanno salutato, Maria$_{obj}$?*
       which girls have greeted Maria
       'Which girls greeted Maria?'

Using number mismatch, the non-ambiguity of (38) is confirmed:

(46) a. *Chi$_{obj}$ è che hanno salutato, le signore$_{subj}$?*
       who is that have greeted the ladies
       'Who is it that the ladies greeted?'
   b. **Chi$_{subj}$ è che ha salutato, le signore$_{obj}$?*
       who is that has greeted the ladies
       Intended meaning: 'Who is it that greeted the ladies?'

To provide the meaning which is ungrammatical in (43b) and (46b), Italian speakers may resort to cleft wh-questions like (47), which contain right-dislocated objects (co-occurring with anticipatory accusative clitic pronouns) instead of marginalized objects:[11]

---

[11] The contrast between (43b)/(46b) and (47) supports the claim that clitic pronouns are not optional. See Cardinaletti (2001), (2002) for tests to distinguish Right-Dislocation and Marginalization – with and without the anticipatory clitic pronoun, respectively.

Right-dislocation of the object also makes simple wh-questions non-ambiguous. Compare (42) with (i), where the accusative clitic pronoun *la* 'her' occurs:

(i) *Chi$_{subj}$ l' ha salutata, Maria$_{obj}$?*
    who her has greeted Maria
    'Who greeted Maria?'

So does the left-dislocation of either the subject (iia) or the object (iib):

(ii) a. *Maria$_{subj}$, chi$_{obj}$ pro ha salutato?*
        Maria who she has greeted
        'As for Maria, who did she greet?'
    b. *Maria$_{obj}$, chi$_{subj}$ l' ha salutata?*
        Maria who her has greeted
        'As for Maria, who greeted her?'

(47) a. *Chi   è   che   l'   ha   salutata, Maria?*
         who   is   that   her   has   greeted   Maria
         'Who is it that greeted Maria?'
    b. *Chi   è   che   le   ha   salutate, le signore?*
         who   is   that   them   has   greeted   the ladies
         'Who is it that greeted the ladies?'

Another strategy to convey the meaning ungrammatical in (43b) is to use the different intonation we saw in (39a), where the object is not marginalized, but receives phrasal stress (being in a post-focal position). As we said above, this strategy gives rise to non-ambiguous sentences; the post-verbal DP can only be the object because of the constraint against two foci:

(48)   *Chi   è #   che   ha   salutato Maria?*
         who   is   that   has   greeted   Maria
    a. *Chi$_{subj}$ è #   che   ha   salutato Maria$_{obj}$?*
         'Who is it that greeted Maria?'
    b. **Chi$_{obj}$ è #   che   ha   salutato Maria$_{subj}$?*
         Intended meaning: 'Who is it that Maria greeted?'

The cleft wh-questions in (43) behave like cleft declaratives (49) and focalizations (50) in that the marginalized constituent can only be the subject; cf. (49a) vs. (49b), (50a) vs. (50b). To convey the other meaning, Right Dislocation of the object is necessary, as shown in (49c)–(50c), or the intonation seen in (40a)–(41a), as shown in (49d)–(50d):[12]

(49) a. *È GIANNI$_{obj}$ che ha salutato, Maria$_{subj}$.*
         'It is Gianni that Maria greeted.'
    b. *$^{??}$È GIANNI$_{subj}$ che ha salutato, Maria$_{obj}$.*
         Intended meaning: 'It is Gianni that greeted Maria.'
    c. *È GIANNI$_{subj}$ che   l'   ha   salutata, Maria$_{obj}$.*
         is Gianni   that   her   has   greeted   Maria
         'It is Gianni that greeted Maria.'
    d. *È GIANNI$_{subj}$ # che ha salutato Maria$_{obj}$.*
         'It is Gianni that greeted Maria.'

---

[12] The strong marginality of (50b) is coherent with the results of Bocci and Avesani's (2015) comprehension experiment, in which a post-verbal DP occurring in a structure with a fronted focus was interpreted as a subject in a very high percentage of the time.

(50) a. GIANNI$_{obj}$ ha salutato, Maria$_{subj}$.
   'Maria greeted Gianni.'
 b. $^{??}$Gianni$_{subj}$ ha salutato, le signore$_{obj}$.
   Intended meaning: 'Gianni greeted the ladies.'
 c. GIANNI$_{subj}$ le   ha   salutate,   le signore$_{obj}$.
   Gianni   them has greeted   the ladies
   'Gianni greeted the ladies.'
 d. GIANNI$_{subj}$ # ha salutato le signore$_{obj}$.
   'Gianni greeted the ladies.'

To understand these contrasts, consider the discussion in section 6 above.

If in object A'-constructions (simple wh-questions included), the verb bears sentential or, when occurring in post-focal position, phrasal stress (Bocci and Avesani 2015), a post-verbal subject is necessarily marginalized (or right-dislocated, see fn. 10). A post-verbal subject phrased together with the verb is necessarily a narrow focus and violates the constraint against two foci occurring in one and the same sentence. Post-verbal objects are instead not necessarily narrow foci and can bear phrasal stress when they are prosodically phrased with the verb. Hence, they do not violate the constraint against two foci and do not need to be marginalized in order to get a grammatical sentence. Their marginalization occurs in another condition, namely when they follow contrastively focalized constituents (Frascarelli 1996).

In subject A'-constructions (simple wh-questions excluded), the presence of marginalized objects indicates that the verb is focalized. These sentences are ungrammatical because focalized verbs are not compatible with preverbal focalized subjects. The constraint against two foci applies here as well. This accounts for (43b), (46b), (49b), and (50b). The only way to destress a post-verbal object is by right-dislocating it, as in (47), (49c), and (50c).

Something special happens in simple subject wh-questions, where the verb bears sentential stress (Nuclear Pitch Accent). This allows the marginalization of the object, as in (42b), and Right Dislocation is not necessary (although possible, see fn. 11). This possibility, as we have seen, is not shared by cleft wh-questions, which can be taken to be another argument for the "embedded" analysis of clefts.

8 Conclusions

In this paper, we have discussed new arguments for the "embedded" cartographic analysis of clefts (Belletti 2009, 2015; Cruschina 2015; Haegeman, Meinunger, Vercauteren 2015). Clefts are complex sentences in which the cleft constituent moves to the left-peripheral focus projection of the clause embedded under the copula. The cleft clause is a reduced clause lacking the highest functional projections, most notably ForceP and IntP, which explains the distribution of the subjunctive Mood in embedded clefts and the ungrammaticality of *perché* in cleft wh-phrases. If the cleft constituent is a wh-phrase, it further raises to the matrix clause, which explains the properties that simple and cleft wh-questions share. These two types of wh-questions however differ in one important respect. Object marginalization is possible in the former but not in the latter type of wh-questions. This is due to the complex syntax-prosody interface, which makes simple wh-questions special among A'-constructions in Italian.

References

Antinucci, Francesco & Guglielmo Cinque. 1977. Sull'ordine delle parole in italiano: L'emarginazione. *Studi di grammatica italiana* 6. 121–146.
Belletti, Adriana. 2001. Inversion as focalization. In Afkte Hulk & Jean-Yves Pollock (eds.), *Subject inversion in Romance and the theory of Universal Grammar*, 60–90. New York: Oxford University Press.
Belletti, Adriana. 2004. Aspects of the low IP area. In Luigi Rizzi (ed.), *The structure of CP and IP. The Cartography of syntactic structures, Volume 2*, 16–51. New York: Oxford University Press.
Belletti, Adriana. 2009. *Structures and strategies*. London: Routledge.
Belletti, Adriana. 2012. Revisiting the CP of clefts. In Günther Grewendorf & Thomas Ede Zimmermann (eds.), *Discourse and grammar. From sentence types to lexical categories*, 91–114. Berlin/ Boston: De Gruyter Mouton.
Belletti, Adriana. 2015. The focus map of clefts. In Ur Shlonsky (ed.), *Beyond functional sequence*, 42–59. Oxford/New York: Oxford University Press.
Bianchi, Valentina, Giuliano Bocci & Silvio Cruschina. 2018. Syntactic and prosodic effects of long-distance wh-movement in Italian. *Journal of Italian Linguistics* 30. 59–78.
Bocci, Giuliano. 2013. *The syntax-prosody interface. A cartographic perspective with evidence from Italian*. Amsterdam/Philadelphia: Benjamins.
Bocci, Giuliano & Cinzia Avesani. 2015. Can the metrical structure of Italian motivate focus fronting? In Ur Shlonsky (ed.), *Beyond functional sequence*, 23–41. Oxford/New York: Oxford University Press.
Bocci, Giuliano & Lucia Pozzan. 2014. Questions (and experimental answers) about Italian subjects. In Carla Contemori & Lena Dal Pozzo (eds.), *Inquiries into linguistic theory and language acquisition. Papers offered to Adriana Belletti*, 28–44. Siena: CISCL Press.
Bocci, Giuliano, Mamoru Saito, & Luigi Rizzi. 2018. On the incompatibility of wh and focus. *Gengo Kenkyu. Journal of the Linguistic Society of Japan* 154. 29–51.
Bocci, Giuliano, Valentina Bianchi & Silvio Cruschina. 2020. Focus in *wh*-questions. Evidence from Italian. *Natural Language and Linguistic Theory* 39. 405–455.
Bonan, Caterina. 2017. Sé or c'est? On the cartography of clefts. *GG@G (Generative Grammar in Geneva)* X. 131–151. https://doi.org/10.13097/cjg3-tfud.

Calabrese, Andrea. 1982. Alcune ipotesi sulla struttura informazionale della frase in italiano e sul suo rapporto con la struttura fonologica. *Rivista di grammatica generativa* 13. 489–526.

Cardinaletti, Anna. 2001. A second thought on emarginazione: Destressing vs. right dislocation. In Guglielmo Cinque & Giampaolo Salvi (eds.), *Current studies in Italian syntax. Essays offered to Lorenzo Renzi*, 117–135. Amsterdam: Elsevier.

Cardinaletti, Anna. 2002. Against optional and zero clitics. Right dislocation vs. marginalization. *Studia Linguistica* 56. 29–57.

Cardinaletti, Anna. 2007. Subjects and wh-questions. Some new generalizations. In José Camacho, Nydia Flores-Ferrán, Liliana Sánchez, Viviane Déprez & María José Cabrera (eds.), *Romance Linguistics 2006: Selected papers from the 36th Linguistic Symposium on Romance Languages (LSRL)*, 57–79. Amsterdam/Philadelphia: John Benjamins.

Cardinaletti, Anna. 2009. On a (wh-)moved Topic in Italian, compared to Germanic. In Artemis Alexiadou, Jorge Hankamer, Thomas McFadden, Justin Nuger & Florian Schäfer (eds.), *Advances in comparative Germanic syntax*, 3–40. Amsterdam/Philadelphia: Benjamins.

Cardinaletti, Anna. 2018. On different types of postverbal subjects in Italian. *Italian Journal of Linguistics* 30. 79–106.

Cardinaletti, Anna. 2021. The position of subjects in Germanic and Romance questions. In Christine Meklenborg & Sam Wolfe (eds.), *Continuity and variation in Germanic and Romance*, 44–69. Oxford: Oxford University Press.

Cruschina, Silvio. 2015. Some notes on clefting and fronting. In Elisa Di Domenico, Cornelia Hamann & Simona Matteini (eds.), *Structures, strategies, and beyond*, 181–208. Amsterdam/Philadelphia: John Benjamins.

Frascarelli, Mara. 1996. *L'interfaccia sintassi-fonologia nelle costruzioni di focalizzazione e topicalizzazione dell'italiano*. Rome: University of Roma Tre PhD dissertation.

Frascarelli, Mara & Francesca Ramaglia. 2013. (Pseudo) clefts at the syntax-prosody-discourse interface. In Katharina Hartmann & Tonjes Veenstra (eds.), *Cleft structures*, 97–138. Amsterdam/Philadelphia: John Benjamins.

Haegeman, Liliane, André Meinunger & Aleksandra Vercauteren. 2015. The syntax of it-clefts and the left periphery of the clause. In Ur Shlonsky (ed.), *Beyond functional sequence*, 73–90. Oxford/New York: Oxford University Press.

Marotta, Giovanna. 2001. I toni accentuali nelle interrogative aperte (wh-) dell'italiano di Lucca. In Camilla Bettoni, Antonio Zampolli & Daniela Zorzi (eds.), *Atti del II congresso di studi dell'Associazione Italiana di Linguistica Applicata*, 175–194. Perugia: Guerra Edizioni.

Rizzi, Luigi. 1996. Residual Verb-second and the Wh-criterion. In Adriana Belletti & Luigi Rizzi (eds.), *Parameters and functional heads. Essays in comparative syntax*, 63–90. Oxford: Oxford University Press.

Rizzi, Luigi. 1997. The fine structure of the left periphery. In Liliane Haegeman (ed.), *Elements of grammar*, 281–337. Dordrecht: Kluwer.

Rizzi, Luigi. 2001. On the position "Int(errogative)" in the left periphery of the clause. In Guglielmo Cinque & Giampaolo Salvi (eds.), *Current studies in Italian syntax. Essays offered to Lorenzo Renzi*, 287–296. Amsterdam: Elsevier.

Rizzi, Luigi. 2010. Some consequences of criterial freezing. In Peter Svenonius (ed.), *Functional structure from top to toe*, 19–54. Oxford/New York: Oxford University Press.

Rizzi, Luigi. 2018. Intervention effects in grammar and language acquisition. *Probus* 30(2). 339–367.

Shlonsky, Ur. 2012. Notes on wh- in situ in French. In Laura Brugè, Anna Cardinaletti, Giuliana Giusti, Nicola Munaro & Cecilia Poletto (eds.), *Functional heads*, 242–252. Oxford/New York: Oxford University Press.

Sabrina Bertollo
2 What is it that requires or constrains clefts? (Dis)Favouring factors for clefting in Germanic and Romance

Abstract: The behaviour of languages with respect to cleft sentences is subject to a great degree of variation. On the one hand there are Romance languages such as some dialects of the Veneto (Italy) in which clefting is the only syntactic strategy to form subject questions (Poletto and Vanelli 1997); on the other languages such as Standard German strongly constrain the availability of clefts (Durrell 2002: 479; Fischer 2009). The aim of the present contribution is to shed some light on the factors which favour clefting and those which inhibit it. On the basis of a thorough analysis of linguistic microvariation observed in Venetan varieties, it will be shown that even in the domain of mandatory clefting some restrictions apply, which enable us to draw a scale for the obligatoriness of clefting depending on the nature of the subject and on its relationship with the lexical verb. On the opposite pole, starting from German data, we will address the extent to which Verb Second, the lack of a specialised preverbal position for the subject, information structure and the availability of other pragmatic strategies may play a role in limiting cleft formation, especially for non-subject constituents. Furthermore, we will consider whether clause-type correlates with the availability of clefting and, more specifically, if wh-questions constitute a vulnerability point for clefting to enter grammatical systems. In this respect a closer look at earlier stages of English (Los 2009) and further Germanic languages such a Norwegian – which, despite being a Verb Second language, makes extensive use of clefts (Gundel 2006; Westergaard, Vangsnes and Lohndal 2017) – will offer some interesting insights to a better understanding of the factors at play.

Keywords: cleft sentences, German(ic), Romance, questions, Verb Second, subject

1 Introduction

Despite long-standing research on their nature, syntactic structure and pragmatic function, cleft sentences still raise a number of intriguing questions which are far

---

Sabrina Bertollo, University of Verona, e-mail: sabrina.bertollo@univr.it

https://doi.org/10.1515/9783110734140-003

from being definitively resolved. One reason for this is their great variability in the languages of the world, which makes it challenging to propose a unified theory which effectively accounts for the different syntactic behaviours of this construction. The widely acknowledged term *cleft* (from the verb *to cleave*) dates back to Jespersen (1937), who first used it to refer to the fact that this kind of clause is split into two parts, as can be seen in (1):

(1) It's Mary who/that broke the window.

Even providing a universally valid definition for clefts, which is not theory-biased, is not trivial. Lambrecht (2001: 466), who built upon Jespersen (1937), defined clefts as "a complex sentence structure consisting of a matrix clause headed by a copula and a relative or relative-like clause whose relativized item is coindexed with the predicative argument of the copula". We will provisionally adopt his definition (see section 2 for critical discussion on the syntactic structure of clefts).

Since theoretical accounts for clefts have varied over time and are still a matter of debate, some of the most influential proposals will be presented and discussed. The aim of this brief review, which will be sketched in section 2, is to address significant aspects of the syntactic derivation, which can be built upon to deal with cleft patterns found in different languages. Following a theoretical background for the syntactic analysis of clefts, section 3 outlines different language typologies which will be explored to understand the factors which favour or disfavour cleft sentence formation. In fact, cross-linguistically it can be observed that languages vary with respect to their clefting behaviour. Some languages such as English can make extensive use of clefts as a pragmatic device, but there are no contexts in which clefts are mandatory: clefting competes with other possible focalization strategies and its use is never required by the syntax as the sole instrument to give rise to a certain clause type. As can be seen from the example in (2), an unmarked sentence (2a) can be rephrased by means of a cleft sentence to focalize a constituent. In the case of (2b) the subject *Joe* is focalized and becomes part of the copular sentence:

(2) a. Joe lives in Brazil
     b. It's Joe who lives in Brazil.

However, this is not the only possible pattern for clefts: languages such as some dialects of the Veneto (North-Eastern Italy) need clefts as a syntactic device to build subject questions (Poletto and Vanelli 1997), the non-cleft counterpart being ruled out. In these varieties, which will be extensively discussed in this article, the question formed by means of a cleft is pragmatically unmarked, as can be seen in

(3), although using clefts for pragmatic purposes is not excluded as in (4) in which a constituent (*Gianni*) is focalized:

(3)   Chi   zé   che   abita   in   Brasile?
       Who   is   that   lives   in   Brazil
       'Who lives in Brazil?'
       (Dialect of Cittadella, Padua)

(4)   Zé   Gianni   che   no   magna   pastasuta
       is   Gianni   that   not   eats   pasta
       'It's Gianni who doesn't eat pasta.'
       (Dialect of Cittadella, Padua)

There are also languages such as Standard German which only allow for limited clefting. As Durrell (2002: 479) points out "with the exception of the type 'Er war es, der mich davon abhielt' [. . .], cleft sentence constructions sound unnatural in German and should be avoided". Fischer (2009) maintains that cleft sentences are much more frequent in English than in German and are often sacrificed in the translations from English into German for the sake of stylistic appropriateness and are replaced by other focusing devices.

     Against this background, different language typologies will be considered in more detail to explore the factors which affect the availability of clefting. Since microvariation is a magnifying lens for the phenomenon to be researched, section 4 draws a fine-grained picture of the Venetan varieties which require clefts for syntactic purposes. We will investigate the extent to which the clause type (+/– declarative) plays a role in requiring clefting and whether the syntactic function of the clefted constituent is a determining factor in the use of clefts. Moreover, as subjects differ depending on the lexical verb they are (thematically) selected by, further aspects such as the position in which the subject is base generated and its relationship with the verb and other possible arguments will be considered. Section 5 focuses on the factors which inhibit clefting in Standard German. In this case, the syntactic function of clefted constituents will be discussed to check whether there is a syntactic correspondence between compulsory clefting and residual clefting possibilities. Moreover, the circumstances which constrain clefting are considered together with potentially competing strategies and alternative focalization devices. In addition, the possibility will be explored that Verb Second and an unspecialised preverbal position may play a role in disfavouring clefting. Some suggestive evidence comes from the information structural change which emerged in Middle English when it lost Verb Second (section 6.1). Finally, section 6.2 deals with apparently puzzling languages such as Norwegian, which is definitely not hostile to clefting despite being a Verb Second language. A closer look at the types of sentences in which clefts can be observed and the analysis of question formation in some Norwegian dialects which are losing Verb Second (Lie 1992; Westergaard, Vangsnes and Lohndal 2017) will offer some interesting insights into determining the rationale behind the use or non-use of clefts. Some concluding remarks and some open questions to be investigated in future research close the paper.

2 Theoretical background: The syntax of cleft sentences

2.1 Specificational and expletive accounts

As a short section cannot do justice to the great deal of literature on clefts, this section will be limited to some influential accounts proposed for this construction. Research on clefts has proceeded from two different perspectives: on the one hand clefts have been treated as paralleling specificational copular sentences;[1] on the other, they have been considered semantically parallel to sentences containing focus fronting. Reeve (2011), who provides a critical overview of the state of the art, labelled the former approach *specificational*. Analyses along these lines have been proposed by Akmajian (1970), Gundel (1977) and Percus (1997). Despite the individual differences which we will not delve into here, all specificational accounts assume a transformational relation between clefts and pseudo-clefts. In other words, (5b) is claimed to be derivationally obtained from (5a). This presupposes that the cleft construction is bi-clausal.

(5)   a.   It's Mary that he calls in the end.
          b.   Who he calls in the end is Mary.

The second set of accounts, which have been labelled *expletive* by Reeve (2011) do not necessarily imply such a relation, but they share the idea that the copula and the expletive pronouns are semantically vacuous and the cleft sentence parallels focus fronting. In all these proposals (Chomsky 1977, Kayne 1994, Meinunger 1998, a.o) the focused constituent is generated within the cleft clause and then moves to its focus position. In particular, Chomsky (1977) proposed that the copula is the

---

[1] The nature and structure of copular sentences have been abundantly dealt with in the literature, see a.o Declerk (1988), Moro (1997), Heycock and Kroch (2002), den Dikken (2006), Heycock (2012).

head of VP which governs a S" node (a CP in modern terms), which symmetrically develops into one NP containing the focus and one adjoined S' (TP), which hosts the subordinate clause from which the focused constituent has started its movement, as if it were a wh- item. Some of these expletive approaches are bi-clausal, other monoclausal, i.e., bi-clausal structures which have become monoclausal. The first radically monoclausal analysis of clefts was proposed by Meinunger (1998). He proposes that the expletive is placed in the Specifier of TopicP, and the copula occupies the head of the same projection, while the clefted constituent targets the Specifier of FocusP. A head in a low portion of the left periphery hosts the complementizer that introduces the cleft clause within which the clefted constituent is generated.

2.2 Third-way proposals for the syntactic derivation of clefts

Over the last fifteen years in particular, "third-way proposals" have been outlined (Belletti 2005, 2015; Frascarelli and Ramaglia 2009, 2013; Reeve 2011; Haegeman, Meinunger and Vercauteren 2013; Pinelli, Poletto and Avesani 2020 a.o.). These are neither completely specificational – in that they do not claim that cleft sentences are transformationally derived from pseudo-clefts – nor expletive, as they attribute a semantic and syntactic function to both the "expletive"[2] and the copula. Rather, the various proposals which reject transformational correspondences and recognise a correlation between focusing and clefting, differ in the way they derive the (dis)continuity which can be observed between the matrix clause and the cleft.

Interestingly, though dispreferred, monoclausal approaches have not been abandoned. Frascarelli and Ramaglia (2009, 2013) want to preserve the similarity between focus and clefts and their isomorphism in the sense that fronted foci and clefted constituents are assumed to target the same landing site. They argue for a monoclausal structure of clefts[3] in which the clefted constituent is generated within a small clause and is claimed to be its predicate, while the subject is *it* (6):

---

2 Reeve (2011) a.o. provides evidence for the semi-argumental status of the pronoun of clefts. One of the relevant cues for the fact that this pronoun is not an expletive is provided by its obligatoriness in Germanic Verb Second languages.
3 Haegeman, Meinunger and Vercauteren (2013) label the analysis by Frascarelli and Ramaglia (2009) as monoclausal although it is technically bi-clausal because the two domains are intertwined.

(6) [IP copula [SC it [NP me]]]⁴

The small clause is licensed by the copula, which merely acts as a linker (den Dikken, 2006). The subject of the small clause moves to the subject position in TP. The subordinate clause instead is base generated in the Specifier of TopicP in CP. The cleft clause is actually a free relative clause, ultimately a DP, containing a small clause in which there is a silent head, which is labelled as *pro*, and the relative clause (7):

(7) [DP [SC [NP pro] [CP that you saw]]]

Thanks to successive leftward movements, all items in the IP layer reach the left periphery of the clause. As pointed out by Haegeman, Meinunger and Vercauteren (2013), this analysis proves to be problematic in various respects, since it does not consider possible locality restrictions and intervention effects. Furthermore, it does not account for the asymmetries between focus fronting and clefts. For instance, main clause phenomena are expected to be possible if the structure is monoclausal, moreover adverbial clauses and complements of factive verbs can be clefted but cannot be fronted (ibidem).⁵ For the purposes of this article, it is also noteworthy that this account does not provide room for fronted clefted constituents, as is the case for wh-questions.⁶ Assuming this account would imply that wh- in regular questions targets a different position to the wh- in clefted questions. In fact, it is assumed that the string *copula + it* is hosted by a Topic position, which is higher than FocP, which is assumed to be hosting wh-. This is not desirable, as it is not supported by semantic or interpretative evidence.

Frascarelli and Ramaglia's (2009, 2013) monoclausal account is based on English and can be adapted to Italian, especially with reference to *pro*-drop. Nonetheless, some elements lead us to believe that biclausal accounts are to be preferred: (i) cyclic remnant movements potentially cause intervention effects; (ii) the outlined filling of the left periphery is problematic, (iii) a formally monoclausal analysis is neither indispensable nor economical,⁷ (iv) inverse clefts such as

---

4 Examples (6) and (7) are cited after Haegeman, Meinunger and Vercauteren (2013: 8).
5 For further discussion on the syntactic asymmetries between clefts and focus see also Pinelli, Poletto and Avesani (2020) who tested parasitic gaps, weak crossover and anaphoric binding. They also showed that these differences do not surface in the prosody.
6 Also this point was already made by Haegeman, Meinunger and Vercauteren (2013).
7 As underlined by Haegeman, Meinunger and Vercauteren (2013) the same drawbacks are shared by all monoclausal analyses, at least for *it*-clefts.

wh-question clefts do not fit into the picture and need to be incorporated in future developments.

Within the cartographic approach, a further proposal for the internal syntax of clefts was outlined by Belletti (2015). She refined some of her previous analyses, arguing for a bi-clausal approach. The core assumptions of her proposal are: (i) the presence of two distinct focus positions, i.e., low vP peripheral Focus (new Information) and High Left Peripheral Focus (contrastive, corrective); (ii) the crucial role played by the copula both to make the different focus positions available and to select a CP as its sentential complement, which is actually a small clause (see den Dikken 2006 and reference cited therein).

With respect to (i), the fact that in Italian New Information Focus appears after the verb, supports the idea that it is low in the structure, as can be seen in (8):

(8) Chi   ha   vinto   la   partita? Ha   vinto   il
    who   has   won-PTCP   the   match   has   won-PTCP   the
    Manchester United
    Manchester United
    'Who won the match? Manchester United won.'

Moreover, a subject cleft can serve as an answer for the same question. On the contrary, an object cleft cannot express new information, since it is corrective and presupposes a context to be contrasted. Unlike new information, contrastive focus is licensed in the left periphery of the clause (9):

(9) La   macchina   mi   hanno   rubato!   (non la bici)
    the   car   me-DAT   have-PRS-3PL   stolen   not the bike
    'They stole my car! (not my bike)'

Belletti (2015: 44) explicitly bases her analysis on the assumption that "subject clefts can express focus of new information", while "object/non-subject clefts can only express corrective/contrastive focus". If we consider that subject clefts can also serve as corrective focus provided that the right context is given, it can be concluded that "subject clefts have one interpretative option more" (ibidem: 46).

As for (ii), the availability of focus projections is due to the selectional properties of the copula, i.e., the copula selects for a reduced CP that lacks the higher focus projection associated with contrastive focus. The structure is represented in (10):[8]

---

8 PredP indicates a relation of predication within the small clause.

(10) be [~~ForceP~~ ..... [~~TopP~~ [$_{FocP}$ Foc [$_{PredP}$ Pred ... [$_{FinP}$che [$_{TP}$ .....

(Belletti 2015: 44, ex. 2)

The result of assuming different focus projections depending on the pragmatic function of the clefted constituent (new information *vs.* correction/contrast) is that two different syntactic derivations have to be proposed:

(11) (7) a Subject clefts, new information

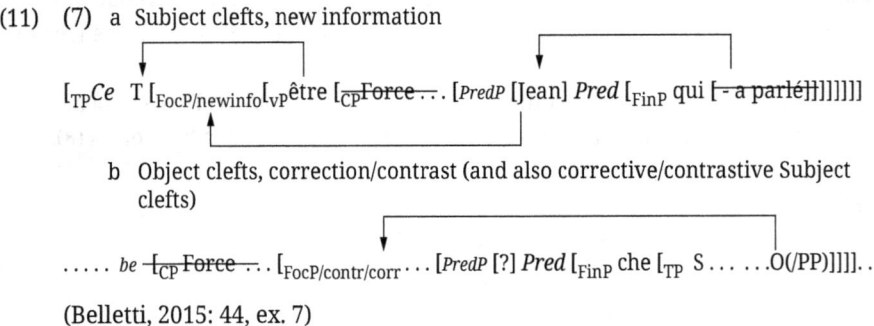

[$_{TP}$*Ce* T [$_{FocP/newinfo}$[$_{vP}$être [~~CP Force~~ ... [$_{PredP}$ [Jean] *Pred* [$_{FinP}$ qui [~~a parlé~~]]]]]

    b Object clefts, correction/contrast (and also corrective/contrastive Subject clefts)

..... *be* [~~CP Force~~ ... [$_{FocP/contr/corr}$ ... [*PredP* [?] *Pred* [$_{FinP}$ che [$_{TP}$ S ...... O(/PP)]]]]..

(Belletti, 2015: 44, ex. 7)

The object cannot cross over the subject, since it would give rise to a strict violation of Relativized Minimality (Rizzi, 1990 and much subsequent work).[9] This is also claimed to explain why an object cleft cannot serve as new information. Further movement is required to account for inverted clefts and to circumvent possible violations of locality. First the clausal predicate FinP has to be extraposed, subsequently the remnant has to move.

The account proposed by Belletti (2015) based on Italian and French is problematic in many respects. For instance, it does not take into account different information structures cross-linguistically. The availability of an unspecified preverbal position as in Verb Second languages, but also rigid non pro-drop languages like English in which the low left periphery is unavailable for new information focus, require the syntactic derivation proposed by Belletti to be re-worked. This goes beyond the goals of this article. Nevertheless, accounting for the factors which favour and disfavour clefting may help shed new light on this construction and provide insights on its internal structure for future research. For the present article, the details of the syntactic derivation are not crucial to investigate the requirements and constraints on clefts.

---

9 Notice that the constraint could be reformulated in terms of Chomsky (2005)'s Minimal Link Condition. See Belletti (2015: 47).

3 The typological distribution of clefts

3.1 Language attitudes towards clefting

On the basis of cross-linguistic observations it can be maintained that clefts vary in many respects: not only in structure, use and interpretation (Hartmann and Veenstra 2013) but crucially also in their availability. In this light, languages can be classified on a scale depending on their attitudes towards clefting. On the top of the scale we find "cleft-friendly languages", i.e., languages which use clefts not only for pragmatic purposes, but also as a syntactic tool, especially to build subject questions. This is typical for many Bantu languages that employ clefts as one of the main focusing devices, because they have a strong constraint against preverbal focus (Lafkioui, Nshemezimana and Bostoen 2016 on Kirundi; Sabel and Zeller 2006 on Nguni). The ban on a focal position in front of the verb also implies that fronted wh- questions are excluded. Sabel and Zeller (2006) deal with clefts in Zulu and describe them as an obligatory strategy for *ex situ* wh-questions to be introduced. Wolof, which belongs to the Niger-Congo language family, uses cleft sentences as the canonical means of forming wh-questions (Torrence 2013). Another case in point is Irish, a VSO language that has a very rich cleft system and a constraint on wh-items sitting alone in front of the verb. As a result, it needs clefts to build well-formed wh-questions. According to Sulger (2009: 574) this is due to the necessity to separate new information (the focused wh-) and given information (the remaining cleft clause). The extensive use of clefts for pragmatic and syntactic purposes is not limited to the above-mentioned linguistic systems: North-Eastern Italian dialects[10] are a window into the phenomenon of clefting, since their microvariation enables us to outline a fine-grained analysis of the different degrees of obligatoriness of clefts in various syntactic contexts. For this reason, these Romance varieties, which definitely deserve the label "cleft-friendly languages", will constitute our object of investigation to detect the factors which favour (or require) clefting (section 4).

If the domain of mandatory clefting represents the top of the scale in the language typology we are sketching based on the attitudes towards this construction, languages such as Standard Italian, English and French can be collocated in the middle of the scale, since clefting is available but never compulsory (neither for the syntax nor at a pragmatic level) and competes with other focusing strategies.

---

[10] It has to be noted that within the landscape of Italian dialects, the phenomenon is not limited to the Northern varieties. Neapolitan also requires clefts to form certain kinds of wh-questions, but it will not be further considered here (for discussion, see Bertollo 2014).

We will label this type "cleft-agnostic languages", since they are indifferent to the construction: they can make use of it, but it is not indispensable. Being in this middle field, these types of languages do not offer insightful contributions to better understand the constraints on or the favouring factors for clefting. The availability of the structure and the possibility to resort to other competing focalization strategies blur the picture, so that the behaviour of these languages is not crucial to shed light on the mechanisms under investigation.

At the bottom of the scale are "cleft-reluctant languages", i.e., languages in which the structure is available but the restrictions on it are very strict. Languages of this type include Sicilian[11] (Cruschina 2015), Old English (Los, 2009), and Standard German, in which the use of clefts is possible, but, as has been mentioned in section 1, subject to many constraints (Lambrecht 2001), which range from actual syntactic impossibility to form a cleft, to sentences which are not strictly ill-formed but also not fully accepted by native speakers (Gundel 2006). Because of the puzzling picture offered by German, which also deserves an in-depth investigation on the possible role played by Verb Second and information structure in inhibiting clefting, this language will be the starting point for the reflections on the factors which strongly reduce the availability of this construction (see section 5).

3.2 Accessibility Hierarchy, relativization, processing and clefting

Before delving into the reasons which make clefts (un)available, it is worth recalling some core notions concerning relativization, and therefore clefting,[12] which are expected to hold cross-linguistically, regardless of the language typology which has been drawn in the previous section. Keenan and Comrie's Accessibility Hierarchy

---

11 In Romance languages it is not very common to find instances of cleft-reluctant languages. As will be discussed in the next sections, the factors which inhibit clefts in Sicilian are possibly compatible with the picture we will sketch on the basis of German.
12 Following influential proposals by Schachter (1973), Hedberg (2000), Reeve (2011) a.o. we assume that the cleft clause is syntactically a relative clause, although there exist cleft constructions in which this seems not to be the case, like in the German colloquial sentence "Es ist mit mir, dass Sie ein Problem haben" literally: "It's with me that you have a problem", in which *dass* is not a relativizer but a declarative complementizer (see Bertollo 2014: 226). However, for these potentially problematic cases which resemble declaratives, it can be argued that complementation is ultimately an instance of relativization (Kayne, 2021). Manzini and Roussou (2021) refine previous proposals in this respect and cite the different implementations of this hypothesis: "modification of a null head (Arsenijevic 2009, Kayne 2010) or a 'content argument' (Kratzer 2006, Moulton 2015), OR a headless relative (Manzini 2010)".

(1977) predicts that limitations apply to the syntactic positions which can be relativized and that a relativization strategy must apply to a continuous segment of the Accessibility Hierarchy.[13] Starting from the left, the syntactic positions are gradually less accessible to relativization:

Subject > Direct Object > Indirect Object > Oblique > Genitive > Object of Comparison

The inherent naturalness of subject relativization is further corroborated by studies on language acquisition (Guasti 2002; Friedmann, Belletti and Rizzi 2009; Adani 2012, a.o.), which consistently show that relative clauses on the subject are easier to process than all other relatives and emerge earlier in language acquisition. This proves to be true both for typical populations and for populations with specific language impairment and dyslexia, who take longer to process object relatives and are less accurate, while subject relatives are well comprehended by all groups. Interestingly, typically developing and atypical populations find it easier to process passive subject relative clauses than object relatives (Arosio et al. 2017). A similar subject-object asymmetry can be argued for in the acquisition of A-bar movement constructions in general, since it can be observed that the movement of objects to an A-bar position is more difficult than the movement of subjects. In fact, the same effects largely investigated for relatives are reported (though to a lesser extent) for wh-questions (Guasti, Branchini and Arosio 2012; Philip et al. 2002). As for clefts, while acquisitional data are scarcer, experimental studies have nevertheless reported increased parsing difficulties for objects, with shorter reading time for subject clefts (Aravind, Hackl and Wexler 2017; Chesi and Canal 2019; Del Puppo 2016). Samo and Merlo (2021) confirm the same asymmetry on the basis of quantitative studies conducted on language corpora. They attribute these differences to intervention effects (Rizzi 2018) taking place for objects and not for subjects. Furthermore, parsing difficulties are shown to increase with the length of the filler gap dependency calculated in terms of the intervening lexical material (Lewis, Vasishth and Van Dyke 2006).

---

13 The Accessibility Hierarchy is the result of evidence gathered through empirical data coming from more than fifty languages. Keenan and Comrie (1977: 63) suggest that the validity of the hierarchy can be extended to other phenomena to explain "the distribution of advancement processes such as passives". It is therefore not necessarily limited to relative clauses. Relatively little attention in the literature has been devoted to the issue of whether the Accessibility Hierarchy can be used for clefts. Luo (1994) was one of the first attempts to investigate 'cleftability' in terms of the Accessibility Hierarchy. His work confirmed the validity of this hierarchy for clefts, which he labelled "Cleftability Hierarchy".

4 Cleft-friendly languages: Mandatory clefting in the Venetan dialects

4.1 Wh- question formation strategies and methodological approach

Clefting is never mandatory in any Venetan dialect as a focusing device – although it is available – while it may be compulsory to form unmarked main interrogative clauses. As has been pointed out in the previous literature (Poletto and Vanelli 1997: 110 a.o.), four different strategies can be described for Northern Italian varieties to form wh- questions: (a) subject-clitic inversion, (b) *in situness*, (c) double introducer, i.e., the coexistence of a wh- pronoun and a complementizer, (d) cleft sentences. We restrict our field of investigation to the Venetan varieties, but all these possibilities are illustrated in (12).[14]

(12) a. Cossa fa-i?
     what   do-PRS.3PL-they
     Campagnola (Padua)
  b. Fa-li   che?
     do-PRS.3PL-they   what
     Chies D'Alpago (Belluno)
  c. Cossa che   i   fa?
     what   that they do-PRS.3PL
     Venezia
  d. Cossa xe   che   i   fa?
     what   is   that they do-PRS.3PL
     Rovigo
     'What do they do?'

The first strategy (a) is the default, although it is not shared with Standard Italian, which does not have subject clitics (Manzini and Savoia 2011). The second one (b) is typical for some Trevisan and Bellunese dialects and has been extensively described (Munaro 1999; Bonan 2019, 2021 a.o.).[15] The third, i.e., the doubly filled

---

14 All the examples provided in (12) come from the ASIt database, which is freely available without registration at the following website: http://svrims2.dei.unipd.it:8080/asit-maldura/pages/search.jsp (accessed 11 April 2022). This question-item is contained in questionnaire 2, position 94.
15 These first two strategies will not be discussed, because they do not contribute to refine the picture of the factors favouring clefting.

complementizer (c) is interesting because in regional substandard Italian it is typical only for embedded interrogatives, whereas it is impossible for main interrogatives. Moreover, this strategy shares some features with clefting and in some varieties directly competes with it. If we now concentrate on the fourth strategy, i.e., clefting (d), Poletto and Vanelli (1997), in their overview of the interrogatives in Northern Italy, already highlighted an asymmetry between the use of mandatory clefts for subject and object questions. In line with the Accessibility Hierarchy and the acquisitional data described in the previous section,[16] they report that if a variety requires clefting for object questions, it requires clefting for the subject as well, but the reverse is not true. This means it may be the case that one variety forms object questions by inverting the verb and the clitic subject while it requires a cleft to form a subject question.

This claim, which is both theoretically and empirically grounded, will be checked against a set of data, firstly to further confirm whether this generalization regarding an asymmetry between subject and object holds as expected, and secondly to have a rough proportion of the number of Venetan varieties which require clefts for objects compared to those which only require it for subjects.[17]

The corpus on which the analysis of the Venetan data is based is ASIt (*Atlante Sintattico dell'Italia Settentrionale*), a collection of dialectal data gathered from written questionnaires.[18] For the purposes of the present research, stimulus sentences, which are representative for the phenomenon under consideration were selected and the corresponding translations in all the collected varieties were manually pulled down. The selected input sentences were translated in nearly all the questionnaires of the Venetan area recorded in ASIt. In case one locality had more than one informant, only one questionnaire has been considered provided that the translations were syntactically homogeneous. In case of discrepancies, the different answers were considered instances of microvariation or competing strategies and are therefore counted as separate. The exclusion of multiple identical questionnaires for the same locality is due to not wanting to distort the general view on the Venetan varieties because of unbalanced data. Although the

---

16 The authors do not mention the Accessibility Hierarchy, which was available at the time, nor acquisitional studies, which, instead flourished only later.
17 Only argumental questions will be considered.
18 The written questionnaires contain translation tasks with stimulus sentences in Italian. Despite the well-known drawbacks of administering dialectal questionnaires with stimuli in a Standard language (Cornips and Poletto 2005, Kasper 2013), it can be argued that the possible negative effects are in this case reduced or even obviated by the fact that the task might be expected to underestimate the contexts in which a cleft is used, as an unmarked question in Italian is never clefted. We can therefore assume that spontaneous clefting is genuine and not induced by the input.

investigation is qualitative in nature, some quantitative tendencies will be drawn. The latter are not claimed to be statistically accurate, since the collected data would need to be further refined and normalized. Nevertheless, the tendencies which emerge are clear enough to outline certain patterns. Macro-tendencies will also constitute the starting point for a subsequent in-depth analysis of syntactic microvariation patterns, which will enable us to better outline the implicational scale in the mandatory use of clefting and to account for possible competing strategies used to circumvent undesired syntactic configurations.

4.2 Questioning an internal argument

Even though diverse input sentences were considered to check that the patterns observed for one verb type were consistent and reliable, for the sake of clarity, in the following sections one example sentence is provided to illustrate each pattern. One representative sentence which has been selected in the ASIt questionnaire to check whether an object question requires clefting in the Venetan varieties is given in (13):

(13) (E io) cosa mangio?
 and I what eat-PRS.1SG
 '(And I) what am I going to eat?'

In a sample of 138 questionnaires, 89% form the question by regularly positioning the lexical verb immediately after the wh-element, regardless of whether the variety is pro-drop or not. The most common translation for (13) is given in (14):

(14) (E mi) cossa magno?
 and I what eat-PRS.1SG
 '(And I) what am I going to eat?'
 Cittadella (Padua)

Less than 4% of the Venetan varieties require a cleft (five localities). A similar low incidence is attested for other competing strategies such as wh- + complementizer. As hypothesized, object questions prove not to be a privileged environment for mandatory clefts to appear, provided that they can be used to form echo-questions or for other pragmatic purposes. Once it has been shown that objects do not require clefting, it is worth investigating whether all subject questions behave alike with respect to mandatory clefting, or if different subjects may affect clefting. The first research question in this respect is whether unaccusativity (Perlmutter 1978) may play a role. In other words, do internal arguments like the subject of unaccusatives pattern with other internal arguments, like objects, which are assigned accusative case, or do they behave like external arguments, with which they share the property of being a subject? To address this issue, input sentences were selected in which the wh-element bears the +animate feature[19] and the verb is unaccusative. Here is an example (15):[20]

(15) Chi   viene   al   posto   tuo?
     Who   comes   at   place   your(2.SG)
     'Who is coming in your place?'

Our data show that subjects of unaccusatives scarcely require clefts and therefore pattern with objects. Although the preference for a non-cleft strategy is confirmed, the number of clefts used to question the subject of unaccusatives is higher compared to objects: 22% of the Venetan dialects require a cleft in this context, as is the case in Arsiero (Vicenza) (16b), while it was scarcely 4% for "true objects". The majority (78%), as exemplified in (16a) by the dialect of Agugliaro (Vicenza), use the strategy of Standard Italian, i.e., wh- + verb:

(16) a. Chi   vien   al   to   posto?
        Who   comes   at   your   place
        Agugliaro (Vicenza)
     b. Chi   sé   che   vien   al   to   posto?
        Who   is   that   comes   at   your   place?
        Arsiero (Vicenza)

According to Levin and Rappaport (1995),[21] the subject of unaccusatives shares the semantic and syntactic properties of direct objects. This may explain why it patterns with objects and not with other subjects in terms of requiring clefting. Moreover, differently from other lexical verbs, unaccusatives lack the vP-layer and do not have an external argument. Our data suggest that subjecthood plays a role, otherwise we could not account for the increase in the number of com-

---

19 The choice to consider only subject questions in which the wh-element bears the +animate feature is due to the fact that it is still debated in the literature whether animacy can play a role in (dis)favouring the compulsory use of clefts. It is also still unclear whether animacy can affect the processing of a subject relative clause. Considering only who-questions avoids the risk of the potentially different properties of inanimate subjects blurring the picture.
20 The input sentence is recorded in the ASIt questionnaire 2, position 22.
21 See also Perlmutter (1978) and Burzio (1986).

pulsory clefts, but this is not the only reason for the evident asymmetry between subjects and objects consistently reported in the literature. Other factors such as the thematic role borne by the subject and the base generation site are also involved.

4.3 Do all subject questions trigger clefting to the same proportion?

We will now explore whether transitive and unergative verbs mark a change in the strategy which is used when their subject is questioned, or whether similar results are obtained for all subjects. To get a fine-grained picture unergatives and transitives were checked separately, as intransitivity is an element of difference between the two classes that may potentially impact on the results.

One input sentence for unergatives is (17):[22]

(17) Chi   piange   di là?
     Who   cries   down-there?
     'Who is crying down there?'

A striking difference emerges for subject questions in which the wh-element is selected by an unergative verb with respect to what has been observed both for objects and unaccusatives. Only 23% of the dialects can form the question without using a cleft: it was exactly the opposite for unaccusatives. In 77% of the questionnaires question formation with unergatives requires a cleft. The pattern is exemplified in (18):

(18) Chi   sé   che   pianse   de là?
     Who   is   that cries   down-there?
     Arsiero (Vicenza)

These data show that the position from which the wh-element is extracted is a deciding factor for clefts to be used: while the subject of unaccusatives can be questioned without a cleft in most varieties, the opposite is true for unergatives. It is certainly to be expected that the subject of transitives, being an external argument, patterns with the subject of unergatives rather than unaccusatives. However, it is not trivial to foresee whether unergatives and transitives show the same degree

---

[22] The input sentence is recorded in the ASIt questionnaire 2, position 28.

of obligatoriness of clefting. In the literature different views on unergatives have been postulated: on the one hand Hale and Keyser (1998) claim that unergatives are concealed transitives which have incorporated their internal object. On the other, Tollan (2018) argues for a non-unified treatment of the subject of transitives and unergatives. Based on evidence from Samoan, she claims the former are merged higher in the structure, in VoiceP, while the latter are introduced in a lower projection, in vP.

To test whether the subject of unergatives and that of transitives behave alike with respect to mandatory clefting, subject questions in which the wh-item is selected by a transitive verb were considered. The sentence here given as (19)[23] will be used to show the obtained results:

(19) Chi porta il pane?
 Who brings the bread?[24]

Interestingly, what we observe for transitives is that a cleft is still required to form a subject question, but to a lesser degree than for unergatives. While 77% of the Venetan varieties require a cleft to form a subject question with unergative verbs, 61% do for transitives.[25]

(20) Chi xe che porta el pan?
 Who is that brings the bread?
 Agugliaro (Vicenza)

These data suggest that the preference for clefts is borne out, but the reduced number of dialects which need a cleft for transitives lets us hypothesize that there must exist dialects in which a cleft is required for unergatives and not for transitives. This possibility will be explored in section 4.4.

Thanks to this first quantitative overview, a scale in the obligatoriness of clefting emerges, which is compatible with the Unaccusativity Hypothesis (Perlmutter 1978), in that it shows that the subject of unaccusatives patterns more with true

---

23 The input sentence is recorded in the ASIt questionnaire 2, position 119.
24 Notice that in out of the blue contexts, the Italian sentence is compatible with two interpretations: (i) Who is going to bring the bread? (ii) Who brings the bread?.
25 Although these data are not claimed to be statistically accurate (see section 4.1), the figures are potentially suggestive. More rigorous statistical testing is required. Nonetheless, the tendency is clear enough to argue in favour of statistical significance, i.e., to maintain that the result is due to some factor of interest rather than to chance. The 5% conventional threshold for statistical significance (Craparo 2007) is abundantly passed.

objects, being an internal argument. Questioning external arguments, like the subject of transitives and unergatives, is instead a deciding factor for clefts to be obligatorily used.[26] The clear tendency which emerges is the following, in which going from left to right the necessity to employ a cleft to form a wh-question increases (21).

(21) object > subject of unaccusatives > subject of transitives > subject of unergatives

Structurally, the scale can be visualized in the following simplified trees which show the different positions in which the wh-element is merged before undergoing feature-checking.[27]

Table 1: Syntactic trees exemplifying the observed scale for different types of lexical verbs.

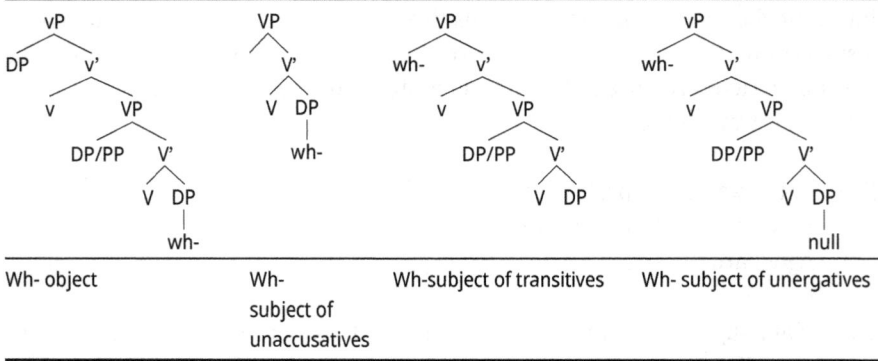

| Wh- object | Wh- subject of unaccusatives | Wh-subject of transitives | Wh- subject of unergatives |

The data show that the broad subject-object asymmetry needs to be refined, since it is not only subjecthood which plays a role, i.e., the fact that the argument is assigned nominative case and ultimately agrees with the inflected verb. Even more crucial is the syntactic position in which the wh-element is generated, and the set of features it bears: although all these arguments will ultimately become subjects, they differ in the thematic role they are assigned by the verb. In fact, the turning point for clefts to become mandatory in most varieties corresponds to

---

[26] The percentages which have been mentioned in the discussion refer to the number of cases in which a cleft sentence is used. Non-cleft strategies used within one and the same locality depending on the nature of the questioned subject are outlined in the subsequent qualitative analysis.
[27] In this simplified representation VoiceP has not been inserted.

the wh-subject bearing a set of features which is not shared by the internal arguments of unaccusatives and accusative objects, which are semantically themes or patients.

4.4 Patterns of mandatory clefting: A qualitative analysis

Once a scale of mandatory clefting has been drawn on the basis of quantitative data, it is now worth seeing whether this hierarchy holds also within single localities and if this set of progressively increasing obligatoriness can be considered an implicational hierarchy in the Venetan varieties. Moreover, it can be insightful to explore what syntactic strategies are used when a cleft is not employed. Single Venetan varieties were explored to carry out a descriptive analysis and classify the different ways in which wh- subject questions are introduced. To guarantee full comparability among different varieties the same set of input sentences used in the previous sections will be employed to outline the different syntactic behaviours. The input sentences in Italian are repeated here for the sake of clarity in (22)

(22) a. Chi viene al tuo posto?
 'Who is coming in your place?'
 b. Chi porta il pane?
 'Who brings the bread?'
 c. Chi piange di là?
 'Who is crying down there?'

Six patterns can be identified (see I–VI in this section), which corroborate and further refine the quantitative picture. Non-cleft alternatives within the same variety can be examined and framed to understand what competing strategies can prevent the dialect from resorting to a cleft.

I. Compulsory clefting for all subject-clefts (not for objects)
The first group is represented by dialects which require clefting to form all subject questions. The pattern is exemplified by Arsiero (Vicenza) in (23). Here no expletive is required. Object or non-argumental questions are regularly formed by subject inversion.

(23) a. Chi sè[28] che vien al to posto?
    Who is that comes in your place?
  b. Chi sé che porta el pan?
    Who is that brings the bread?
  c. Chi sé che pianse de là?
    Who is that cries down-there
    Arsiero (Vicenza)

II. Compulsory clefting for all external arguments

The second pattern comprises all the varieties in which the subject of unaccusatives is not clefted to form a main interrogative, but external arguments must be questioned by means of a cleft. Depending on whether the variety is pro-drop or not, a third-person subject clitic pronoun may be inserted, as is the case for Agugliaro (Vicenza) – see (24) – or must be inserted, as in Cesiomaggiore (Belluno) – see (25). Interestingly, the availability of a clitic subject also allows for inverse orders in which the wh-element is not fronted but appears after the copula (25b). This order, with a low wh-element, is excluded in the copular sentences of pro-drop varieties which use a cleft.

(24) a. Chi vien al to posto?
    Who comes in your place?
  b. Chi xé che porta el pan?
    Who is that brings the bread?
  c. Chi xé che pianse de là?
    Who is that cries down-there
    Agugliaro (Vicenza)

(25) a. Chi vien lo al to posto?
    Who comes it in your place?
  b. E-lo chi che porta el pan?
    Is-it who that brings the bread?
  c. Chi e-lo che pianse de là?[29]
    Who is-it that cries down-there
    Cesiomaggiore (Belluno)

---

[28] In the transcription of the sentence on the ASIt platform the copula is spelled as sè. However, there is no element to imply that there is a grammatical distinction reflected by the quality of the vowel. It could just be a typo.

[29] The informant also suggests "Elo chi..." as an alternative.

III. Compulsory clefting only for unergatives

The third type is represented by varieties in which all subject questions, with the exception of questions on the subject of an unergative verb, can be formed without resorting to a cleft. Even though it is not obligatory, some varieties belonging to this group, such as that spoken in Illasi (Verona), require a cleft for the subject of unergatives but use an existential construction in the copular clause of the cleft, as can be seen in (26c).[30] Notice that (26b) shows right dislocation of the object, which is resumed by the object clitic *le*.

(26) a. Ci   ven   al   to   posto?
        Who comes in   your place?
    b. Ci   le   porta   el   pan?
        Who it   brings   the   bread?
    c. Ci   gh'è   che   pianse   de là?
        Who there-is that   cries   down-there
        Illasi (Verona)

IV. Wh + C° / (existential) cleft

As pointed out by Poletto and Vanelli (1997) a possible strategy to form a main question is to use the same structure normally employed in the Venetan varieties and in substandard regional Italian for all embedded interrogatives, i.e., the co-occurrence of a wh-element and a declarative complementizer, as can be seen in (27):

(27) No   so   chi   che   vien
     Not   know who   that   comes
     'I don't know who is coming.'
     Cittadella (Padua)

Interestingly, some varieties such as the dialect of Monselice (Padua) exhibit a pattern in which unaccusatives use wh- + C° (28a), transitives require a cleft (28b), while unergatives require a cleft in which the copular clause is formed via wh+ C° and is existential, since it inserts the existential pronoun *ghe*, the same as in Illasi (26). The use of an overt existential structure is not totally surprising if we con-

---

30 (26c) is a non-canonical cleft, i.e., an existential cleft, in which the copular sentence contains an existential expletive pronoun of the type "there" in English or "ci" in Italian ("ghe" in the Venetan varieties in which the construction is attested). The same holds also for (28c). For English existential clefts, see Collins (1992), on *il-y-a*-clefts in French and *c'è*-clefts in Italian, see Karssenberg (2018).

sider that exhaustiveness and existentiality are claimed to be some of the main features of clefts (Hedberg 2000: 891).

(28) a. Chi che ven ciò al posto tuo?
   Who that comes PRT in place your
   b. Chi sé che porta el pan?
   Who is that brings the bread
   c. Chi che ghe xe che pianse de a?
   Who that there- is that cries down-there
   Monselice (Padua)

It can be observed that both in the wh- + C° and the cleft strategy the lexical verb does not raise to C. This strategy seems to be further reinforced if wh- + C° is also used for the matrix copular clause in (28c), so that even the copula does not have to raise to C to form a main interrogative.

V. Wh + C° for all kinds of partial questions

Even with unergatives, which are the lexical verbs most likely to require clefts to form a question on their subjects, some varieties use a non-cleft strategy. They can simply resort to the standard strategy for all lexical verbs, or, like the varieties here exemplified by Pramaggiore (29), the adopted strategy requires that all subject questions are introduced by co-occurring wh- + C°. As highlighted for type IV, this structure, typical of embedded interrogatives, proves to be effective to prevent the lexical verb from raising to C.

(29) a. Chi che vien al to posto?
   Who that comes in your place
   b. Chi che (el) porta el pan?
   Who that he brings the bread
   c. Chi che pianze de a?
   Who that cries down-there
   Pramaggiore (Venice)

VI. Filling of gaps / wh + C° /clefts (on a scale)

A puzzling mix of strategies is used by varieties such as that spoken in Motta di Livenza (Treviso). The subject of an unaccusative or transitive verb can be questioned in two different ways, which are apparently equivalent and in competion with each other. One possibility is to fill the gap. This means a subject clitic appears after the lexical verb and the wh-element is regularly fronted; the lexical verb raises to C as normally happens for interrogatives. The second possibility to form a question is to use the already discussed wh- + C° strategy. In the latter case no overt subject clitic is used. For questions in which the wh-element is the subject of an unergative, only one structure is attested, i.e., a cleft sentence. Also in this case, the copular clause requires a subject pronoun (the same used for verb-clitic inversion).

(30) a. Chi   vegne-o   al posto tuo? / chi che vien   al
        who   comes-he   in place your / who that comes in
        posto tuo
        place your
     b. Chi   porte-o   el pan   ?   / chi che porta el pan?
        Who   brings-he the bread   / who that brings the bread
     c. Chi   e-o   che   pianze par de' à
        Who   is-it that cries   for down-there
        Motta di Livenza (Treviso)

4.5 Intermediate remarks on Venetan

The distribution of mandatory clefting in the Venetan dialects shows that clause-type is a deciding factor on the type of cleft to be used. In varieties which can resort to clefting for pragmatic purposes in declarative contexts to focalise a phrase, clefting may also be mandatory only for wh-questions. The fact that in -Q contexts clefting is never compulsory, while it may be syntactically needed to form unmarked wh-questions proves that focusing and wh-movement are similar but differ in some respects. Generalized wh-fronting required by questions and the obligatory overt movement of the lexical verb to C do not happen for -Q, i.e., declaratives, in the Romance varieties under investigation.

The patterns of wh-subject question formation emerging from the analysis of the individual Venetan varieties are consistent with evidence coming from the preliminary quantitative analysis: the scale showing an increase in the need for clefts starting from object questions, followed by the subjects of unaccusatives, the subjects of transitives and finally by the subjects of unergatives is respected throughout the dialects and no attestation has been found in the corpus in which discontinuous segments of the scale follow the same rule. It can be inferred that the scale is hierarchically regulated. Incidentally, the four syntactic configurations shown in Table 1 can be schematized as giving rise to questions on an internal argument on the one hand (true objects and subjects of unaccusatives) and on an external argument on the other (subjects of transitives and unergatives). The fact that the subject of unaccusatives patterns with the object of transitives in the scarce attestation of mandatory clefts suggests that the traditional subject-object asymmetry needs to be further refined, since the position from which the wh-element is extracted plays a crucial role in determining whether a cleft sentence is preferred or if other strategies have to be applied. The residual difference between object wh-questions and subject questions in which the verb is unaccusative can be explained in terms of feature checking: true objects are not assigned nominative case, they do not agree with the lexical verb and can remain lower in the structure before being fronted. However, even external arguments do not behave identically. The higher likelihood of unergatives requiring clefts leads us to think that unergatives are not actually concealed transitives, as was traditionally hypothesized (Hale and Keyser 1998). This could be due to the possible involvement of VoiceP for transitives, but also to the semantic and structural relationship the subject holds with the object position: unergatives are often "internally caused" (Levin and Rappaport 1995) and do not have an overt object (with the exception of possible cognate objects). These aspects need to be further investigated and can shed more light on the different nature of subjects.

Another question still needs to be addressed: if forming a relative clause and therefore a cleft sentence causes high processing load, as was discussed in section 3.2, why is clefting used as a default unmarked strategy to build subject wh-questions? Clefting offers the certain advantage of not having to move the lexical verb to CP, which is lexically filled by the wh-element[31] (SpecCP) and by a copula (C°). Depending on the variety and its pro-drop status, we may also find a subject clitic within the cleft, otherwise a clitic can be used as a gap-filler in a main question structure, thus reducing the burden of long distance processing. However, even the gap filling may prove to be insufficient to prevent a variety from building a cleft to question the subject of unergatives, i.e., the type of verb most likely to require clefting (see type VI). The strategy of blocking the lexical verb out of the CP-layer is consistent with the cleft-competing mechanisms used by some varieties (see type V) that attain the same objective by inserting a complementizer after the wh-element giving rise to the structure of an embedded interrogative. The second advantage of using a cleft rather than a regular interrogative clause is a clear separation of Focus and Ground, which is provided by the syntax and makes processing easier. As for subject clefts, disjointness (Friedmann, Belletti and Rizzi 2009), i.e., the lack of intervention effects, is ensured so that no difficulties concerning this aspect are expected. The cost of using a cleft for the subject is therefore well counterbalanced.

---

31 If we deliberately leave *in-situness* apart, the wh-element has to obligatorily reach the left periphery.

The benefits of resorting to a subject cleft have been described for acquisition. Clear cues come from the fact that in children's immature grammar cleft questions on the subject are used more frequently than by adults (Guasti 2002). If processing and producing a cleft were costlier than building a regular question, we would expect the opposite. Unlike subject wh-questions, wh-questions on the object are not rephrased as clefts, since the advantages of clefting would not effectively counterbalance the derivational complexity of object relative clauses, which emerge much later in acquisition and cause worse performance in comprehension tasks. As Friedmann, Belletti and Rizzi (2009) effectively pointed out, potential locality violations and Relativized Minimality (Rizzi 1990) combined with long distance make clefting a less competitive strategy in this syntactic context, since it would add further syntactic complexity, which is not desirable. What is observed instead, especially in child grammar are circumvention strategies and the search for alternative utterances with lower derivational complexity. Wh-subject clefts even in the passive are sometimes used by children (but also by adults) as an escape to overcome intervention (Del Puppo 2016: 144).

5 Cleft-reluctant languages: The case of German

5.1 The availability of clefts in German: Between syntactic and pragmatic constraints

The availability of clefts ranges from the domain of "graded" syntactic obligatoriness, as has been described in section 4 – which does not affect the pragmatic possibilities in declaratives – to the very limited availability of the construction as a focalization device as is the case for some Germanic varieties like German.

Unlike many Romance languages, German strongly constrains the use of clefts. As was anticipated in section 1, according to some authors like Durrell (2002), clefts are only acceptable in German if the subject is focalized and the relative pronoun introducing the subordinate clause bears nominative case, all other cases such as dative being ruled out. Descriptive grammars like Duden (2006) consider clefts as a subtype of relative clause and warn readers about their comparative scarcity with respect to other languages. Moreover, Duden (2006: 1044) gives an example of an incorrect cleft sentence in which the focalized item bears dative case (31):

(31) *Es war einem Journalisten, dem   er den Hinweis
     It was a.DAT Journalist   whom.DAT he the hint
     verdankte.
     owed
     'It was to a journalist that he owed the hint.'

(31) is factored out because both the focalized item and the relative pronoun are marked for dative. However, while (31) is unacceptable, given a felicitous context, some configurations which are considered impossible by Durrell (2002) are not totally excluded, as grammaticality judgments collected among native speakers show. For instance, cleft sentences in which the focalized item has an object function are possible as shown in (32), cited after Cruschina (2015: note 13):

(32) HANS war es, den   ich getroffen habe
     Hans was it whom.ACC I   met   have.PRS.1SG
     'It was Hans whom I met.'

If one considers the description contained in the grammis-platform made available by the *Institut für Deutsche Sprache Mannheim* (Vorderwülbecke 2018), clefts are cited among the pragmatic devices which realize emphasis. Grammis provides an example of a corrective cleft, here reported as (33), in which a whole prepositional phrase is clefted and the subordinate clause is introduced by *wo* (literally 'where').[32] The context in answer to which the cleft sentence is uttered is that someone says that she had an accident in Bonn.[33]

(33) Nein, es war <in Mainz>, wo   sie den Unfall hatte.
     No   it was in Mainz   where she the accident had
     'No, it was in Mainz that she had the accident.'

As (33) shows, cleft sentences are not syntactically ruled out, not even if prepositional phrases are clefted. Provided that DPs not governed by a preposition are in the nominative in the copular clause, non-subjects are also admitted as clefted con-

---

[32] Notice that *wo* is used in many colloquial varieties as a relativizer not bearing Case and phi-features. Pittner (2004) reports it can be used to relativize a head which bears nominative or accusative case as in "Der Mann, wo ich getroffen habe" (lit. the man, *wo* I met have). *Wo* can also be found in clefts even though the clefted constituent is not locative (Bertollo 2014), as in "Du warst es, wo immer an mich geglaubt hat" (lit. you were it, *wo* always in me believed has).

[33] The original sentence which was given to create the appropriate context for the cleft to be felicitous is the following: "Sie hatte einen Unfall in Bonn".

stituents. However, it seems that the contexts in which a cleft sentence is felicitous are far less frequent in German than in many other Germanic and Romance languages. By comparing different languages, Lambrecht (2001) convincingly shows that German does not require a syntactic shift to provide a corrective answer to a question. In the context in which the question "Is your knee hurting?" has to be negatively answered, Italian can resort either to prosodic devices or to a cleft, while a cleft, though grammatically possible, would sound unnatural and hence infelicitous in German. Consider (34a) for German and (34b-c) for Standard Italian[34] from Lambrecht (2001: 486)[35] which show that left-peripheral focus in German serves the pragmatic domain in which a cleft is used in languages such as Italian:

(34) a. Nein, mein FUSS tut weh
       No   my   foot makes-pain
    b. No,   mi   fa   male   il PIEDE.
       No   me   makes pain   the foot
    c. No,   è   il   PIEDE che mi   fa   male.
       No   is   the   foot   that me makes pain
    'No, my FOOT hurts. / No, it's my FOOT that hurts.'

5.2 Focus fronting and clefts

Under careful scrutiny, it emerges that German clefts and focalization are not mutually exclusive and do not really compete for the same pragmatic contexts. Moreover, focus fronting can be felicitously combined with clefts, as clefted DPs or clefted pronouns preferably appear in pre-copular position, with the dummy pronoun *es* after the copula, as is shown in (32). Especially for clefts in which a personal pronoun other than third-person singular is focalized, the acceptability of the cleft sentence decreases considerably if the clefted pronoun is post-copular and does not serve as a syntactic subject for the copula triggering agreement (Bertollo 2014: 211).[36] See example (35):

---

[34] The same pattern would also hold for most Venetan varieties.
[35] The same set of examples is also cited by Cruschina (2015).
[36] Notice that the subordinate clause exhibits third person agreement if the introducer is a *d*-relative pronoun in the nominative. In many Romance varieties such as French, Standard Italian and Venetan dialects the lexical verb in the cleft clause agrees in number with the clefted personal pronoun.

(35) Du   bist   es,   der   immer   lügt.
     You   are   it   who   always lies
     'It's you who always tells lies.'

Interestingly, a preference for focus fronting within clefts is shared by the varieties in which the preverbal position is often used to host focus.[37] Cruschina (2015: 194) based on his experiment on Sicilian, a Romance cleft-reluctant variety, empirically observes the same. In particular, he points out that: "FF [focus fronting] with clefts is in fact possible (and sometimes preferred over postverbal focalization) in those Romance varieties where the preverbal focus position is generally much more active, such as Sicilian and Sardinian, as well as some dialects of Catalan".[38] If, along the lines of Rizzi (1997) and Cruschina (2015), we posit a parallelism between fronted wh-phrases[39] – which incidentally trigger compulsory clefting in some Romance varieties – and fronted foci, it does not come as a surprise that clefts also show a preference for the syntactic prominence of the wh- or of the focalized constituent. Furthermore, the similarity between German and other cleft reluctant varieties in this respect suggests that the internal syntax of the cleft sentence is in a strict relation with the information structure of the language. As also pointed out by Lambrecht (2001), Cruschina (2015: 181) a.o. postulates a pan-Romance generalization according to which "languages resorting to FF [focus fronting] as a generalized focus strategy only marginally admit CC [cleft constructions]". Building upon this postulate for Romance, it is worth investigating whether the constraint on clefts due to the availability of focus fronting in the left periphery (which serves most of the pragmatic contexts in which a cleft is used in cleft-friendly languages) can be further refined to account for the scarcity of clefts in German.

---

37 This is also valid for New Information Focus.
38 It is noteworthy that the fronting of the clefted constituent is unavoidable for subject questions in Venetan varieties in which *in-situness* is excluded. In Standard Italian and in the Venetan varieties under investigation, in -Q contexts focus fronting within the copular clause of the cleft is only compatible with a contrastive interpretation. Compare (i) New Information Focus and (ii) Contrastive Focus in the following Italian example:

(i)	È	Mario	che	mi	ha	detto	questo
	is	Mario	who	me	has	told	this
(ii)	Mario	è	che	mi	ha	detto	questo
	Mario	is	who	me	has	told	this

'It's Mario who told me this.'

39 Bocci, Bianchi and Cruschina (2021), based on evidence from Italian, argue for a focus feature bundled within the wh-element in direct questions.

5.3 Clefting and Verb Second

Verb Second is ubiquitous in Germanic languages, with the evident exception of modern English. It has been postulated in the literature that different kinds of Verb Second exist, depending on its symmetric *vs.* asymmetric status, the complementizer system and the possibility of circumventing linear restrictions (Poletto, Tomaselli and Giorgi 2021). If we focus on German and look at its left periphery, it is clear that the C domain is not only available for all kinds of foci, but it can host any constituent, regardless of its pragmatic markedness. This is due to its status as an "unconditioned V-to-C language" (Holmberg 2015; Walkden 2016; Woods and Wolfe 2020, a.o.), which distinguishes it from other Verb Second structures, which are instead criterial.[40] Being a Verb Second language has two implications: (i) the lexical verb obligatorily raises to C in all matrix clauses, regardless of the clause-type, and (ii) the preverbal position is not specialized for the subject, which provides for a looser word order on condition that the inflected verb is the second constituent of the clause.

As for (i), this is an obvious difference with respect to all Romance languages which do not require overt V-to-C in declaratives. In German, since the inflected verb in matrix clauses always sits in C, there is no advantage to prefer a cleft over other strategies to prevent the lexical verb from raising to C, producing a more complicated structure. From an economy perspective, creating a bi-clausal construction, containing a relative clause, whose processing is computationally costly, would not prove effective to circumvent the raising of the lexical verb to C, which is the default strategy in main clauses.

As for (ii), the multifunctionality of the pre-verbal position of German allows for an information structure in which the prominence of the subject is not positionally marked. The focalization of a phrase as well as the distribution of presupposition and topicality can be encoded in various ways by the Verb Second syntax. One possible strategy on which German can rely is scrambling, which is typically associated with OV languages. A-scrambling is typically utilized to mark specificity, while A-bar-scrambling can be triggered by the need to check focus discourse-features (see Hinterhölzl 2006 and references cited therein). As pointed out by Haider (2020: 375), scrambling "matches the preferred partitioning of an utterance in given vs. new or background vs. focus areas", which is a function typically performed by clefts. See (36) cited from Haider (2020: 375, example 1d in the original).

---

[40] Criterial V-to-C means that the trigger of verb movement has to be parametrized in terms of features. Languages of this type are Armenian (see Poletto, Tomaselli and Giorgi 2021).

(36) Heute regiert das Land   eine   korrupte Clique
     Today governs the country one   corrupt clique
     'It's a corrupt clique who governs the country nowadays.'[41]

Furthermore, German has a rich modal particle system containing items such as *ja, eigentlich, schon, doch*, which can serve as focus markers, but can also encode illocutionary force and express the attitude of the speaker towards their utterance (Bayer and Trotzke 2013). Part of these uses is covered in some languages by cleft constructions. Hence, the availability of modal particles in German further reduces the number of contexts in which a cleft is pragmatically needed. As has been described, focus fronting is perfectly compatible with clefts; similarly, also modal particles and cleft constructions are not mutually exclusive, as can be seen in the following German example in which a question on the subject containing a modal particle is clefted (37).

(37) Wer ist es wohl, der diese hier so schillernd
     Who is   it PRT   who this   here so blinkingly
     beschriebene Immunotherapie produzieren [..] will?
     described   immunotherapy   produce.INF   wants
     'Who is it who wants to produce this beautifully described immunotherapy?'
     https://forum.spiegel.de, 19th February 2013

As suggested by Bayer and Trotzke (2013), *wohl* expresses uncertainty about the answer. In this case the pragmatic value is also reinforced by labour division between given (presupposed) and new (wh-), which is in the copular clause of the cleft. The non-cleft equivalent "Wer will wohl diese. . ." would be felicitous as well.

5.4 Subject – object asymmetries

It is now appropriate to investigate whether the preference for subjects rather than objects to be clefted, which has been described for cleft-friendly languages like some Romance dialects of the Veneto region, also holds for German. On the basis of cross-linguistic data, as well as acquisitional data, it is to be expected that even in cleft-reluctant languages subjecthood is a favouring factor for clefting to be employed. Nominative Case is the easiest to be relativized and a relative clause

---

41 My translation.

on the subject is easier to process and produce than a structure with object A-bar extraction involving intervention effects (see section 3.2).

Recent quantitative studies on German clefts (Tönnis, Fricke, and Schreiber 2018; Tönnis 2018) confirm – *contra* Durrell (2002) – that clefts are not only available for subjects but also for other arguments. Nevertheless, corpus-based research on German (ibidem) clearly highlights a subject-object asymmetry in the frequency of use of clefts. Tönnis, Fricke, and Schreiber's (2018) study does not only measure the frequency of subject clefts with respect to their object counterpart, but it also checks the frequency against the overall number of subjects and objects attested in the whole corpus.[42] This additional step is methodologically necessary to guarantee the reliability of the research, since subjects are comparatively more frequent than objects and this could have an impact on the number of subject clefts which appear in the corpus (Tönnis, Fricke and Schreiber 2018: 232–233). The number of occurrences the authors of the study report for subject clefts in their corpus is 249, while object clefts are only 24, which is different from the proportion attested for subject and object arguments in their regular positions (ibidem). Whereas object clefts are about one tenth of all cleft occurrences, non-clefted objects are 93 *vs.* 193 non-clefted subjects.

These data confirm the robust prediction that even in languages in which clefts are not frequently employed and only serve pragmatic purposes, the subject is the preferred syntactic position on which a cleft sentence can be formed. Tönnis, Fricke and Schreiber (2018) associate this preference with the greater range of pragmatic devices for emphasising the object (displacement, prosodic marking etc.). Conversely, signalling the prosodic and pragmatic prominence of the subject is assumed to be a key factor for clefts to be used. According to their intuition as native speakers of German, clefts are used more frequently in the written language than in the spoken,[43] which they impute to the impossibility of prosodically marking prominence in the written form.

---

[42] The corpus consists of 300 sentences drawn from a subcorpus of the DeReKo corpus (Das Deutsche Referenz Korpus: ⟨http://www.ids-mannheim.de/kl/projekte/korpora, accessed 08 February 2022). The authors declare having cross-checked their data by statistically considering that only one constituent per sentence at a time can be clefted. In case of sentences containing more than one potentially 'cleftable' constituent, the probability for the subject to be the target of clefting diminishes.

[43] Reliable quantitative accounts on this still lack.

5.5 The disputed role of agentivity

The investigation of the Romance varieties spoken in the Veneto suggests that one of the factors which play a role in the obligatoriness of clefting to form subject questions is the nature of the subject, i.e., not only its base-generation site but also its featural array, which involves thematic information. Specifically, it was highlighted that the subject of unaccusatives – a non-agent argument – is least likely to require a cleft. It is therefore worth understanding whether the thematic role of the focalized argument has an influence on the availability of clefting in German as well.

Interestingly, Tönnis, Fricke and Schreiber (2018) do not find any animacy effect in their quantitative study on German clefts. This means that clefted inanimate subjects are claimed to pattern with clefted animate subjects without any relevant difference.[44] Furthermore, the quantitative analysis provided on the basis of the same dataset does not support the hypothesis that agentivity is a crucial property of clefted subjects. According to Tönnis, Fricke and Schreiber's (2018) account, the proportion of clefted subjects bearing the Theta-role of agent is not significantly different from the proportion of non-clefted agent subjects (33% *vs.* 37%). In other words, agents are not more likely to be clefted than non-agents.

However, this assumed unrelatedness between clefting and agentivity is controversial. So-called DO-clefts, i.e., wh-clefts using the verb "do" (*tun* in German)[45] are traditionally used in the literature as a test to diagnose agentivity (see Jackendoff 2007 and references cited therein; more recently, specifically on German, see Kretzschmar and Brilmayer 2020). Even though it has to be pointed out that wh-clefts and "regular" clefts do not behave alike in all respects and that DO-cleft-tests do not imply that agents are more prone to be clefted in all types of clefts, the issue of a potential role of agentivity as a favouring factor for this construction is not trivial and deserves further investigation. A question to be addressed in the first instance, which could directly affect the results, is how agentivity is conceived. A binary division between agents and non-agents may be problematic: a simplistic approach which generically considers agentivity "as the capacity to

---

[44] We will not address the animacy issue, which would deserve further investigation, and will remain rather agnostic with respect to it. It is not to be *a priori* excluded that it may be a factor at play. For the animacy hierarchy, in a transitive sentence in a prototypical flow of information the agent is high in animacy, while the patient is low, giving rise to a subject-preference for the animate (see Comrie 1989: 185). The interpretation of potentially ambiguous relative clauses takes advantage of featural disjointness and presupposition when the subject is human and the object is inanimate (see Wang 2011: 35 a.o.).

[45] An example of DO-cleft is the following: "What he did was to set up a company".

control a situation" (Verhoeven 2017: 5) is incompatible with the many different properties of agentive participants in an event (Wang 2011, Verhoeven 2017). In the light of a gradient notion of agentivity, seminal works such as Dowty (1991) have identified a set of features which are typically associated with it: volition, intention, sentience, instigation, causation and action. Agent participants involved in an event do not obligatorily bear all these features, which are dependent on the relation between the argument and the verb. As a consequence, not all agents are equally representative of the class. Expanding Dowty's (1991) framework, Tollan (2018: 1) proposes that the subjects of unergatives "encompass a subset of the semantic properties of full-fledged transitive [. . .] agents". If, along these lines, we assume that the subjects of unergatives are "less agentive" than the subjects of semantically transitive verbs[46] (Wiltschko 2001), hypothesising a direct involvement of agentivity in allowing for cleft formation should imply that subject clefts in which the lexical verb is a fully-fledged transitive are more likely to appear than clefts in which the lexical verb is unergative.

If we consider the data from the Romance dialects spoken in the Veneto, it emerges that the likelihood of requiring clefting for a question on the subject of an unergative is greater than for a question on the subject of a transitive verb. The implicational scale observed for the Venetan varieties (see section 4.2) together with the data discussed by Tönnis, Fricke, and Schreiber (2018), which do not reveal any increase in the number of clefts if the clefted argument is an agent, suggest that agentivity is not a key factor, neither in favouring nor in inhibiting clefting.

5.6 Intermediate remarks on German

By analysing the behaviour of German with respect to clefts, it emerges that some crucial factors play a role in constraining clefting. An overarching factor is information structure and therefore the functions of the CP-layer. Languages such as German, but also Sicilian, in which the left periphery is freely available for focus fronting (including new information focus), generally avoid resorting to clefting to pragmaticize a constituent. Moreover, being a Verb Second language, German requires that the lexical verb always reaches a C-head and the pre-verbal position is not necessarily filled by the subject, even in unmarked contexts. In contrast to Romance languages, which frequently use clefts, in German the overt activation of the left periphery of the clause is a generalized phenomenon which takes place

---

[46] It is well-known that transitive constructions do not necessarily imply semantic transitivity. Transitive psych-verbs, for instance, involve no agent.

regardless of clause-type and pragmatic purposes. Furthermore, the availability of scrambling as well as the use of modal particles provide tools to pursue the same pragmatic goals which cleft-friendly languages attain through clefting. In addition, since V-to-C is the regular movement of the verb, building a more complex structure would not be effectively counterbalanced by the fact that the lexical verb remains low in the clausal spine. As in Romance, consistent with the predictions for relative clauses, if a cleft is built, it is preferably on the subject, which is according to Durrell (2002) the only possibility for clefting, all other arguments allegedly being excluded. Although the restrictions on other arguments are not so strict, empirical investigations on corpus data highlight a clear asymmetry with subject-clefts being favoured over object-clefts. Within subject-clefts it is still unclear whether the lack of agentivity of certain subjects can further constrain clefting in German: previous studies do not offer uncontroversial data which allow us to exclude or accept this possibility. Similarly, studies on the impact of clause-type in favouring or inhibiting clefting in German (and in other cleft-reluctant varieties) are still lacking.

6 Verb Second but cleft-friendly? Some cues from diachrony and the puzzle of Northern Germanic languages

6.1 The loss of Verb Second in Middle English and the rise of clefts

Jespersen (1937: 86) already noted the link between rigid SVO and the rise of clefting and claimed that clefts are a means to obliviate the disadvantages of rigid word order. His idea was reproposed by Traugott (1972) for English. In more recent times, Los (2009) offered some interesting insights to a better understanding of the relation between the loss of Verb Second in favour of rigid SVO orders and the emergence of clefts, by investigating earlier stages of English and specifically the phase in which Verb Second was progressively lost. Los (2009) documents that, at the stage in which English was still a Verb Second language and therefore the pre-verbal position was not specialized for the subject, attestations of clefts were extremely scarce. Before the loss of Verb Second, the preverbal position was multifunctional and could host marked and unmarked constituents. When the syntactic structure turned to a rigid SVO order, the preverbal position had to be filled by the subject but could also encode pre-subject constituents. Clefts are claimed to be an Early Modern English innovation to compensate for the change in information structure caused by the loss of Verb Second (ibidem: 99). The change is attested in corpus studies which show that in Middle English objects started to be less frequently preposed. Speyer (2005) argues that this is strictly connected with the loss of Verb Second, as the verb did not raise to C° anymore. The fact that the preverbal position was gradually allotted to the subject led to a disruption of the previous information structure. This hypothesis is corroborated by translations in late Middle English in which passages which had been translated by means of new information focus fronting started to be translated with a cleft (Ball 1991: 157 here cited after Los 2009: 112).

To summarize, the data point to an emergence of clefts in Early Modern English. This coincided with Verb Second loss, the specialization of the preverbal position for the subject and the decline of pre-posed objects, which gave rise to a re-organization of information structure and determined a subversion of the functions of the left periphery. These are strong cues suggesting that Verb Second (and symmetrically its loss or absence) is a factor in determining whether a language is cleft-friendly or cleft-reluctant. It is worth mentioning that languages such as Swedish, which is typically cited as a counterexample to the involvement of Verb Second syntax in inhibiting clefting, significantly differs from Verb Second cleft-reluctant languages (like German and Old English) in that it has a strong preference for pre-verbal subjects: corpus studies cited by Los (2009: 105) show that 73% of first constituents are subjects, while the number of subjects in the first position ranges between 51% and 54% in German and Old English. This suggests that the first position in Swedish tends to be specialized for the subject, thus signalling that this language is inclined to a more rigid word order, which typically correlates with the emergence of clefts.

6.2 Clefts in Norwegian

Based on corpus analysis, Gundel (2006) reports that the number of clefts in Norwegian is triple the number of clefts in English. She claims that the high frequency of clefts is due to information structure reasons and specifically to a preference to encode all presupposed information in the cleft clause and to present new information in the matrix clause. Søfteland (2014) investigated the distribution of clefts in Norwegian in relation to clause-type, i.e., whether the occurrences of clefts in questions and in declarative contexts are statistically similar. Her results show that 4.9% of declarative clauses contain clefts, but the proportion increases significantly in wh-matrix questions where clefts make up 16% of the total.[47] Further corroboration of the asymmetry between clause-type comes from other Northern Germanic Verb Second languages such as Swedish, for which Brandtler (2019) describes a similar distribution between clefts and non-clefts. Moreover, in both languages the preference for clefts does not equally involve all wh-, but seems to be specialized for argumental interrogatives.

The correlation between clause-type and clefting deserves further investigation. It has been observed in section 4 that in non-Verb-Second cleft-friendly languages like the Romance varieties spoken in the Veneto, the only context in which clefting is compulsory are main interrogatives in which the clefted wh-element is argumental. Against this background, Norwegian offers an insightful perspective on the relation between clefting and word order on the one hand, and clefting and clause-type on the other. This can potentially form a bridge between cleft-friendly languages and the typical Verb Second reluctance towards clefting. The picture is all the more interesting, if we consider that, other than Standard Norwegian, many Norwegian dialects allow for non-Verb-Second orders in main wh- questions starting from the subject (see Westergaard and Vangsnes 2005 a.o.). Westergaard, Vangsnes and Lohndal (2017: 18), on the basis of updated questionnaires among native speakers, confirm Nordgård's (1988) condition according to which "a dialect may have non-inverted word order in matrix wh- questions iff the dialect allows insertion of the complementizer *som* under extraction of the embedded subject".[48] In other words, the insertion of a relative complementizer triggers the blocking of Verb Second and the verb remains lower in the clause, as exemplified in Northern Norwegian in (38) (Westergaard, Vangsnes and Lohndal 2017: ex. 13a):

(38) Kem   som   sæll   fiskeutstyr   her   i   bygda?
      who   SOM   sells fishing.gear here in   village.DEF
      'Who sells fishing gear in this village?'

This is reminiscent of the wh + C° structure common to some of the Romance varieties in the Veneto discussed above as a possible strategy to introduce subject questions. Crucially, Lie (1992)[49] offers an account for the emergence of the relative complementizer *som* within matrix questions and argues that non-Verb-Second syntax in Norwegian dialects has diachronically developed along the following

---

47 These data are cited after Hauge (2018).
48 Nordgård (1988) is cited entirely after Westergaard, Vangsnes and Lohndal (2017: 18).
49 Here entirely cited after Westergaard, Vangsnes and Lohndal (2017).

pattern, here exemplified in (39) after Westergaard, Vangsnes, and Lohndal (2017: ex. 23). The data come from the Hedalen dialect.[50]

(39) a. Hå va de som skjedde?
       what was it SOM happened
       'What was it that happened?'
   b. Hå va som skjedde?
       what was SOM happened
       'What was it that happened?'
   c. Hå som skjedde?
       what SOM happened
       'What happened?'

Three stages of development can be identified in (39): the starting point (39a) is a regular cleft in which the subordinate clause is introduced by the relative complementizer *som*;[51] the next step (39b) is the loss of the expletive in the copular clause; the last stage is represented by (39c) in which the copula is lost and the lexical verb fails to raise to C°.

If Lie (1992) and Westergaard, Vangsnes, and Lohndal (2017) are right, this would imply that wh-questions are a vulnerability point: the formation of root wh-interrogatives allows for competing strategies, one of them being clefting. If a cleft is used, it first leads to a disruption of the information structure (separation between new and given) which has consequences for the verb in the subordinate clause of the cleft as the complementizer prevents the verb from raising to C°.

Evidently, this analysis has strong implications both for Verb Second varieties not allowing for clefting (their reluctance towards the use of this construction could be interpreted as an indirect cue of the "robustness" of Verb Second), and for non-Verb-Second languages such as the Romance varieties spoken in the Veneto, which diatopically perform all three possibilities outlined in (39), i.e. (i) cleft with expletive pronoun, (ii) cleft with no expletive, and (iii) wh- + relative complementizer.

---

[50] Precisely, the data come from the variety spoken in the district of Valdres, about 140 km to the northwest of Oslo, "inner" western part of eastern Norway.
[51] The declarative complementizer is *at*.

7 Final remarks

The careful analysis of the attitudes towards clefting of "cleft-friendly" and "cleft-reluctant" languages has helped shed light on the factors which favour and constrain this construction. The investigation of the microvariation displayed by the Romance varieties spoken in the Veneto region (Italy) clearly indicates that clause-type plays a role in encouraging the use of clefts. Specifically, wh-questions are the only domain in which clefts are not optional but a syntactic device (i.e. not used only for pragmatic purposes).

Closer scrutiny of the +Q contexts in which a cleft is mandatory enabled us to draw a fine-grained picture of the phenomenon. In line with previous research, clefts are preferred for subject questions, while other strategies tend to be employed to question non-subjects. Nevertheless, the broad asymmetry subject *vs.* object does not fully capture the complex distribution of this construction. Specifically, not all subjects behave alike: the subject of unaccusatives, as an internal argument, patterns more with true objects, while external arguments are more likely to require a cleft to be questioned. Even among external arguments, the subject of unergatives and transitives do not behave exactly alike, since subject questions in which the lexical verb is unergative are more likely to require clefts. This suggests that a significantly different featural array has to be postulated even within the class of external arguments, reinforcing the hypothesis that unergatives are not concealed transitives.

The strategies other than clefting used in Venetan varieties to form a question without employing the standard strategy all point in the same direction, i.e., they all achieve the goal of preventing the lexical verb from raising to C: one case in point is the use of the wh-+ C° strategy, as if the question were embedded. These points suggest that the critical layer determining the availability/necessity or unavailability of clefting is CP, i.e., the landing site of focus and A-bar movement. Although building a cleft is costly from a processing perspective, data from acquisition as well as the dialectal data observed, suggest that the cost of building a cleft on the subject is counterbalanced by a clear separation of focus and ground and the prevention of the raising of the verb to C. In contrast, intervention effects, locality and therefore an increased processing load, which are typical of A-bar dependences involving an object, would not be solved by forming a cleft, which would instead require further syntactic complexity. Against this background, the clefting of the object is a disfavoured option to build a question.

Once the factors which favour clefting (to the point that they make it mandatory) had been identified, our perspective was reversed. Starting from a prototypically cleft-reluctant language like Standard German, attention was paid to the aspects which constrain clefting and make it unavailable. Previous studies on clefts in German suggest that two types of constraints apply: syntactic and pragmatic. The latter refer to the fact that the contexts in which a cleft sentence is felicitous are not the same as it is in other languages, although no syntactic ban applies. On the other hand, at a syntactic level, the reported acceptability of the construction ranges from very restrictive interpretations (clefts only admitted for subjects, as maintained by Durrel in his 2002 work) to more liberal ones (the platform Grammis considers also clefted PPs grammatical). For Romance (see Belletti 2015) it has been argued that clefts directly correlate with the availability of low (vP) and high (left peripheral) focus. Interestingly, in languages such as German and Sicilian which resort to generalized focus fronting (see Cruschina 2015 for Romance), the use of clefts is inhibited: in many pragmatic contexts in which a cleft is used in cleft-friendly languages, focus fronting is employed instead in German. The unrestricted availability of a preverbal position, which is not specialized for the subject, reduces the necessity to use a cleft. Focus fronting is possible in cleft-friendly languages like the observed Venetan varieties; however, it is a marked strategy which involves the overt activation of the CP and the raising of the lexical verb to C°, which is not required in clefts. Nevertheless, clefts and focus fronting are not mutually exclusive, since even within the marginal use of clefts, inverse copular clauses with a fronted constituent are far more frequent than the sequence *es* + copula + clefted DP. The fronted constituent within the copular clause triggers agreement and therefore serves as the syntactic subject of the clause, which guarantees prominence.

The internal structure of the cleft sentence is also strictly related to the information structure of the language. The lack of a specialized preverbal position in German correlates with the fact that it is a Verb Second language of the type "unconditioned V-to-C". The direct consequence of this is that the left periphery is always active and lexically filled regardless of pragmatic necessities. While the advantage provided by clefts in cleft-friendly languages like the Venetan varieties is that the lexical verb does not need to be moved to the CP-layer, no such advantage would be found in German where the raising of the lexical verb to C is the unmarked strategy for all main clauses. The increased syntactic complexity of building a cleft sentence is therefore not counterbalanced by shorter movement of the lexical verb. Moreover, the availability of further pragmatic devices such as modal particles and scrambling providing for a clear partitioning of given *vs.* new information further diminishes the need for clefts.

After considering information structure and word order factors, attention was paid to the extent to which the graded necessity for clefting observed for the Venetan varieties is also found in cleft-reluctant languages like German. Relying on previous corpus studies (Tönnis 2018 a.o.) it emerged that the Acessibility Hierarchy and specifically a preference for subject clefts over non-subject clefts is also valid for German. This points to the fact that subjecthood is cross-linguistically a favouring factor for clefts to be used. Nonetheless, future research needs to clarify whether the broad asymmetry between subjects and non-subjects in the availability of clefts can be further refined for German. It would be interesting to investigate whether the picture emerging from the Venetan data with respect to the featural array of the subjects which favour clefting is paralleled by German. This would not only contribute to a better understanding of the factors involved in clefting, but also to a more refined notion of subjecthood in relation to the lexical verb.

Finally, the analysis of cleft patterns in Verb Second cleft-friendly languages, like Norwegian and Swedish, and some cues from diachrony offered an insightful link between what can be observed in the Venetan varieties and in German, providing support to some of the points made above. As for the role of Verb Second inhibiting clefting, the progressive loss of Verb Second in the history of English clearly shows that the specialization of a preverbal position for subjects and the increased rigidness of word order coincided with the emergence of clefts (Los 2009). As for Norwegian, which despite being Verb Second makes extensive use of clefts, quantitative data show that the privileged environment for clefts to appear is questions as in the Venetan varieties. Furthermore, data coming from Norwegian dialects seem to suggest that the use of clefts to form a (subject) question is a way towards the loss of Verb Second, cleft questions and the relative element that introduces the subordinate clause being an effective instrument to prevent the lexical verb from raising to C. This offers new, still unexplored, perspectives, which make clefts a further diagnostic test to verify whether a weakening of Verb Second is taking place or whether it remains robust.

References

Adani, Flavia. 2012. Some notes on the Acquisition of relative clauses: New data and open questions. In Valentina Bianchi & Cristiano Chesi (eds.), *ENJOY LINGUISTICS! Papers offered to Luigi Rizzi on the occasion of his 60th birthday*, 6–13. Siena: CISCL Press. http://www.ciscl.unisi.it/gg60/papers/adani.pdf (accessed 8 January 2022).

Akmajian, Adrian. 1970. *Aspects of the grammar of focus in English*. Massachusetts Institute of Technology PhD dissertation.

Aravind, Athulya, Martin Hackl & Kenneth Wexler. 2017. Syntactic and pragmatic factors in children's comprehension of cleft constructions. *Language Acquisition*. 1–31. https://dspace.mit.edu/handle/1721.1/112930 (accessed 8 January 2022).

Arosio, Fabrizio, Francesca Panzeri, Bruna Molteni, Santina Magazù & Maria Teresa Guasti. 2017. The comprehension of Italian relative clauses in poor readers and in children with Specific Language Impairment. *Glossa: A Journal of General Linguistics* 2(1). 1–25. https://doi.org/10.5334/gjgl.107

Arsenijević, Boban. 2009. Clausal complementation as relativization. *Lingua* 119. 39–50. https://doi.org/10.1016/j.lingua.2008.08.003

Ball, Catherine N. 1991. *The historical development of the* it-*cleft*. Pennsylvania: University of Pennsylvania ProQuest dissertation Publishing.
Bayer, Joseph & Andreas Trotzke. 2013. Discourse particles, successive-cyclic movement, and the nature of derivations. Paper presented at the Workshop *"The Role of Modal Particles in Diverse Speech Acts"*, Ca' Foscari University, Venice, 3–4 October.
Belletti, Adriana. 2005. Answering with a 'cleft': The role of the Null Subject Parameter and the VP periphery. In Laura Brugè, Giuliana Giusti, Nicola Munaro, Walter Schweikert & Giuseppina Turano (eds.), *Contributions to the thirtieth Incontro di Grammatica Generativa*, 63–82. Venice: Cafoscarina.
Belletti, Adriana. 2015. The focus map of clefts. Extraposition and predication. In Ur Schlonsky (ed.), *Beyond functional sequence. The cartography of syntactic structures volume 10*. 42–59. Oxford & New York: Oxford University Press. https://doi.org/10.1093/acprof:oso/9780190210588.003.0003
Bertollo, Sabrina. 2014. *On relatives with a null head. German free relative clauses and clefts*. Padua: University of Padua dissertation. http://paduaresearch.cab.unipd.it/6883/1/Bertollo_Sabrina_tesi.pdf (accessed 25 April 2022).
Bocci, Giuliano, Valentina Bianchi & Silvio Cruschina. 2021. Focus in *wh*-questions. Evidence from Italian. *Natural Langugage & Linguistic Theory* 39. 405–455. https://doi.org/10.1007/s11049-020-09483-x
Bonan, Caterina. 2019. *On clause-internally moved wh-phrases. Wh-to-Foc, nominative clitics, and the theory of Northern Italian wh-in situ*. Geneva: University of Geneva PhD dissertation. DOI: 10.13097/archive-ouverte/unige:119060
Bonan, Caterina. 2021. *Romance interrogative syntax. Formal and typological dimensions of variation*. Amsterdam: John Benjamins. https://doi.org/10.1075/la.266
Brandtler, Johan. 2019. The question of form in the forming of questions: The meaning and use of clefted wh-interrogatives in Swedish. *Journal of Linguistics* 55(4). 755–794. https://doi.org/10.1017/S0022226718000634
Burzio, Luigi. 1986. *Italian syntax. A Government-Binding approach*. Dordrecht: D. Reidel Publishing Company.
Chesi, Cristiano & Paolo Canal. 2019. Person features and lexical restrictions in Italian clefts. *Frontiers in Psychology* 10. 2105. http://doi.org/10.3389/fpsyg.2019.02105
Chomsky, Noam. 1977. On wh-movement. In Peter Culicover, Thomas Wasow & Adrian Akmajian (eds.), *Formal syntax*, 71–132. New York: Academic Press.
Chomsky, Noam. 2005. Three factors in language design. *Linguistic Inquiry* 36. 1–22.
Collins, Peter. 1992. Cleft existentials in English. *Language Sciences* 14(4). 19–433. https://doi.org/10.1016/0388-0001(92)90024-9
Comrie, Bernard. 1989. *Language universals and linguistic typology: Syntax and morphology*. Chicago: University of Chicago press.
Cornips, Leonie & Cecilia Poletto. 2005. On standardising syntactic elicitation techniques (part I). *Lingua* 115 (7). https://doi.org/10.1016/j.lingua.2003.11.004
Craparo, Robert M. 2007. Significance level. In Neil J. Salkind (ed.), *Encyclopedia of measurement and statistics*. Vol. 3, 889–891. Thousand Oaks, CA: SAGE Publications.
Cruschina, Silvio. 2015. Some notes on clefting and fronting. In Elisa Di Domenico, Cornelia Hamann & Simona Matteini (eds.), *Structures, strategies and beyond: Studies in honour of Adriana Belletti*, 181–208. Amsterdam: John Benjamins. https://doi.org/10.1075/la.223.09cru
Declerck, Renaat. 1988. *Studies on copular sentences, clefts and pseudoclefts*. Berlin: Mouton De Gruyter.
Del Puppo, Giorgia. 2016. *On the acquisition of focus: Elicited production of cleft sentences and wh-questions by school-aged, Italian-speaking children*. Venice: University of Ca' Foscari dissertation.

Den Dikken, Marcel. 2006. *Relators and linkers*. Cambridge, Massachusetts: MIT Press.
Dowty, David. 1991. Thematic proto-roles and argument selection. *Language* 67. 547–619.
Duden. 2006. *Die Grammatik*. Volume 4. Berlin: Dudenverlag
Durrell, Martin. 2002. *Hammer's German grammar and usage*. 4th edn. London: Arnold.
Fischer, Klaus. 2009. Cleft sentences: Form, function, and translation. *Journal of Germanic Linguistics* 21(2). 167–191. doi:10.1017/S1470542709000257.
Frascaralli, Mara & Francesca Ramaglia. 2009. (Pseudo) clefts and information structure at the syntax-phonology interface". *Lingbuzz*. http://ling.auf.net/lingBuzz/000841 (accessed 05 Januar 2022).
Frascarelli, Mara & Francesca Ramaglia. 2013. (Pseudo)clefts at the syntax-prosody-discourse interface. In Katharina Hartmann & Tonjes Veenstra (eds.), *Cleft structures*, 97–137. Amsterdam: John Benjamins.
Friedmann, Naama, Adriana Belletti & Luigi Rizzi. 2009. Relativized relatives: Types of intervention in the acquisition of A-bar dependencies. *Lingua* 119. 67–88. https://doi.org/10.1016/j.lingua.2008.09.002
Guasti, Maria Teresa. 2002. *Language acquisition: The growth of grammar*. Cambridge: MA: MIT Press.
Guasti, Maria Teresa, Chiara Branchini & Fabrizio Arosio. 2012. Interference in the production of Italian subject and object wh-questions. *Applied Psycholinguistics* 33(1). 185–223. https://doi.org/10.1017/S0142716411000324
Gundel, Jeanette. 1977. *Role of topic and comment in linguistic theory*. Bloomington: Indiana University Linguistics Club.
Gundel, Jeanette. 2006. Clefts in English and Norwegian: Implications for the grammar-pragmatics interface. In Valéria Molnár & Susanne Winkler (eds.), *The Architecture of focus*. Berlin/Boston: Mouton de Gruyter, 517–548. https://doi.org/10.1515/9783110922011.517
Haegeman, Liliane, André Meinunger & Aleksandra Vercauteren. 2013. The architecture of *it*-clefts. *Journal of Linguistics* 50(2). 1–28. https://www.leibniz-zas.de/fileadmin/Archiv2019/mitarbeiter/meinunger/2014_Meinunger-Haegeman-Cleft.pdf (accessed 7 September 2023).
Haider, Hubert. 2020. A null theory of scrambling. *Zeitschrift für Sprachwissenschaft* 39(3). 375–405. https://doi.org/10.1515/zfs-2020-2019 .
Hale, Ken & Samuel Jay Keyser. 1998. The basic elements of argument structure. *MIT Working Papers in Linguistics* 32. 73–118.
Hartmann, Katharina & Tonjes Veenstra (eds.). 2013. *Cleft structures*. Amsterdam: John Benjamins.
Hauge, Anne Helene. 2018. *Clefts in Norwegian wh-questions. Their use and meaning*. Oslo: University of Oslo MA thesis.
Hedberg, Nancy. 2000. On the referential status of clefts. *Language* 76. 891–920.
Heycock, Caroline. 2012. Specification, equation, and agreement in copular sentences. *Canadian Journal of Linguistics/Revue canadienne de linguistique* 57(2). 209–240.
Heycock, Caroline & Anthony Kroch. 2002. Topics, focus and syntactic representations. In Line Mikkelsen & Christopher Potts (eds.), *WCCFL 21: Proceedings of the 21st West Coast Conference on Formal Linguistics*. 141–165. Somerville, Massachusetts: Cascadilla Press.
Hinterhölzl, Roland. 2006. *Scrambling, Remnant movement and restructuring in West Germanic*. Oxford: Oxford University Press.
Holmberg, Anders. 2015. Verb Second. In Tibor Kiss & Artemis Alexiadou (eds.), *Syntax – theory and analysis: An international handbook*, 342–382. Berlin/Boston: De Gruyter Mouton. https://doi.org/10.1515/9783110377408.342
Jackendoff, Ray. 2007. *Language, consciousness, culture: Essays on mental structure*. Cambridge, Massachusetts: MIT Press.

Jespersen, Otto. 1937. *Analytic syntax*. London: Allen and Unwin.
Karssenberg, Lena. 2018. *Non-prototypical clefts in French: A corpus analysis of* il y a *clefts*, Berlin/Boston: De Gruyter. https://doi.org/10.1515/9783110586435
Kasper, Simon. 2013. Attributional praxis and linguistic stability. In Alena Barysevich, Alexandra D'Arcy & David Heap (eds.), *Proceedings of methods XIV. Papers from the Fourteenth International Conference on Methods in Dialectology, 2011*, 80–89. Frankfurt am Main: Peter Lang.
Kayne, Richard. 1994. *The antisymmetry of syntax*. Cambridge, Massachusetts: MIT Press.
Kayne, Richard. 2010. Why isn't this a complementizer?. In Richard Kayne (ed.), *Comparisons and contrasts*, 188–231. New York: Oxford University Press.
Kayne, Richard. 2021. On complementizers and relative pronouns in Germanic vs. Romance. In Sam Wolfe & Christine Meklenborg (eds.), *Continuity and variation in Germanic and Romance*. Oxford Scholarship Online. DOI:10.1093/oso/9780198841166.003.0016.
Keenan, Edward L. & Bernard Comrie. 1977. Noun phrase accessibility and Universal Grammar. *Linguistic Inquiry* 8(1). 63–99.
Kratzer, Angelika. 2006. Decomposing attitude verbs. Paper presented at the conference *"Honoring Anita Mittwoch on her 80th birthday"*, The Hebrew University of Jerusalem, 4 July. https://semanticsarchive.net/Archive/DcwY2JkM/attitude-verbs2006.pdf (accessed 12 January 2022).
Kretzschmar, Franziska & Ingmar Brilmayer. 2020. Zooming in on agentivity: Experimental studies of DO-clefts in German. *Linguistics Vanguard* (6)1. https://doi.org/10.1515/lingvan-2019-0069
Lafkioui, Mena B., Ernest Nshemezimana & Koen Bostoen. 2016. Cleft constructions and focus in Kirundi. *Africana Linguistica* 22. 71–106. https://hal.science/hal-01486747/document (accessed 8 January 2022).
Lambrecht, Knud. 2001. A framework for the analysis of cleft constructions. *Linguistics* 39(3). 463–516.
Levin, Beth & Malka Rappaport Hovav. 1995. *Unaccusativity: At the syntax-lexical semantics interface*. Cambridge, Massachusetts: MIT Press.
Lewis, Richard L., Shravan Vasishth & Julie A. Van Dyke. 2006. Computational principles of working memory in sentence comprehension. *Trends in Cognitive Sciences* 10(10). 447–54. doi: 10.1016/j.tics.2006.08.007.
Lie, Svein. 1992. Ka du sei? [what are you saying] *Maal og Minne 1992*. 62–77.
Los, Bettelou. 2009. The consequences of the loss of verb-second in English: Information structure and syntax in interaction. *English Language and Linguistics* (13)1. 97–125. doi:10.1017/S1360674308002876.
Luo, Cheng. 1994. *The accessibility hierarchy and clefting*. Manitoba: University of Manitoba PhD dissertation. https://mspace.lib.umanitoba.ca/bitstream/handle/1993/19752/Luo_The_Accessibility.pdf?sequence=1 (accessed 9 April 2022)
Manzini, M. Rita. 2010. The structure and interpretation of (Romance) complementizers. In Phoevos Panagiotidis (ed.), *The complementizer phase*, 167–199. Oxford: Oxford University Press.
Manzini, M. Rita & Anna Roussou. 2021. Sentential complementation: Nominalization and other strategies. Paper presented at the Incontro di Grammatica Generativa 46 (IGG46), Siena 23-26/02/2021. http://www.ciscl.unisi.it/igg46/23/roussou_manzini.pdf (accessed 9 January 2022).
Manzini, M. Rita & Leonardo M. Savoia. 2011. Wh-in situ & wh-doubling in Northern Italian Varieties: Against remnant movement. *Linguistic Analysis* 37(1). 79–113.
Meinunger, André. 1998. A monoclausal structure for (pseudo-)cleft sentences. In Pius N. Tamanji & Kiyomi Kusumoto (eds.), *Proceedings of the 28th Annual Meeting of the North East Linguistics Society*, 283–298. Amherst, Massachusetts: Graduate Linguistics Student Association.

Moro, Andrea. 1997. *The raising of predicates*. Cambridge: Cambridge University Press.
Moulton, Keir. 2015. CPs: Copies and compositionality. *Linguistic Inquiry* 46. 305–342. https://doi.org/10.1162/LING_a_00183
Munaro, Nicola. 1999. *Sintagmi interrogativi nei dialetti italiani settentrionali*. Padua: Unipress.
Nordgård, Torbjørn. 1988. Omkring ordstilling i hv-spørsmål i norske dialekter. [About word order in hv- questions in Norwegian dialects]. *Writing series from the Department of Phonetics and Linguistics 33*, 26–37. Bergen: University of Bergen.
Percus, Orin. 1997. Prying open the cleft. In Kiyomi Kusumoto (ed.), *Proceedings of the 27th Annual Meeting of the North East Linguistics Society*, 337–351. Amherst, Massachusetts: Amherst, Massachusetts: Graduate Linguistics Student Association.
Perlmutter, David M. 1978. Impersonal passives and the unaccusative hypothesis. *Proceedings of the Berkeley Linguistics Society* 4. 157–189. https://doi.org/10.3765/bls.v4i0.2198
Philip, William, Peter Coopmans, Wouter van Atteveldt & Matthijs van der Meer. 2002. Subject-Object asymmetry in child comprehension of wh-questions. In Anna H.-J. Do, Laura Domínguez & Aimee Johansen (eds.), *BUCLD 25: Proceedings of the 25th annual Boston University Conference on Language Development*, 587–598. Somerville, Massachusetts: Cascadilla Press. https://vanatteveldt.com/files/BUCLD25.pdf (accessed 7 September 2023).
Pinelli Maria Cristina, Cecilia Poletto & Cinzia Avesani. 2020. Does prosody meet syntax? A case study on standard Italian cleft sentences and left peripheral focus. *The Linguistic Review* 37(2). 309–330. https://doi.org/10.1515/tlr-2019-2045
Pittner, Karin. 2004. *Wo* in Relativsätzen – eine korpusbasierte Untersuchung. *Zeitschrift für germanistische Linguistik* 32(3). 357–375.
Poletto, Cecilia, Alessandra Tomaselli & Alessandra Giorgi. 2021. A crosslinguistic perspective on the relationship between information structure and V2. Paper presented at the *35th Comparative Germanic Syntax Workshop, University of Trento, 23–25 June*. https://event.unitn.it/cgsw35/CGSW_35_paper_27_poletto_et_al.pdf (accessed 7 September 2023).
Poletto, Cecilia & Laura Vanelli. 1997. Gli introduttori delle frasi interrogative nei dialetti italiani settentrionali. In Paola Benincà & Cecilia Poletto (eds.), *Strutture interrogative dell'Italia settentrionale*. Padua: Quaderni di lavoro ASIt. http://asit.maldura.unipd.it/papers.html (accessed 10 February 2022).
Reeve, Matthew. 2011. The syntactic structure of English clefts. *Lingua* 121(2). 142–171. https://doi.org/10.1016/j.lingua.2010.05.004
Rizzi, Luigi. 1990. *Relativized minimality*. Boston: MIT Press.
Rizzi, Luigi. 1997. The fine structure of the left periphery. In Liliane Haegeman (ed.), *Elements of grammar*. Dordrecht: Springer. https://doi.org/10.1007/978-94-011-5420-8_7.
Rizzi, Luigi. 2018. Intervention effects in grammar and language acquisition. *Probus* 30(2). 339–367. https://doi.org/10.1515/probus-2018-0006.
Sabel, Joachim & Jochen Zeller. 2006. Wh-question formation in Nguni. In John Mugane, John P. Hutchison & Dee A. Worman (eds.), *Selected proceedings of the 35th Annual Conference on African Linguistics*, 271–283. Somerville, MA: Cascadilla Proceedings Project. http://www.lingref.com/cpp/acal/35/paper1316.pdf (accessed 8 January 2022).
Samo, Giuseppe & Paola Merlo. 2021. Intervention effects in clefts: A study in quantitative computational syntax. *Glossa: A Journal of General Linguistics* 6(1). https://doi.org/10.16995/glossa.5742
Schachter, Paul. 1973. Focus and relativization. *Language* 49. 19–46.
Søfteland, Åshild. 2014. *Utbrytingskonstruksjonen i norsk spontantale*. [The cleft construction in Norwegian spontaneous speech]. Oslo: University of Oslo dissertation.

Speyer, Augustin. 2005. A prosodic factor for the decline of topicalisation in English. In Stephan Kepser & Marga Reis (eds.), *Linguistic evidence: Empirical, theoretical and computational perspectives*, 485–506. (Studies in Generative Grammar 85). Berlin/New York: Mouton de Gruyter.

Sulger, Sebastian. 2009. Irish clefting and information-structure. In Miriam Butt & Tracy Holloway King (eds.), *Proceedings of the LFG09 Conference*, 562–582. Stanford: CSLI Publications. https://web.stanford.edu/group/cslipublications/cslipublications/LFG/14/papers/lfg09sulger.pdf (accessed 21 February 2022).

Tollan, Rebecca. 2018. Unergatives are different: Two types of transitivity in Samoan. *Glossa: a journal of general linguistics* 3(1). https://doi.org/10.5334/gjgl.223

Tönnis, Swantje. 2018. Investigating the distribution of clefts in Written and Spoken German. The role of prosody. Paper presented at the conference of the *"Deutsche Gesellschaft für Sprache" on the relation between prosodic and referential structure*. Stuttgart, 7–9 March. https://idsl1.phil-fak.uni-koeln.de/sites/IDSLI/dozentenseiten/Heusinger/Konferenzen/Praesentationen_DGfS_2018/To__nnis-DGfS2018.pdf (accessed 10 February 2022).

Tönnis, Swantje, Fricke Lea M. & Alexander Schreiber. 2018. Methodological considerations on testing argument asymmetry in German cleft sentences. In Eric Fuß, Marek Konopka, Beata Trawinski & Ulrich H. Waßner (eds.), *Grammar and corpora 2016*, Heidelberg: Heidelberg University Publishing. 231–240. https://doi.org/10.17885/heiup.361.c4703

Torrence, Harold. 2013. A promotion analysis of Wolof clefts. *Syntax* 16(2). 176–215.

Traugott, Elisabeth. 1972. *The history of English syntax: A transformational approach to the history of English sentence structure*. New York: Holt, Rinehart and Winston.

Verhoeven. Elisabeth. 2017. Scales or features in verb meaning? Verb classes as predictors of syntactic behavior. *Belgian Journal of Linguistics* 31(1). 164–193. https://doi.org/10.1075/bjl.00007.ver

Vorderwülbecke, Klaus. 2018. Gewichtung bei Fokuspartikeln, Negation, Spalt- und Sperrsätzen. In Leibniz-Institut für Deutsche Sprache (eds.), *Systematische Grammatik. Grammatisches Informationssystem grammis*. https://grammis.ids-mannheim.de/systematische-grammatik/2361 (accessed 15 January 2022).

Walkden, George. 2016. *V2*. University of Manchester, June–August. http://walkden.space/V2.pdf (accessed 10 February 2022).

Wang, Luming. 2011. *The influence of animacy and context on word order processing: Neurophysiological evidence from Mandarin Chinese*. Leipzig: Max Planck Institute for Human Cognitive and Brain Sciences. https://pure.mpg.de/rest/items/item_858568/component/file_861031/content (accessed 10 February 2022).

Westergaard, Marit & Øystein Vangsnes. 2005. Wh-questions, V2, and the left periphery of three Norwegian Dialect types. *Journal of Comparative Germanic Linguistics* 8. 117–158. https://doi.org/10.1007/s10828-004-0292-1

Westergaard, Marit, Øystein Vangsnes & Terje Lohndal. 2017. Variation and change in Norwegian wh-questions. The role of the complementizer *som*. *Linguistic Variation* 17 (1). 8–43. https://doi.org/10.1075/lv.17.1.02wes

Wiltschko, Martina. 2001. The syntax of transitivity and its effects. Evidence from Halkomelem Salish. In Karine Megerdoomian & Leora Anne Bar-el (eds.), *WCCFL 20: Proceedings of the 20th West Coast Conference on Formal Linguistics*. 593–606. Somerville, Massachusetts: Cascadilla Press.

Woods, Rebecca & Sam Wolfe (eds.). 2020. *Rethinking Verb Second*. Oxford: Oxford University Press.

Adriana Belletti and Giuliano Bocci

3 Subject versus object clefts: A fresh perspective on a robust asymmetry

Insights from French answering strategies

Abstract: Cleft sentences constitute a form of focalization cross-linguistically. They come in different guises, though: either as new information clefts/NIC, or as contrastive/corrective clefts/CC. Explicitly expressed in cartographic terms, this distinction corresponds to the different (specifier of) focus position that the clefted constituent occupies, either in the low vP-periphery or in the high left periphery of the clause. As for their linear word order, the two types of clefts are not distinguishable. New experimental evidence based on French highlights this fundamental distinction, thus confirming insights from previous work: whereas subject clefts can be NIC, object clefts cannot, even in a language like French, which widely exploits clefts as an answering strategy to new information questions. Intervention locality expressed in featural Relativized Minimality terms is the fundamental principled reason accounting for this robust asymmetry.

Key words: New information clefts/NIC, contrastive/corrective clefts/CC, subject clefts, object clefts, focalization, featural Relativized Minimality/fRM

1 Introduction: Two types of clefts

Our point of departure in this article is the following insight drawn from previous work (Belletti & Bennati & Sorace 2007; Belletti 2009; 2012; 2015 and references cited therein): Cleft sentences constitute a form of focalization, cross-linguistically; however, cleft sentences come in different guises depending on the type of focalization that they express. They may express straight new information focus (new information clefts, henceforth NIC) or they may express a contrastive/corrective focus (Corrective clefts, henceforth CC). Explicitly expressed in cartographic terms, this distinction corresponds to the different positions that the clefted constituent occupies within the clause. Based on the quoted references, these positions correspond to either the Specifier of the clause-internal low, vP-peripheral Focus posi-

---

Adriana Belletti, Università di Siena, e-mail: adriana.belletti@unisi.it
Giuliano Bocci, Università di Siena, e-mail: giuliano.bocci@unisi.it

tion characteristically dedicated to new information focus, or the clause-external left peripheral focus position characteristically dedicated to contrast/correction (see references quoted for detailed discussion in a crosslinguistic perspective).

Given this fundamental insight from previous work, we assume that clefts sentences[1] of both types share the same fundamental property whereby the copula selects a small clause complement (as is always the case, Moro 1997) which, in this case, corresponds to a portion of the CP area. This small clause complement is a reduced CP structure. Given the map of the left periphery in (1) from Rizzi & Bocci (2017), the selected CP is a reduced structure truncated at the level of the FocP, as illustrated in (2):[2]

(1) Force > Int > Top > Q/Foc > Mod > Fin > IP

(2) .....[FOCP(NI) Foc *be* [ForceP.....[TopP [FOCP(CC) Foc [TopP ...[FinP [TP

As indicated in (2), the focus position hosting in its Spec the new information constituent (NI, in 2) is located in the immediate periphery of the matrix copula, whereas the focus position hosting in its Spec the correctively/contrastively focalized constituent (CC in 2) is located in the reduced left periphery of the CP-small clause complement of the copula. Hence, the vP-peripheral NI Spec/FocP is targeted by the focalized constituent of NICs, the left peripheral CC Spec/FocP is targeted by the focalized constituent of CCs.

Interestingly, in terms of their linear word order, the two types of clefts are not distinguishable. Consider the case of a subject cleft like (3):[3]

(3) C'est   Marie/MARIE   qui   a   parlé
     It is   Marie/MARIE   that has   spoken

---

[1] 'It-clefts' in the literature on English (Belletti 2015 and references cited therein; den Dikken 2013; Bonan 2021a; 2021b).
[2] (2) adapts the relevant structure, based on the references quoted in the text from previous work; details that are not crucial for the present discussion are omitted in order to focus only on the aspects that are relevant in the present investigation. See in particular Belletti (2015) and references cited therein for discussion of the status of *ce* in French and its integration in the structure which also involves the process of extraposition, and Belletti (2012; 2013b) on closer discussion of the low location of the complementizer in the *Fin* head, based on comparative considerations with Japanese *no*, the low complementizer of clefts in Japanese.
[3] We illustrate with French examples, as this is the main language of investigation in the present work.

The cleft in (3) may either correspond to a NIC or to a CC, with no difference in word order. However, the crucial difference lies in the position occupied by the clefted subject, corresponding to Spec/FocP(NI) or Spec/FocP(CC), explicitly expressed in cartographic terms as in (4)a-b, respectively:

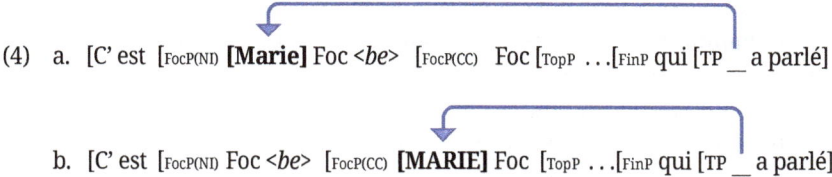

(4) a. [C' est [FocP(NI) **[Marie]** Foc <be> [FocP(CC) Foc [TopP …[FinP qui [TP __ a parlé]

b. [C' est [FocP(NI) Foc <be> [FocP(CC) **[MARIE]** Foc [TopP …[FinP qui [TP __ a parlé]

Different prosodic properties are associated with the different types of focus, once their representations are read at the phonological interface (Bocci 2013; Bianchi & Bocci & Cruschina 2016); whence the different writing of 'Marie' in (3), (4).[4]

This summarizes and spells out our fundamental analytical assumptions.

1.1 New information clefts as an answering strategy

A related further insight which will drive the investigation of the present article is the following: descriptive and experimental evidence on answering strategies has shown that, depending on the language, questions asking for the identification of the subject (e.g. *Who has brought these flowers?*) may be answered with a NIC (in e.g. French, Japanese, Norwegian…). A first manifestation of the existence of this type of characteristic answer has emerged from the particular angle of experimental work on the L2 acquisition of Italian undertaken by Belletti & Leonini (2004).[5] In the answers to questions asking for the identification of the subject expressed in their L2 Italian, L1 speakers of French answered with a cleft sentence, as in the following exchange:

---

[4] The derivations in (4) are somewhat simplified. For the sake of clarity we directly locate the quasi expletive subject 'ce' in the subject position, and directly move the clefted constituent, here the subject, into Spec/FocP(NI). See Belletti (2012; 2015) for further elaboration on the first merge position of 'ce' and the presence of an EPP/subject-like position within the (reduced) CP (as in the CP pseudo-relative complement of perception verbs, along the same lines originally discussed in Guasti (1993). Nothing hinges on this simplification, which will make the reading smoother, highlighting the fundamental insight.
[5] See Belletti (2018) for recent reassessment.

(5) Q: Chi ha portato questi fiori?   (from Belletti & Leonini 2004:(7))
         'Who has brought these flowers?'
     A: È la mamma che ha portato i fiori. (from Belletti & Leonini 2004:(8b))
         'It is the mother who has brought the flowers.'

The other L2 speakers tested, with German as their L1, did not resort to this type of answer, but rather to SV answers; similarly to L1 English speakers (at the *near native* level) later tested in Belletti et al. (2007). Belletti & Leonini's (2004) experiment eliciting answers to questions on the identification of the subject[6] has also been utilized as a controlled descriptive device: it has been doubled in a number of languages to test for the preferred answering strategy in the relevant language, given the same discourse conditions.[7]

In this article we will present new results from the newly adapted version of the experiment to French. As was to be expected given the first results from the L2 Italian answers provided by the L1 French speakers tested in Belletti & Leonini's original experiment, the answers provided by the French speakers for questions on the identification of the subject show ample use of NIC in their native French (Section 2.1).

1.2 Subject vs object clefts: New information clefts vs corrective clefts

However, a question concerning the identification of the object cannot be answered with a NIC. Contrasts like the following in French illustrate the point:

(6) Subject Question – Answer
     Q: Qui est parti/a parlé?
         'Who has left/has spoken'?
     A: C'est Jean (qui est parti/qui a parlé)
         'It is Jean (that has left/has spoken).'

---

[6] See Belletti & Leonini (2004) for detailed description, and the other references quoted above.

[7] Languages tested with the same design include: Brazilian Portuguese, Finnish, Croatian, English (Guesser 2011; Dal Pozzo 2011; 2015; Belletti 2013a for an overview). For newly tested results on French see Section 2.1. For further consistent results on different multilingual populations, see the already mentioned Belletti et al. (2007) on near native speakers and Caloi et al. (2018) on heritage speakers.

(7) Object Question – Answer
   Q: Qu'est-ce que t'as acheté / Marie a acheté ?
       'What have you bought / What has Mary bought?'
   A: ∗C'est un livre (que j'ai acheté / Marie a acheté).
       'It is a book (that I/Marie bought).'
   Q': Qui as-tu rencontré / est-ce-que Marie a rencontré ?
       'Whom have you met / whom has Marie met?'
   A': ∗C'est Pierre (que j'ai rencontré / que Marie a rencontré).
       'It is Pierre (that I have met /that Marie has met).'

Contrasts of this type have been discussed in Belletti (2009; 2015) based on grammaticality judgments provided by native speakers.[8] In the present article we provide new controlled experimental evidence strongly confirming this robust asymmetry.

But why should such an asymmetry exist to start with? We now spell out what our assumptions are to account for it, which in turn unveils the very clear prediction of the assumed approach, now corroborated by the new experimental results to be presented in Section 2.

1.2.1 Only subject clefts can express new information

The object cleft in (7)A is clearly a possible word by word well-formed sentence in French. It just cannot be used as an answer to the preceding question (7)Q. It can, instead be used as a corrective cleft, as in the exchange in (8), with the associated appropriate prosody:

(8) Context: Tu as finalement acheté un journal.
                'You have finally bought a newspaper.'
     Reply: No, no.   C'est   UN   LIVRE   que   j'ai   acheté
              No, no. It is   A   BOOK   that I have   bought

Given the analysis sketched in (4) for NIC and CC, the contrast between (7) and (8) amounts to saying that an object cleft can only be of the CC type, with the object displaced in the left periphery of the complement of the copula as illustrated in (9):

---

8 Both (7)A/A' are given as an illustration also indicating that the animate vs inanimate character of the preposed object does not play any role in modulating the unacceptability of the NI-object cleft. In the material used in the experiments presented in Section 2.1 the preposed object was always animate, as in (7)A'.

(9) [C' est [FOCP(NI)   Foc <be> [FOCP(CC) **[UN LIVRE]** Foc [TOPP . . .[FINP que [TP je/Marie ai/a acheté _]

In contrast, a subject cleft can be a NIC, witness the very existence of the NIC answering strategy discussed in 1.1 and in (6). The exchange in (10) shows that a subject cleft can also be of the CC type:

(10) Context: Marie est finalement partie.
              'Marie finally left.'
      Reply: No, no. C'est JOËLLE qui est partie.
              'No. It is JOËLLE who left.'
      Reply: No, no. C'est   JOËLLE   qui   est   partie.
              No   no. It is   JOËLLE   that have left

The derivation of the reply in (10) will have the subject displaced in the same left-peripheral Spec/FocP in the complement of the copula as in (9). (11) illustrates the derivation of the reply in (10).

(11) [C' est   [FOCP(NI)   Foc <be> [FOCP(CC) **[JOËLLE]** Foc [TOPP . . .[FINP qui [TP __ est partie]

In (4)a the derivation of the NIC subject cleft of the type in (6)A was illustrated, with the subject moved into the Spec/FocP position in the low vP periphery of the matrix copula. The question as to why an object cleft cannot be a NIC thus amounts to asking why a direct object cannot reach the low Spec/FocP position in the vP periphery of the matrix copula. The line of argument towards an explanation that we adopt here is presented in Section 1.3.

1.3 Intervention locality and the lack of object clefts expressing new information

Consider the derivation (4)a, repeated in (12)a for convenience, compared with the analogous derivation of a potential NIC involving the focalization of the direct object into the vP- peripheral Spec/Foc$_{(NI)}$ position illustrated in (12)b/b' for sentences (7)A/A':

3 Subject versus object clefts: A fresh perspective on a robust asymmetry — 87

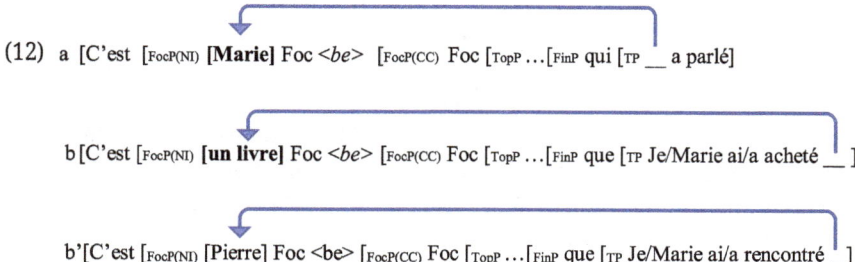

(12) a [C'est [FocP(NI) [**Marie**] Foc <*be*> [FocP(CC) Foc [TopP ...[FinP qui [TP __ a parlé]

b [C'est [FocP(NI) [**un livre**] Foc <*be*> [FocP(CC) Foc [TopP ...[FinP que [TP Je/Marie ai/a acheté __]

b'[C'est [FocP(NI) [**Pierre**] Foc <*be*> [FocP(CC) Foc [TopP ...[FinP que [TP Je/Marie ai/a rencontré __]

Assume, as in the previous quoted work, that the target NI Spec/FocP position shares properties with the subject position of the clause (Spec/TP). In terms of the A/A' distinction, such a position is computed as an A position.[9] Hence the NI Spec/FocP, while being a criterial position (Rizzi 2015a; 2015b), has the status of an A position.[10] This being the case, the reason for the impossibility of object-NICs finds an immediate answer: it is the consequence of a locality violation, specifically intervention locality expressed through the featural Relativized Minimality/fRM principle. In a nutshell, according to fRM the dependency between X (target) and Y (origin) in (13) cannot be established if Z (intervener) structurally intervenes, and Z and X are positions of the same type, sharing relevant features (Rizzi 1990; 2004; Starke 2001; Friedmann & Belletti & Rizzi 2009; Chomsky's 2001 Minimal search):

(13)
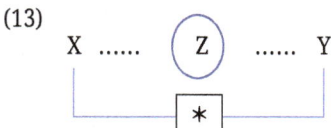

In (12)b/b' in its movement from its first merge position within the embedded TP (the base position, Y in 13) into the matrix Spec/FocP$_{(NI)}$ position (the target position, X in 13) the direct object (*un livre/Pierre*) crosses over the subject (*Je/Marie*, the intervener, Z in 13) in the embedded TP. Hence, a NI object cleft cannot be derived since it inevitably gives rise to an intervention locality problem, i.e. to a violation of fRM. Whence the strong judgement given by native speakers to answers such

---

9 Relevant in this respect is the fact that in a language like Italian, new information postverbal subjects filling the low Spec/Foc$_{(NI)}$ position give rise to verbal agreement (much as preverbal subjects do). As mentioned in previous work, the A/A' distinction may be a too coarse distinction. We continue to assume it here in the lack of a possibly better and more nuanced notion.
10 Akin in this respect to the Spec/SubjP position (Rizzi & Shlonsky 2007).

as those in (7)A/A'. The contrast between (12)a, a well-formed NI subject cleft, and (12)b/b' an impossible NI object cleft directly confirms, in turn, the crucial role played by the grammatical principle: a NI subject cleft can be properly computed since in its derivation no violation of fRM is produced. In its movement from its merge position within the embedded TP (the base position, Y in 13)[11] into the matrix Spec/FocP$_{(NI)}$ position (the target position, X in 13) the subject (*Marie*) does not cross any intervener (Z in 13).

In conclusion, it is for principled reasons that subject clefts can be realized both as NICs and as CCs whereas object clefts only admit the computation of CCs. This conclusion has the direct consequence that only subject clefts can function as answering strategies to questions of new information. Thus, even in languages that privilege the use of clefts in NI focus answers, such as French, only subjects can be properly clefted in the Spec/FocP$_{(NI)}$ position in the low vP-periphery of the matrix copula.

2 Experimental evidence

On the basis of the analysis presented in Section 1, we have concluded that (i) Subject clefts in French are a very natural and productive way to express a new information focus interpretation on subjects, e.g. in answers to subject wh-questions (Section 1.1). (ii) In contrast to subject clefts, object clefts cannot be used as a way to express a new information focus interpretation on objects (Section 1.2.1). This contrast between subject and object clefts holds true only in case of clefts conveying new information focus. (iii) In case of clefts that express corrective focus, both subject and object clefts are fully acceptable (Section 1.2). In this section, we discuss novel experimental evidence that supports these three points.

---

11 This position may be identified with vP-internal first merge, as in Rizzi & Shlonsky (2007), building on Rizzi (1982); a silent expletive-like *pro* thus fills the higher subject/EPP position; given its expletive nature and being in relation with the subject, it does not count as an intervener; see the cited previous work and much related literature on this aspect. Since nothing hinges on this particular detail, in order to provide a smoother presentation, the derivation of a subject cleft is illustrated with movement of the subject from the Spec/TP position (4b, 12a).

2.1 Elicitation experiment

To verify that subject clefts constitute a natural and productive answering strategy to subject questions, we adapted the elicitation experiment originally conducted by Belletti and Leonini (2004) in (L2) Italian to French.

2.1.1 Procedure, materials, and participants

As in its original version, this production experiment was run as a PowerPoint presentation. It consisted of 22 short videos illustrating a scene from everyday life. The videos were presented individually. After each video, participants were asked to answer prerecorded questions concerning the scene (from 1 to 3 questions per scene). The target questions included 34 subject wh-questions, aimed at inducing in the answers a new information focus interpretation on the subject. The original questions used by Belletti & Leonini (2004) were translated from Italian into French carefully ensuring that verbs of the same class were used: the subject wh-questions we tested included 6 wh-questions with unaccusative verbs, 10 with intransitive verbs, and 18 with transitive verbs. Besides these target questions, the experiment included 25 questions as distractors.[12]

51 native French speaker participants were recruited through internal advertising at the University of Geneva and the experiment was administered in a quiet room.[13] Their participation was not compensated. Each session started with the presentation of the experimental task. Then a short questionnaire concerning their linguistic background was presented to the participants. At the beginning of the experimental session, participants were instructed to answer the questions using sentences that contained a verb, in the way they felt was the most natural. The first trial presented to the participants was always a filler trial in which they were invited to describe the scene. The answers obtained were recorded, and subsequently transcribed and coded with respect to their syntactic structure.

---

[12] For the sake of completeness, the 25 fillers included 3 wh-questions with an existential construction, 5 polar questions, 3 object wh-questions, and 11 adjunct wh-questions. The 3 remaining questions were aimed at eliciting a description of the scene.
[13] Out of the 51 native speakers we tested, 15 reported to be early bilingual. The responses provided by these participants were in line with those of the 36 monolingual speakers.

2.1.2 Results

After the 34 experimental trials (i.e. subject wh-questions), we collected a total of 1730 answers, plus 4 null answers (the participants were unable to recall the scene). Besides 4 null answers, 189 answers had the form of nominal fragments (i.e. 10.9% of the data) and these datapoints were removed for the analysis. The remaining 1541 answers were all full sentences containing a verb.

Table 1: Elicitation experiment: types of structures collected in answers to subject wh-questions.

	Subject clefts	SV structures	Other structures	TOT
#	841	690	10	1541
%	54.61%	44.63%	0.75%	100%

Table 1 reports the types of structures we collected in answers to wh-subject questions. Subject clefts constitute the most frequent type of structure (54.61%), followed by SV sentences (44.63%). The other cases are very marginal (0.75%).[14]

These findings show that subject clefts are a natural and fully productive way of answering subject wh-questions in French. Furthermore, it may be revealing to compare them with those obtained from the L1 Italian speakers tested in Belletti & Leonini (2004) and those tested with the same material in Belletti et al. (2007). Consider Table 2.

Table 2: Answers to subjects wh-questions in French and Italian.

	Subject clefts	SV structures	VS structures	Other
French (L1)	54.61%	44.63%	0%	0.75%
Italian (L1) from Belletti & Leonini (2004)	0%	1%	98%	1%
Italian (L1) from Belletti et al. (2007)	0%	7%	93%	0%

As can be observed in Table 2, Italian native speakers virtually always expressed new information focus on subjects by producing structures in which the subject

---

14 More specifically, the category "other structures" includes 4 passive structures in which the subject of the wh-question appears as the "by-phrase" in the passive answer, and 6 cases of answers introduced by *il s'agit* "it is a question of".

appears in postverbal position (cf. Belletti 2004 and related work). It must be remembered, though, that subject clefts are perfectly acceptable in Italian, as no formal properties rule out their derivation (cf. Belletti 2009: Chapter 10). Still, they are not a productive way of answering subject wh-questions, as VS is the preferred answering strategy. By contrast, in French – where postverbal subjects cannot be licensed as they are in Italian – subject clefts are a natural and very productive way to express new information on subjects. Moreover, the new results from L1-French are perfectly in line with those originally obtained in the L2 Italian answers provided by French native speakers (69% of subject cleft answers in L2 Italian), and thus corroborate the analysis of these answers proposed in Belletti & Leonini (2004) as directly mimicking the L1.

2.2 Forced choice experiments

The results of the elicitation experiment fully confirm the use of subject clefts to convey new information on subjects in French. Let us now consider the other empirical predictions discussed in section 1. In contexts expressing new information focus, in contrast to subject clefts, object clefts are expected to be infelicitous. Furthermore, this asymmetry between objects and subjects should disappear in contexts in which the clefted element associates with a corrective focus import. In this section (2.2) and in the following one (2.3), we report the results of two forced choice experiments (FC experiments) that we carried out to test these predictions. In both FC experiments we compared the preference for cleft over SVO sentences in relation to the syntactic role of the clefted element (subject vs object), and to the focus interpretation at play (new information vs corrective focus).

2.2.1 FC experiment 1

2.2.1.1 Procedure and participants

FC experiment 1 was set up as a web-based experiment on PCIbex featuring a two-alternative forced choice task. Stimuli were presented in the form of short written dialogues between two fictional characters (speaker A and speaker B). Each exchange was introduced by a short description of the scene in which the dialogue takes place. At end of each exchange, speaker B could reply with two alternative sentences (presented in blue on the screen). Participants were asked to take speaker B's role and to select the alternative that sounded more natural within the dialogue. Once the sentence was selected with the mouse, a button appeared in order to confirm the selection and to move to the next trial. Each stimulus/exchange was presented individually.

45 participants were recruited via Prolific.co (https://www.prolific.co/) and paid 2.00 GPB for their participation. The campaign was profiled to recruit participants that reported to be native speakers of French, raised monolingual, born and living in France, and with no experience of language and hearing disorders, aged between 18 and 40. The entire experiment lasted on average 12–15 minutes.

The experiment started with a brief description of the task, followed by the consent form. To double-check the recruitment conditions specified on Prolific.co, participants were then asked to answer a short preliminary questionnaire (if they were native speakers of French, where they currently live in France, where they grew up, if they are bilingual, and their age). After the questionnaire, a page with detailed instructions was presented. Participants were instructed to imagine the dialogues as ordinary conversations, to keep in mind how they use language in their everyday life, and to read the sentences with the intonation that they found more natural. The experiment continued then with a short familiarization session (4 trial) that preceded the experimental phase. A debriefing page closed the experiment.

2.2.1.2 Design and materials

The design included four conditions, resulting from crossing two binary independent factors. Both factors were manipulated within participants and between items. The first factor (*focus type*) concerned the discourse context which introduced speaker's B alternative continuations: we manipulated the content of speaker A's turn, and the beginning of speaker B's turn to induce the presence of either a (narrow) corrective focus or a (narrow) new information focus interpretation in speaker B's alternatives. More specifically, in one case, speaker B corrected a previous sentence asserted by speaker A, while, in the other, speaker B answered an information seeking wh-question asked by speaker A. Notice that in the conditions inducing new information focus, speaker A's wh-questions featured the interrogative element *est-ce que/qui* in both object and subject wh-questions. We will come back to this point in Section 2.2. The second factor (*focused element*) concerned the syntactic role of the focused element in B's alternatives: either the subject or the direct object in transitive clauses.

The two alternatives proposed to the participants were unreduced sentences: a cleft sentence and a SVO sentence. An item illustrating the four conditions is reported in (14)–(17).

(14) *Corrective focus on the subject*
Context:
Hier soir, il y a eu la réunion mensuelle de l'association de ton quartier. Le président de l'association était absent et tu es en train de lui raconter ce qui s'est passé. Il y a eu des disputes entre les membres présents: un projet que l'association avait présenté à la ville a été refusé, et la responsabilité de cet échec a échauffé les esprits. Au final, des insultes ont même été proférées.
'Last night, the monthly meeting of your neighborhood association took place. The president of the association wasn't there, and you are reporting to him what happened. There was some arguing among the members: the city hall rejected a project presented by the association and the responsibility of this failure got people worked up. Eventually, some insults were exchanged.'

a. <u>The president (i.e. speaker A):</u>
Je n'aurais jamais imaginé qu'ils en arrivent là. C'est incroyable que Sandrine ait insulté la I.
'I would never have imagined that they would get to that point. It is incredible that Sandrine insulted the manager.'

b. <u>You (i.e. speaker b):</u>
Mais non ! C'est pas du tout ça !
'This is not what happened!'

C'est la trésorière qui a insulté la responsable !   *(CC) Cleft alternative*
'It was the treasurer who insulted the manager!'

La trésorière a insulté la responsable !   *SVO alternative*
'The treasurer insulted the manager!'

(15) *Corrective focus on the object*
Context as in (14)

a. <u>The president:</u>
Je n'aurais imaginé qu'ils en arrivent là. C'est incroyable que la trésorière ait insulté Sandrine.
'I would never have imagined that they would get to that point. It is incredible that the treasurer insulted Sandrine.'

b. <u>You:</u>
Mais non ! C'est pas du tout ça !
'This is not what happened!'

C'est la responsable que la trésorière a insultée ! *(CC) Cleft alternative*
'It was the manager whom the treasurer insulted!'

La trésorière a insulté la responsable ! *SVO alternative*
'The treasurer insulted the manager!'

(16) *New information focus on the subject*
Context as in (14)

a. The president:
Je n'aurais jamais imaginé qu'ils en arrivent là. Qui est-ce qui a insulté la responsable ?
'I would never have imagined thate they would get to that point. Who insulted the manager?'

b. You:
C'est la trésorière qui a insulté la responsable. *(NI) Cleft alternative*
'It was the treasurer who insulted the manager.'

La trésorière a insulté la responsable- *SVO alternative*
'The treasurer insulted the manager.'

(17) New information focus on the object
Context as in (14)

a. The president:
Je n'aurais jamais imaginé qu'ils en arrivent là. Qui est-ce que la trésorière a insulté ?
'I would never have imagined that they would get to that point. Who did the manager insult?'

b. You:
C'est la responsable que la trésorière a insultée. *(NI) Cleft alternative*
'It was the manager whom the treasurer insulted.'
La trésorière a insulté la responsable. *SVO alternative*
'The treasurer insulted the manager.'

We tested 16 items consisting each of 4 different versions, corresponding to the 4 experimental conditions (cf (14)–(17)), for a total of 64 experimental stimuli. Each item was introduced by the same short description. In all of the items, the target sentences (speaker B's alternative sentences) featured transitive verbs, and both the subject and the object were human and singular. In a half of the stimuli (8 items), the subject and the object were both realized by proper names, while in the other half (8 items), they were both realized by definite descriptions, always matching for gender (i.e. masculine in a half of the items, female in the other half).

Following a Latin square procedure, the 64 experimental stimuli were divided into 4 lists, consisting each of 16 experimental trials, in which each item appeared only once. Participants were randomly assigned to one of the 4 lists. Experimental trials were then interspersed with 16 filler trials, featuring exchanges analogous to the experimental trials. In the fillers, the alternatives consisted of pairs of wh-questions with the wh-element occurring in situ and ex situ.[15] With the function of attention check, we included in the fillers 4 trials with indirect wh-questions. In these structures, wh-in situ is ungrammatical: see (18), where the second alternative is flagrantly unacceptable (* omitted from the example).

(18) *Alternatives in an attention check trial*
Toi:
Tu sais quoi ? Elles ont oublié à qui Pierre a menti.   *Ex situ alternative*

Tu sais quoi ? Elles ont oublié Pierre a menti à qui.   *In situ alternative*

'You know what? They forgot to whom Pierre lied.'

The presentation order of the stimuli was pseudo-randomized and the order in which the alternatives were displayed was counterbalanced.

2.2.1.3 Results

Out of the 45 participants that took part in the experiment, 8 participants failed at least one attention check trial (expressing their preference for the *in situ* counterpart of the indirect wh-question), and their data were thus removed for the analysis. The analysis of the preliminary questionnaires confirmed that, in line with the recruitment criteria, all the 37 remaining participants were native speakers of French, raised monolingual, born and currently living in France.

The data we collected were fitted with a multi-level mixed effects regression with log odds of preferring cleft sentences over SVO sentences as the dependent variable, and *focus type* and *focused element* as fixed factors. The model was specified with a dummy coding schema with corrective focus and object as the reference category. The most complex random effect structure justified by the data included

---

[15] For the sake of completeness, fillers included 4 monoclausal (direct) wh-questions, 4 biclausal (direct) wh-questions with short-distance movement, 4 biclausal (direct) wh-questions with long-distance movement, and 4 indirect questions (used as an attention check). All the pairs of alternatives differed with respect the position of the wh-element (in situ vs. ex situ).

by-item and by-participant intercepts and slopes for both factors. A summary of the statistical model is reported in Table 3. The probabilities of selecting cleft over SVO sentences extracted from the model are plotted in Figure 1.[16]

Table 3: FC Experiment 1. Summary of the statistical model.

Predictors	Preference for Cleft over SVO		
	Odds Ratios	C.I.	p
(Intercept) [new information focus; Object]	0.40	0.22 – 0.71	**0.002**
focus type [corrective focus]	9.59	4.19 – 21.96	**<0.001**
focused element [Subject]	20.67	7.48 – 57.14	**<0.001**
focus type [corrective focus] * focused element [Subject]	0.57	0.17 – 1.94	0.369

The statistical analysis revealed that in case of new information focus on objects (the intercept in the model), the preference for cleft sentences over SVO is significantly much lower than chance. To put it in other words, participants significantly prefer SVO sentences over object cleft in answering object wh-questions, as the reader can observe in Figure 1. This contrasts with the condition in which new information is associated with the subject of the clause: in case of subject wh-questions the probability of answering with a subject cleft is significantly much higher.

Notably, object cleft sentences are not always dispreferred over SVO sentences: when the object expresses corrective focus rather than new information focus, the preference for object clefts is significantly higher, to a rate equivalent to the condition of corrective focus on subjects (as indicated by the lack of a significant interaction in the model).

In conclusion, all the predictions were borne out. In new information focus contexts subject clefts are highly chosen (and preferred over SVO) whereas object clefts are not. In contrast, when the context prompts correction, both subject and object clefts are preferred.

---

[16] The reader may wonder whether the nature of the clefted element (a definite description vs a proper name) may have an impact on the preference for clefts. We explored this hypothesis by building a model analogous to the one described in the main text with 3 independent factors: besides *focus type* (corrective vs new information) and *focused element* (object vs subject), we added *XP type* (proper name vs. definite description). The model revealed that the type of XP did not play any significant role (not even in interaction with the other factors).

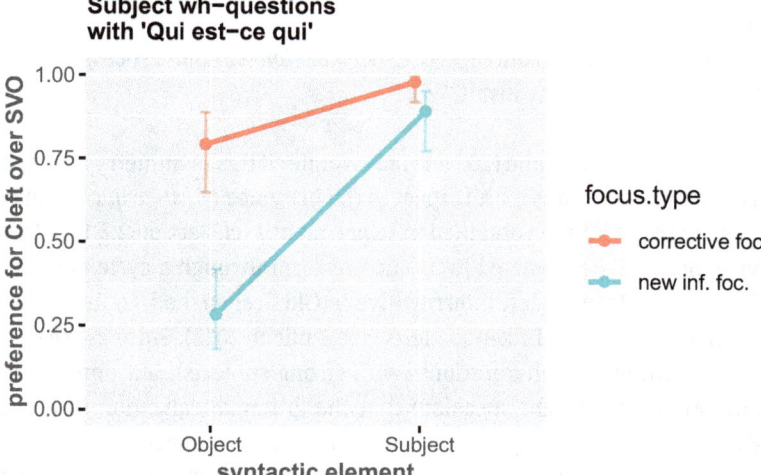

Figure 1: FC experiment 1: estimated probability of selecting clefts over SVO sentences (C.I. =.95).

2.2.2 FC experiment 2

In FC experiment 1, we induced a new information focus interpretation on the relevant constituent (either the subject or the object) by using information seeking wh-questions. A question that may come to mind is then whether the way wh-questions are formulated might impact on the preference for clefts in the answers.

In FC experiment 1, both subject and object wh-questions included the interrogative element *est-ce qui/que*. However, wh-question formation in French displays an asymmetry between subject and object questions. Subject wh-questions are acceptable with and without this element, and its presence seems to be related more to register variation, rather than structural requirements. This is not the case in object wh-questions when the intervening subject is a proper name or a definite description, as in our examples: in these structures, the absence of *est-ce que* leads to a perceivable degradation. Compare (19) and (20).

(19) a. Qui est-ce qui a insulté la responsable ?   *S-wh question with 'est-ce qui'*
      b. Qui a insulté la responsable ?   *S-wh question without 'est-ce qui'*
         'Who insulted the manager?'

(20) a. Qui est-ce que la trésorière a insulté ?   *O-wh question with 'est-ce que'*
   b. ??Qui la trésorière a insulté ?   *O-wh question without 'est-ce que'*
   'Who did the treasurer insult?'

Given the contrast between (19) and (20), one may wonder if this asymmetry between subject and object wh-questions with respect to the presence of *est-ce que/qui* may have an impact on the results we obtained in Experiment 1 (cf. Section 2.2.1.3). This interrogative expression has evolved to its current form through a cycle of grammaticalization starting from a cleft interrogative in Old French, and, in this sense, *est-ce que/qui* is diachronically linked to clefts (see Tailleur 2013). Since *est-ce que/qui* is obligatory with object wh-questions (with strong subjects), but optional in subject wh-questions, one might speculate that the grammaticalization of *est-ce que/qui* might be at a different stage in object and in subject wh-questions: the presence of *est-ce qui* in subject wh-questions could be perceived as marked, priming and boosting thus the preference for clefts over SVO sentences. In contrast, the presence of *est-ce que* in object wh-questions – which is mandatory – would not be perceived as marked and, in this sense, it would not induce a preference for clefted alternatives. If this line of hypothesis were correct, the observed preference for answering subject wh-questions with a cleft rather than with a SVO sentence might be induced by the presence of *est-ce qui* in the subject wh-questions condition.

In order to test if the way subject wh-questions are formulated may impact on the way participants answered in our task and provide thus an alternative account for our findings, we carried out a second forced choice experiment: FC experiment 2.

2.2.2.1 Procedure, design, and materials

The procedure and the design of FC experiment 2 were identical to FC Experiment 1. We tested the very same materials with the relevant exception of the subject wh-questions that introduced the alternatives in the new information focused subject condition: 'est-ce qui' did not occur in speaker's A question. Compare (16.a) from FC experiment 1 with (16'.a) tested in FC experiment 2.

(16')   New information focus on the subject
. . .

   a. The president:
   Je n'aurais jamais imaginé qu'ils en arrivent là. Qui a insulté la responsable ?
   'I would never have imagined that they would get to that point. Who insulted the manager?'

45 Participants (none of them tested in FC experiment 1) were recruited via Prolific. co with the same compensation and the same screening criteria (they were raised monolingual, born and living in France, aged between 18 and 40).

2.2.2.2 Results

Out of the 45 native French speakers tested in FC experiment 2, 8 participants failed at least 1 attention check trial and their datapoints were removed. The remaining data were fitted as described for FC experiment 1. As before, the most complex random effect structure justified by the data included by-item and by-participant intercepts and slopes for both factors. A summary of the statistical model obtained for FC experiment 2 is reported in Table 4 and the probabilities of selecting cleft over SVO sentences are plotted in Figure 2.

Table 4: FC Experiment 2. Summary of the statistical model.

Predictors	Preference for Cleft over SVO		
	Odds Ratios	C.I.	p
(Intercept)	0.32	0.14 – 0.73	**0.006**
[new information focus; Object]			
focus type [corrective focus]	21.91	7.28 – 65.96	**<0.001**
focused element [Subject]	25.16	8.19 – 77.24	**<0.001**
focus type [corrective focus] * focused element [Subject]	0.30	0.07 – 1.29	0.105

The statistical model output results that perfectly replicate those of FC experiment 1 as is clear by comparing Tables 3 and 4, and Figures 1 with 2. As before, in contexts that induce a new information focus on the object, object clefts are significantly dispreferred over SVO sentences, while the same type of focus interpretation on subjects strongly favors subject clefts over SVO sentence. The contrast between new information focus on objects and on subjects is significant (p=.006).

In conclusion, the comparison between FC experiment 1 and 2 shows that the strong preference for subject clefts in answers to new information subject wh-questions is unrelated to the presence of *est-ce qui* in the preceding wh-questions: subject clefts are overwhelmingly preferred to express new information focus on subjects, independently of how the subject wh-questions is formed.

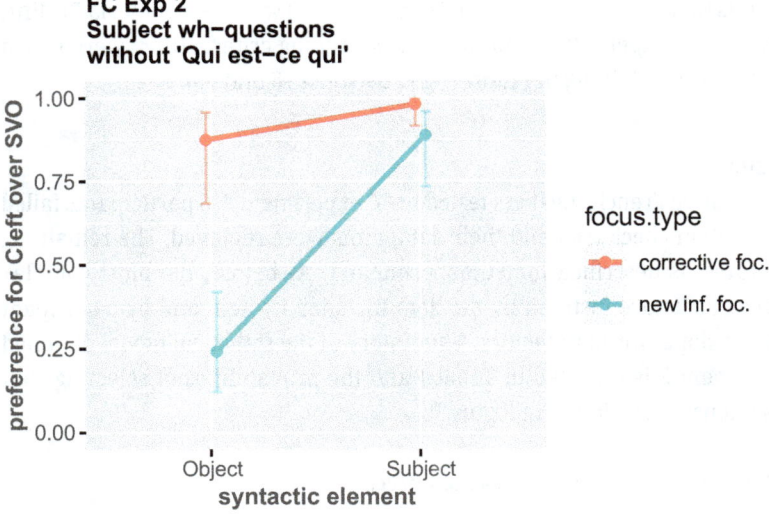

Figure 2: FC experiment 2: estimated probability of selecting clefts over SVO sentences.

3 Summary and concluding remarks

In this paper we have reported novel experimental evidence that meets the predictions on the conditions that license declarative clefts in French proposed in Belletti (2009; 2012; 2015 and related work) on the basis of judgments from native speakers and experimental results in L2. In contexts in which the subject qualifies as new information focus – as in answers to subject wh-questions – or as corrective focus, subject clefts are perfectly natural. In contrast, when it is the object that qualifies as the focus, a distinction between the two types of focus emerges. In contexts in which the object expresses new information focus, object clefts are not felicitous, while they are natural if the object conveys a corrective focus interpretation.

According to the analysis developed in Belletti (2009; 2012; 2015 and related work), cleft sentences expressing new information and corrective focus feature different syntactic derivations, despite the fact that they display the same word order. The clefted element in new information focus clefts targets the Specifier of a New Information Focus Projection located in the immediate periphery of the matrix copula, while the clefted element in corrective clefts targets the Specifier of the left peripheral Focus Projection in the (reduced) CP of the small clause, which is the complement of copula.

Besides their positional difference (and their interpretative import), the two focus positions also differ with respect to another relevant aspect: unlike the left peripheral Corrective Focus Projection, the Specifier of the New Information Focus Projection qualifies as an A position, analogously to the subject position of the clause (i.e. Spec;TP). As a result, a clefted object that moves to the NIF projection crossing a preverbal subject gives rise to a featural Relativized Minimality/fRM violation, from which the deviant status of object NICs follows. In contrast, a similar violation is not generated when an object moves to the left peripheral Corrective Focus Projection crossing a subject in Spec;TP. Analogously, no fRM violation obtains when a clefted subject is moved to the Specifier of the New Information Focus Projection or to the Specifier of the left peripheral Corrective Focus position.

In order to test the conditions that license cleft sentences by means of controlled techniques, we carried out an elicitation experiment and two web-based forced choice experiments. The experimental results we obtained fully support the above-mentioned analysis. First, subject clefts are a natural answering strategy to express new information subjects in French, while object clefts are not equally felicitous to express new information focus objects. This asymmetry between objects and subjects, however, disappears when clefts are used to express a corrective focus interpretation on the clefted element: in these contexts, both object and subject clefts appear to be equally natural. The robust asymmetry between subject and object clefts is thus sharply corroborated by new results presented here.

References

Belletti, Adriana. 2004. Aspects of the low IP area. In Luigi Rizzi (ed.), *The structure of CP and IP. The cartography of syntactic structures, volume 2*, 16–51. New York: Oxford University Press.
Belletti, Adriana. 2009. *Structures and strategies*. London/New York: Routledge.
Belletti, Adriana. 2012. Revisiting the CP of clefts. In Günther Grewendorf & Thomas Ede Zimmermann (eds.), *Discourse and Grammar. From Sentence Types to Lexical Categories*, 91–114. Berlin/New York: de Gruyter.
Belletti, Adriana. 2013a. Contributing to linguistic theory, language description and the characterization of language development through experimental studies. In Misha Becker, John Grinstead & Jason Rothman (eds.), *Generative linguistics and acquisition: Studies in honor of Nina M. Hyams*, 309–324. Amsterdam: John Benjamins.
Belletti, Adriana. 2013b. On Fin: Italian che, Japanese no and the selective properties of the copula in clefts. In Yoichi Miyamoto, Daiko Takahashi, Hideki Maki, Masao Ochi, Koji Sugisaki & Asako Uchibor (eds.), *Deep insights, broad perspectives. Essays in honor of Mamoru Saito*, 41–55. Tokyo: Kaitakusha.
Belletti, Adriana. 2015. The focus map of clefts: Extraposition and predication. In Ur Shlonsky (ed.), *Beyond functional sequence. The cartography of syntactic structures*, Vol. 10, 42–59. Oxford: Oxford University Press.

Belletti, Adriana. 2018. Revisiting the cartography of (Italian) postverbal subjects from different angles with reference to canonicality considerations. *Italian Journal of Linguistics* 30(2). 37–58. DOI: https://doi.org/10.26346/1120-2726-123

Belletti, Adriana, Elisa Bennati & Antonella Sorace. 2007. Theoretical and developmental issues in the syntax of subjects: Evidence from near-native Italian. *Natural Language & Linguistic Theory* 25(4). 657–689. DOI: https://doi.org/10.1007/s11049-007-9026-9

Belletti, Adriana & Leonini, Chiara. 2004. Subject inversion in L2 Italian. In Susan Foster-Cohen, Michael Sharwood Smith, Antonella Sorace & Mitsuhiko Ota (eds.), *EUROSLA Yearbook: Volume 4.*, 95–118. Amsterdam: John Benjamins.

Bianchi, Valentina, Giuliano Bocci & Silvio Cruschina. 2016. Focus fronting, unexpectedness, and evaluative implicatures. *Semantics and Pragmatics* 9(3). DOI: https://doi.org/10.3765/sp.9.3

Bocci, Giuliano. 2013. *The syntax–prosody interface: A cartographic perspective with evidence from Italian*. (Linguistik Aktuell/Linguistics Today Vol. 204). Amsterdam: John Benjamins Publishing.

Bonan, Caterina. 2021a. *Romance interrogative syntax*. (Linguistik Aktuell/Linguistics Today Vol. 266). Amsterdam: John Benjamins.

Bonan, Caterina. 2021b. The periphery of vP in the theory of wh-in situ. *Glossa: A Journal of General Linguistics* 6(1). 103. DOI: https://doi.org/10.16995/glossa.5714

Caloi, Irene, Adriana Belletti & Cecilia Poletto. 2018. Multilingual competence influences answering strategies in Italian–German speakers. *Frontiers in Psychology* 9(1971). doi: 10.3389/fpsyg.2018.01971. PMID: 30429806; PMCID: PMC6220047.

Chomsky, Noam. 2001. Derivation by phase. In Michael Kenstowicz (ed.), *Ken Hale: A life in language*, 1–50. Cambridge, MA: MIT Press.

Dal Pozzo, Lena. 2011. *Testing the acquisition of new information subjects: Evidence from Italian and Finnish*. Siena: University of Siena PhD dissertation.

Dal Pozzo, Lena. 2015. *New information subjects in L2 acquisition: Evidence from Italian and Finnish*. Florence: Florence University Press. Retrieved from 10.36253/978-88-6655-870-5

den Dikken, Marcel. 2013. Predication and specification in the syntax of cleft sentences. In Katharina Hartmann & Tonjes Veenstra (eds.), *Cleft structures*, 35–70. Amsterdam: John Benjamins Publishing Company. DOI: https://doi.org/10.1075/la.208.02dik

Friedmann, Naama & Belletti, Adriana & Rizzi, Luigi. 2009. Relativized relatives: Types of intervention in the acquisition of A-bar dependencies. *Lingua* 119(1). 67–88. DOI: https://doi.org/10.1016/j.lingua.2008.09.002

Guasti, Maria Teresa. 1993. *Causative and perception verbs*. Turin: Rosenberg and Sellier.

Guesser, Simone. 2011. *La sintassi delle frasi cleft in portoghese brasiliano*. Siena: University of Siena PhD dissertation.

Moro, Andrea. 1997. *The raising of predicates: Predicative noun phrases and the theory of clause structure*. Cambridge: Cambridge University Press.

Rizzi, Luigi. 1982. *Issues in Italian syntax*. Dordrecht: Foris.

Rizzi, Luigi. 1990. *Relativized minimality*. Cambridge, MA: The MIT Press.

Rizzi, Luigi. 2004. Locality and left periphery. In Adriana Belletti (ed.), *The cartography of syntactic structures*, Vol. 3: *Structures and beyond*, 223–251. Oxford University Press: New York.

Rizzi, Luigi. 2015a. Cartography, Criteria, and Labeling. In Ur Shlonsky (ed.), *Beyond functional sequence. The cartography of syntactic structures*, Vol. 10, 314–338. Oxford University Press.

Rizzi, Luigi. 2015b. Notes on labeling and subject positions. In Elisa Di Domenico & Cornelia Hamann & Simona Matteini (eds.), *Structures, strategies and beyond. Studies in honour of Adriana Belletti*, Vol. 223, 17–46. Amsterdam: John Benjamins Publishing Company. Retrieved from https://benjamins.com/#catalog/books/la.223/main

Rizzi, Luigi & Bocci, Giuliano. 2017. Left periphery of the clause: Primarily Illustrated for Italian. In Martin Everaert & Henk Van Riemsdijk (eds.), *The Wiley Blackwell companion to syntax* (2nd Edn.). Oxford: Wiley-Blackwell. https://doi.org/10.1002/9781118358733.wbsyncom104

Rizzi, Luigi & Shlonsky, Ur. 2007. Strategies of subject extraction. In Hans Martin Gärtner & Uli Sauerland (eds.), *Interfaces + recursion = language? Chomsky's Minimalism and the view from syntax-semantics*, 115–160. Berlin/New York: Mouton de Gruyter.

Starke, Michal. 2001. *Move dissolves into merge: A theory of locality.* Geneva: Université de Genève dissertation.

Tailleur, Sandrine. 2013. *The French wh interrogative system: Est-ce que, clefting?* Toronto: University of Toronto PhD dissertation.

Charlotte Bourgoin and Kristin Davidse
4 Making the case for distinguishing information structure from specification in English *it*-clefts

Abstract: In this chapter, we argue against the view that the syntax of clefts codes focus-presupposition semantics. Theoretically, we assume that grammar and prosody code distinct types of functional organisation, while descriptively, we ground the proposed account in corpus study of contextualised spoken data. We argue that *it*-clefts are specificational constructions, whose relative clause and antecedent represent an open proposition and its filler, i.e. the variable and value, related to each other by the identifying matrix, which triggers an implicature of exhaustiveness. Onto the specificational relation, a great variety of prosodically coded information structures can be mapped. We classify and quantify the informational patterns attested in our dataset in terms of Halliday's (1967a) influential distinction between unmarked presenting and marked contrastive focus. We establish that the most common information structure of *it*-clefts, if we take full and reduced clefts together, is that in which contrastive focus relates to presupposed information. However, in a significant minority of cases, full *it*-clefts manifest the information structure in which recoverable information precedes a presenting focus, while, most commonly, full *it*-clefts involve a combination of the contrastive focus pattern on the matrix and presenting foci on the cleft relative clause. We show that these patterns can also account for the neglected phenomenon of selective focus on an element of the value, and we discuss how this interacts with the implicature of exhaustive specification.

Keywords: clefts, information structure, English, specificational constructions

1 Introduction

At the risk of simplifying somewhat, it seems fair to say that *it*-clefts are often seen as the paradigm example of a construction whose syntax expresses information structural meaning. On this view, a cleft like *It was Doom who framed Roger Rabbit* expresses a simple proposition, *Doom framed Roger Rabbit*, but unpacks it into

---

Charlotte Bourgoin, University of Leuven, e-mail: charlotte.bourgoin@kuleuven.be
Kristin Davidse, University of Leuven, e-mail: kristin.davidse@kuleuven.be

the pragmatic constituents of an exhaustive focus, *Doom*, and a presupposition, *x framed Roger Rabbit*. Subject *it* and verb *be* are viewed as semantically empty elements whose only function is focus marking.

(1) Who framed Roger Rabbit? It was Doom who framed Roger Rabbit.

This view has a long tradition in both formal (e.g. Chomsky 1971, Akmajian [1973] 1979, Kiss 1998) and more functional approaches (e.g. Prince 1978; Hedberg 1990, 2000, 2013; Lambrecht 1994, 2001). With it, have come specific predictions about the prosodic realisation of the focus and presupposition constituents.

(2) It was DOOM who framed Roger Rabbit.

(3) It was DOOM who was in fact the MURDERER.

(4) It was not DOOM who vanquished ROGER. It was ROGER who vanquished DOOM.

According to Lambrecht (2001), an example like (2) illustrates the typical prosodic pattern of English *it*-clefts, in which the focus phrase is "necessarily accented" (2001: 493) while the presupposition is typically "unaccented" (2001: 479). If the presupposition is not "sufficiently salient in the discourse" (Lambrecht 2001: 480), as in (3), then it can carry an accent, which Lambrecht analyses as a topic accent because he views the presupposition as inherently topical. By contrast, Hedberg (2013) allows for the possibility of focus accents on the presupposition constituent, amongst others, in case of complex focus, i.e. two foci related to one focus operator, as illustrated in (4).

In this chapter, we will argue for an alternative account of *it*-clefts, which does not view them as a construction dedicated solely to the expression of information structural meaning. Rather, we advocate a 'non-derivational' structural analysis (Davidse 2000; Huddleston and Pullum 2002), according to which they are specificational constructions. Their identifying matrix specifies a value, e.g. *Doom* in (1), for a variable, i.e. the gap in the proposition expressed by the relative clause, *x who framed Roger Rabbit*. Onto these grammatical constituents, a much greater variety of focus assignment patterns can be mapped than recognised in the pragmatic account.

A few of these non-recognised patterns are illustrated in (5)–(7), with the preceding discourse given in brackets.

(5) (that's Tony Dunn -- Dunn down the line now -- aiming for Best -- or Aston -- missed them both) and it's Derby that take up the COUNT (LLC)[1]

(6) (and within about ten or fifteen years -- people are going to be asking) why on earth it WAS that Britain was allowed to get beHIND (LLC)

(7) (because there's not the same pressure on the material) it's the POP material that counts (LLC)

In (5), the postverbal complement does not carry a focal accent, which is problematic for the pragmatic approach which analyses it as inherently focal, but not for our analysis which analyses this constituent as the value of the specificational relation. In (6), the focal accent on the copula in the matrix is motivated by the interrogative mood, which we will incorporate in our account. Finally, in (7), it is only the premodifier *pop* of the value NP, which is focal. Importantly, the presupposition in this example is *x material that counts*, which does not coincide with the grammatical constituent of the relative clause. Again, this is problematic for approaches that ascribe information structure semantics to the syntactic constituents of clefts.

The main thesis of this chapter is the need to distinguish the specificational semantics construed by the lexicogrammatical structure of *it*-clefts from the very diverse information structural patterns coded by prosody which may be mapped onto the specificational relation.

The alternative account that we develop is motivated by the empirical evidence from spontaneous spoken dialogue as illustrated in (5)–(7), which casts doubt on the enterprise to explain the intonation in terms of the alleged focus–presupposition semantics of the grammatical constituents (see Bourgoin, O'Grady and Davidse 2021). Our account is also motivated by different theoretical views on the nature of the grammatical sign. We assume that grammatical meaning is naturally symbolised by the grammar and prosody of a language (Bolinger 1977; Halliday 1967a, 1994; Langacker 1987, 1991, 2021). This is incompatible with the idea of semantically empty elements and form-meaning mismatches, which are invoked in the pragmatic account of *it*-clefts.

This chapter will be structured as follows. In Section 2, we outline our theoretical-descriptive framework, focusing in particular on the semantics and prosodic realisation of information structure. In Section 3, we make our case for ascribing

---

[1] Cited examples were extracted with the proper licences: those followed by (WB) from WordbanksOnline and those followed by (LLC) from the first London Lund Corpus, as included in ICE-GB-2.

specificational semantics to *it*-clefts. In Section 4, we describe the compilation of our dataset from the London Lund Corpus and our prosodic annotation of the sound files. In Section 5, we present our corpus-based study of the prosodically coded focus assignment in our cleft data, which we interpret in terms of the unmarked and marked information structures distinguished by Halliday (1967a, 1994). In Section 6, we home in on the neglected issue of selective focus illustrated in (7), which shows particularly clearly that the focus–presupposition organisation is associated with the prosodically coded information structure of clefts. In Section 7, we offer conclusions and discuss perspectives for future research.

2 Theoretical-descriptive framework

2.1 Theoretical premises

The primordial tenet of Halliday's (1994) functional linguistic theory is that the grammatical meaning of linguistic signs is *naturally* symbolised by the grammar and prosody of a language. The meaning and form of a grammar cannot be separated from each other. They constitute the two sides of the same symbolic relation. Grammatical meaning is language-specific, not universal. From language-specific usage, the semantics of grammar can be derived in basically two ways: firstly, by cracking the coding relation between form and meaning, and, secondly, by generalising from specific usage tokens to increasingly schematic structural representations.[2]

The second crucial tenet in Halliday's (1967a, 1994) theory is that utterances convey three main types of functional meaning, which are all naturally coded by grammatical and phonological form, and which, very roughly, can be summarised as follows. The *representational*[3] organisation of the clause is concerned with *representing* experienced processes in the world as well as processes within our consciousness in terms of process-participant structures. This organisation is coded

---

[2] This does not mean that Halliday rejects, for instance, a logical approach to language. He merely states that logic does not capture language-specific meaning, and is, of its nature, not concerned with the symbolic relation defining linguistic signs. He does recognise a type of meaning, referred to by Hjelmslev ([1947]1961) as the 'purport' of utterances, which is "intertranslatable" between different languages and "could, for example, be analyzed from one or another logical, or . . . psychological, point of view" (1961: 51) or within (social) anthropology (1961: 78).

[3] Halliday (1967a, 1994) in fact uses the term "ideational" for this layer of organisation, rather than "representational" (Hengeveld 1989). We use the latter term as it has wider currency and seems more transparent to us.

by what are often referred to as verb-argument structures (Halliday 1967a, 1994). The *interpersonal* organisation of the clause moulds these representations into *speech acts* coded by mood and modality. The *textual* organisation signals relations internal to the messages being communicated as well as relations with both the co-text and situational context, through word order and prosodic choices.

It has sometimes erroneously been thought that Halliday's three-level organisation of the clause is equivalent to the traditional distinction between semantics, syntax and pragmatics, as is indeed assumed by Lambrecht (1994: 6–7). This is emphatically *not* the case. The traditional distinction assumes that syntax is concerned with purely structural combinatory relations, semantics with logical or conceptual representations of meaning, and pragmatics with how context contributes to meaning. At first sight, the non-adherence to this traditional distinction might appear surprising, but the alternative view of grammatical signs as symbolic form-meaning pairings, also advocated by Bolinger, has in fact been gaining ground in such theories as Langacker's (1991, 2021) Cognitive Grammar and a number of Construction Grammars. The specific Hallidayan take on grammatical signs has been most significantly developed in McGregor's (1997, 2021) Semiotic Grammar, while it has arguably gained the greatest common currency in Traugott's (1982, 1989, 2010) work on language change. The first formulation of her hypothesis about subjectification as a process of change referred directly to the three types of functional structure distinguished by Halliday: change was predicted to start from representational "meanings situated in the described external or internal (evaluative / perceptual / cognitive) situation" over "meanings situated in the textual situation" to "interpersonal [meanings] . . . such as expressions of speech function, exchange structures, and attitude" (Traugott 2010: 31). Importantly, Traugott (2010: 46–49) stresses that one can only speak of change if the new meaning has become conventionally associated with a specific form, yielding a new form-meaning pairing. In other words, in this strain of linguistics, it is also assumed that representational, interpersonal and textual meaning *all* involve conventionalised *form-meaning pairings*.

2.2 Information structure and focus

According to Halliday (1967a: 200–201), the information structure which English speakers impose on their discourse in real time is "realized directly in the phonological organization". Information structure is not determined by, but mapped onto, grammatical structure.

To bring to consciousness the semantics of information structure, linguists have to (i) interpret its prosodic *realisation* (Halliday 1963), which is characterised by "inherent iconism" (Bolinger 1985), e.g. between intonational and informational prominence, and (ii) derive semantic *generalisations* from actual contextualised usage by studying how prosody expresses the speaker's communicative purposes and their awareness of what information is already shared with the hearer, and what information is added as new to the hearer.

The first type of choice speakers continuously make is that of dividing their discourse into *information units*. This is done by marking off units by melodic contours (Halliday 1963), which are falling or rising tones (transcribed by \ and /), or combinations of these.[4] Tone boundaries are transcribed by double slashes. English speech progresses as a succession of melodic units, which "represents the speaker's blocking out of the message into quanta of information, or message blocks" (Halliday 1967a: 202). Information units correspond to a clause in about 60 % of cases (O'Grady 2014), being smaller or larger than a clause in the remaining percentage.[5]

The second type of speaker choice is concerned with the *internal structure* of the information units, which is based on the contrast between focal and non-focal information. The information focus, i.e. what the speaker selects as the most salient information the hearer has to attend to, is signalled by the tonic syllable within the tone unit, which "carries the main pitch movement" (Halliday 1994: 296). The perceived nuclear prominence is "primarily a matter of pitch (pitch movement, not pitch level) and secondarily one of duration and intensity" (Halliday 1994: 203).[6] In transcriptions, the tonic syllable is bolded or capitalised. The domain of the information focus is typically not just the tonic syllable as such but the larger constituent it is part of (Halliday 1967a: 204). Information structures consist of an obligatory focal domain and optional non-focal segments.

Halliday (1967a: 203–9, 1994: 295–9) distinguishes two main types of focus and information structure: the unmarked type, which can itself be subdivided into two subtypes, and a marked type.

---

4 In this approach, breaks are secondary in the signalling of information units. On the one hand, there may, but need not, be pauses *between* tone units. On the other hand, spontaneous speech often features breaks *within* tone units, when the speaker hesitates or is looking for words. These do not interfere with the hearer's perception of the tone (p.c. Halliday).
5 The number of information units that speakers divide clauses into is tied to different text types. For instance, the loud-reading of news bulletins, which pack much new lexical information into clauses, typically has more information units per clause than spontaneous dialogue, in which clauses feature many anaphoric grammatical items (Halliday 1967a: 205).
6 In support of the point that the pitch movement on the tonic syllable, not loudness, is the main marker of focus, O'Grady (p.c.) points out that, irrespective of whether speakers whisper, shout or speak normally, hearers pick up the information focus.

The most typical, or *unmarked*, information structure starts off with recoverable information and continues with non-recoverable information, which partly or wholly coincides with an information focus marking the *most salient new* information, whereby 'new' means information 'freshly' introduced in the discourse (Halliday 1994: 295–299). An unmarked information focus occurs unit-finally, that is to say, it is marked by a tonic on the last lexical element of the information unit. The actual domain of the focus (underlined in the examples) is the constituent containing the tonic syllable, like the whole NP with its NP-internal restrictive relative clause in // I'm looking for the caretaker who looks after this **block** // (Halliday 1967a: 207). The unmarked information structure tends to have a left to right form of organisation with given information, if present, preceding new information (Halliday 1967a: 205). If the lexical element is followed by an anaphoric grammatical constituent, then it is not part of the focus because it is inherently recoverable, e.g. // I **saw** her //. What precedes the focal domain may be entirely recoverable, or it may be recoverable shifting into non-recoverable information without being focal, as is the case in the caretaker example, where *I* is situationally recoverable, but *'m looking for* is not. This creates a certain indeterminacy. This is, in fact, why unmarked focus "may be ambiguous" (Halliday 1967a: 208), and why a second subtype needs to be distinguished, where the whole unit contains non-recoverable information, as is often the case at the beginning of a story. In this subtype, the focal domain is "the whole of the information unit" (Halliday 1967a: 208).

The marked type of information structure, then, contains a focus that is "informationally contrastive [. . .] within a closed system or lexically" (Halliday 1967a: 207). The notion of 'contrastive focus' subsumes both contrast with, and addition to, another option from a finite set (Halliday 1967a: 226). This marked focus is, through its shared set membership with another element, semantically cohesive (Halliday 1994: 295–299). A marked focus always relates to a block of presupposed information (Halliday 1967a: 206). This entails that marked information structures *imply* a question pertaining to *one specific* constituent like a *wh*-question or an echoic polar question (Halliday 1967a: 207–211). By contrast, unmarked information structures correspond simply to general questions like *what is happening?* (Halliday 1967a: 208). A marked focus need not, and often does not, form the final element of the tone unit. The domain of a marked focus relation may be a clause constituent, as in // John painted the **shed** yesterday //, which implies the *wh*-question *What did John paint yesterday?*, which presupposes that John painted something yesterday (Halliday 1967a: 207–208). Contrastive focus may also be a constituent of a phrase, as in // I've seen **bett**er plays //, which presupposes that the speaker has seen at least some plays, or a constituent of a word, as in // the damage was only **ex**ternal//, which presupposes that there was some sort of damage (Halliday 1967a: 208). Finally, marked focus may also involve contrast with options of grammatical systems, as in // he d\id take it //, which implies the echoic polar question // **d/id** he take it // (Halliday 1967a: 211).

The basic contrast just outlined between unmarked and marked focus is referred to in Kiss (1998: 249) as a "neglected distinction", which yet has "been present in the literature for a long time (see, for example, Halliday 1967; Rochemont 1986), although the interpretations attributed to the two focus notions (variously called CONTRASTIVE FOCUS versus PRESENTATIONAL FOCUS, NARROW FOCUS versus WIDE FOCUS, or, in this article, IDENTIFICATIONAL FOCUS versus INFORMATION FOCUS) have not always been exactly the same". In the remainder of this chapter, we will use the terms "contrastive focus" versus "presenting focus".

Verstraete (2007: 81) has pointed out the *prima facie* similarity between the three types of focus distinguished by Halliday (1967a) and Lambrecht's (1994, 2001: 485) ternary typology of predicate-focus, sentence-focus and argument-focus. In cases where the information unit as defined by Halliday coincides with a clause, his and Lambrecht's three types of focus may in practice roughly coincide. Halliday's unmarked information structure whose focus presents the most salient new resembles Lambrecht's predicate focus, and the structure whose focus domain is formed by the whole information unit resembles sentence-focus. Halliday's marked information structure with a contrastive/additive focus relating to a presupposed message block resembles Lambrecht's argument focus. However, there are fundamental differences regarding the (elements of) structure that focal meaning is ascribed to: Halliday's notion of focus is an element of the tone unit while Lambrecht's theory of focus is tied to sentence syntax. Halliday's framework also allows for greater information structural variation in that information unit and clause do not coincide in a large number of cases, and the contrastive/additive focus may be anything from a clause over a phrase and word to a morpheme.

A final caveat to be made about Halliday's (1967a: 204, 1994: 301) approach to information structure is that he stresses that speakers' *representation* of information as (non)recoverable or presupposed may not correspond to the actual state of the discourse, and may be manipulated for rhetorical aims, as illustrated in (8). The first move by A is an interpellation centred on contrastive focus *b/ack*, which presupposes that B has been away. B recognises the attack and counters the presupposition with contrastive focus on (not) /**out**.

(8) A: // Are you coming **b/ack** into circulation? //
    B: // I didn't know I was /**out** // (Halliday 1994: 300)

Speakers may "play with the system" ... "to produce an astonishing variety of rhetorical effects" (Halliday 1967a: 301).

3 *It*-clefts as specificational constructions

In this section, we present our account of the representational meaning coded by *it*-clefts, which, in accordance with the theoretical tenets set out in Section 2, we analyse compositionally (Davidse 2000, Davidse and Kimps 2016, Davidse and Njende 2019). *It*-clefts consist of a copular matrix and a specific type of relative clause with features distinctive to clefts, henceforth referred to as a cleft relative clause (CRC).

The "cleft relative clause. . . is not syntactically part of the subject [*it*]" and "does not form a constituent with its antecedent" (Huddleston and Pullum 2002: 1416). Importantly, the antecedent of the CRC is the full complement NP, e.g. *the boy* in (9), in contrast with restrictive relative clauses (RRCs), whose antecedent is the nominal head, e.g. *boy* in (10). As a consequence, the antecedent of the CRC refers to a fully determined instance, viz. *the boy* whom the hearer is presumed to be able to identify in (9) (Davidse 2000: 1107–1113). By contrast, the antecedent of an RRC is a mere entity-type. The information added to it by the RRC creates a contextually unique description, *boy who caused all the trouble*, which can, therefore, receive definite determination.

(9) Who caused all the trouble? — It was [the boy] [who caused all the trouble]. (Huddleston 1984: 460)

(10) Who was that on the phone? — It was [the [boy who caused all the trouble]]. (Huddleston 1984: 460)

The relative clause in a cleft formulates an open proposition whose semantic gap is represented by a relative marker, *x who caused all the trouble*, in (9). In pseudo-clefts, e.g. (11), the relative clause likewise formulates an open proposition, but its semantic gap is represented more explicitly by the general head noun like *person* or *one* heading the relative clause, resulting in the NP *the one ('x') who caused all the trouble*. This NP, *the one/person who caused all the trouble*, construes a 'superscriptional' entity (Higgins 1979), or, as Declerck (1988) puts it, a definite description used attributively in the sense of Donnellan (1966), i.e. used essentially, specifying the necessary properties of "whatever or whoever fits that description" (Donnellan 1966: 46). The concrete person fitting the definite description in (11) is referred to by the postverbal NP, *the boy*. These semantics of pseudo-clefts are accounted for in the literature by analysing them as specificational-identifying constructions, in which the main verb *be* expresses a relation of *identification* between the value of a variable (Higgins 1979; Huddleston and Pullum 2002). The variable is the superscriptional entity, the x with the role marked by the relative pronoun in the state-ofaffairs of the relative clause, and the value is the concrete entity that fills the open proposition, i.e. *the boy* in (11).

(11) The one/person who caused all the trouble was the boy.

It-clefts likewise express a specificational-identifying relation (Davidse 2000; Huddleston and Pullum 2002: 1416–7) and a relation between the open proposition conveyed by the relative clause and the NP filling the semantic gap. But the structural assembly of these two relations is different. In *it*-clefts, e.g. (9), the value *the boy* is related to the variable *x who caused all the trouble* by being inserted directly into the antecedent position of the CRC. The value can be related to the variable in this way because the CRC "does not form a constituent with its antecedent" (Huddleston and Pullum 2002: 1416): antecedent and CRC are structurally 'binarised' (p.c. Karel Van den Eynde) in clefts. It is the matrix that relates its postverbal NP as antecedent to the relative anaphor, thus specifying the value for the semantic gap in the CRC's open proposition. The matrix is an identifying clause (Huddleston and Pullum 2002: 1416–1417) with definite subject *it*, or occasionally *that* (Hedberg 2000), as in (12), which construes the value NP as an 'identifier' (Halliday 1967a: 224; Davidse 2000: 1120). The definite pronominal subject *it* or *that* triggers an implicature of exhaustive specification to the effect that the individuals referred to by the value NP *coincide* with the set of all instances corresponding to the variable. If the value NP is singular, then it is taken to be the only one filling the semantic gap, and if it is plural, then it is taken to exhaustively state the entities that correspond to the variable. This is a conversational implicature as it can be cancelled without causing any incongruence (Horn 1981, Declerck 1988, De Cesare and Garassino 2015), as illustrated by (13).

(12) A: I knew the maternity hospital had closed.
B: Yeah. *That's Fulford that's closed* yeah but now they're gonna close Naburn I think (WB)

(13) A. He-he saved my life ...
B. ... *It was the Italian that saved your life*
A. Oh, but he [the American] did too. (from de Mille, J. 1871. *The American Baron*, quoted in Schwenter and Waltereit 2010: 90)

The matrix of a cleft construction can also be an existential clause (Davidse 2000; Lambrecht 2001), as in (14). As in *it*-clefts, the entities filling the gap in the open proposition conveyed by the relative clause are inserted directly in the antecedent position of the CRC, and it is the matrix which relates the structurally binarised antecedent and CRC. As we have an existential matrix here, it merely states that instances corresponding to the variable exist. The existential matrix in (14) has an *enumerative* meaning (Davidse 1999, 2000), which triggers a conversational implicature of non-exhaustive specification (Lambrecht 2001: 205). It is implied that the individuals referred to in the postverbal complement, *Paul and his wife*, do *not* exhaust the set of instances that fill the open proposition *x (who) were there*.

(14)   A: And were they...were they well-received these visits? Erm were there a lot of people interested in them?
            B: Well I suppose there were about I've got photographs actually if you'd be interested to see. There must have been about nine of us altogether. *There's Paul and his wife were there.* (WB)

The proposed compositional analysis sheds light on so-called reduced clefts (Declerck & Seki 1990) or truncated clefts (Hedberg 2000; Huddleston & Pullum 2002; Collins 2006). Importantly, as argued by Davidse (2000: 1121, Davidse & Njende 2019), both *it*-clefts and *there*-clefts can be 'reduced' in the sense that they can presuppose the variable from the preceding discourse without realising it overtly as a CRC, as in (15), where the hearer is instructed to infer the variable from the preceding discourse, i.e. '(which is) for supper'. Examples like (15) can naturally be accounted for as monoclausal constructions that are, in their own right, specificational constructions. The construction in (15a), with subject *it*, verb *be* and postverbal complement expresses as such identifying-specificational semantics with exhaustiveness implicature, while that with existential *there* as subject (15b) expresses enumerating-specificational semantics with non-exhaustive implicature.

(15)   a.   What's for supper? It's spaghetti! (WB)
           b.   What's for supper? There's spaghetti! (WB)

We will return to these issues, when we turn to the information structure of full and reduced clefts in section 5.

4 Data and methodology

This study draws on the prosodic analysis of 238 tokens of *it*-clefts extracted from the 100 texts of the first London-Lund Corpus (LLC) (Svartvik 1990). The LLC consists of a collection of dialogues between two or more speakers and a limited number of monologues recorded in the UK between 1953 and 1987. To retrieve all occurrences of full and reduced specificational *it*-clefts from the LLC, we queried the written transcription of the corpus with the sequence *it* + form of copula *be*. The resulting dataset was then manually analysed so as to retain clefts only. With this maximalist approach, our goal was to ensure the retrieval of full clefts as well as reduced clefts. Excluded instances include all constructions realised by superficially similar syntagms such as copular sentences with a restrictive relative clause (as in 10 above). Our final dataset comprises 238 occurrences of specificational *it*-clefts, among which 143 are full clefts and 95 are reduced clefts. The overall distribution is shown in Table 1.

Table 1: Overview of the LLC dataset.

	Full clefts	Reduced clefts	Total
Raw count (%)	143 (60%)	95 (40%)	238

We completely reviewed the already existing prosodic coding of the corpus[7] by a mix of auditory and instrumental analysis, running all sound files of clefts through the software Praat (Boersma 2001) and comparing our own inter-rated annotation to that of the compilers. This is possible because Halliday's (1963, 1967a b, Halliday and Greaves 2008) and Crystal's (1969) approach are both rooted in the British School of intonation. We made three types of changes to the original.

Firstly, the analysis of the tones was corrected in a number of cases. For instance, in (16a) the original coding had a rise on *w/ork*, which was changed into the fall on *w|ork* (16b) that is clearly shown in the Praat image in Figure 1.

(16) a. he said you're sure it's Marks and **Sp\arks** you're going to **w/ork** for // (LLC)
b. he said you're sure it's Marks and **Sp\arks** // you're going to **w\ork for** //

Secondly, the LLC annotation assumes the existence of compound tones, as in (16a), defined by Halliday (1967b) as involving two fused tones, each with a tonic, between which no pre-tonic material can be inserted. However, Tench (1990) has shown contra Halliday (1967b) that a pre-tonic segment can in fact be inserted before the second tonic, which justifies adding a tone unit boundary breaking the compound tone into two, as in (16b).

---

7 The LLC was originally annotated according to Crystal's (1969) model of prosodic and paralinguistic systems and offers a full and a reduced transcription. For this study, we used the reduced transcription of the LLC (see Svartvik 1990) which omits any kind of paralinguistic annotations and only includes prosodic coding. We, however, removed annotations that were not of interest for our analysis such as indications of boosters, duration of pauses and degrees of stress.

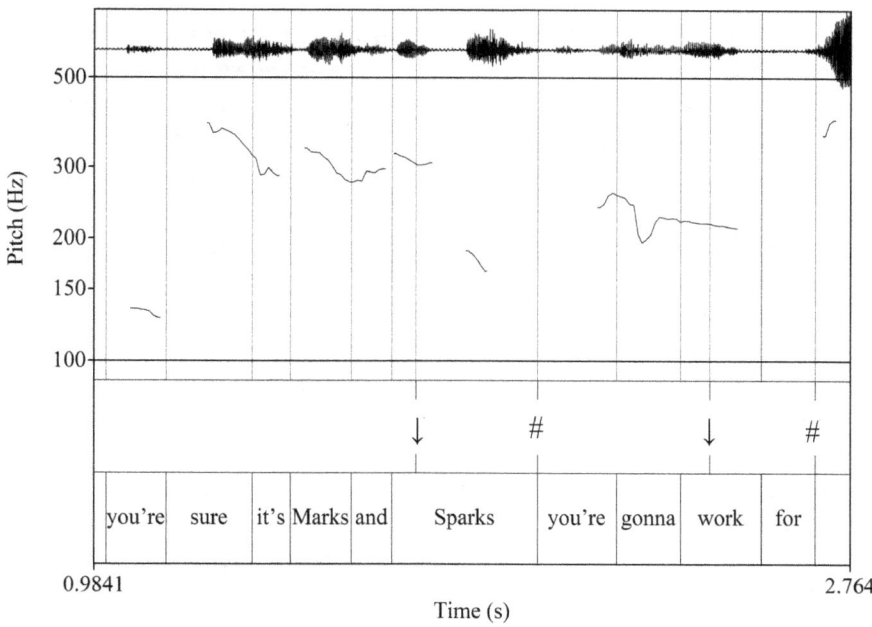

Figure 1: Praat image of (16).

Thirdly, the LLC transcription assumes the existence of subordinate tones, indicated by squiggly brackets in (17a). In view of the flat nature of phonological patterning, O'Grady (2013) has argued against the idea that a secondary tone unit can be embedded in a primary tone unit. Hence, where LLC marked a subordinate tone, one of two options was followed. The secondary tone unit was either removed if it was considered not prominent enough, or recoded as a primary tone, adding a boundary, as in (17b), if the tone contour was judged to be sufficiently prominent according to both the auditory and instrumental analysis.

(17) a. **n\o** // it's the **\Union** // - - as dist**\/inct** from SRC {that runs **th/at** //} // (LLC)
 b. **n\o** // it's the **\Union** // - - as dist**\/inct** from SRC // that runs **th/at** //

The goal of the prosodic annotation was to establish an empirical base against which to assess hypotheses and predictions in the literature about prosodic prominences and their relation to focus marking in *it*-clefts. While some studies have posited that the value NP carries the only information focus coded by a pitch accent (Clark and Haviland 1977; Givón 2001; Lambrecht 2001), others have claimed that it carries the main information focus marked by the 'strongest' of multiple accents (Prince 1978; Declerck 1984, Patten 2012). Studies in the Hallidayan tradition (e.g.

Halliday 1967a; Collins 1991, 2006) have pointed out the existence of multiple information patterns, in some of which the value NP is non-focal, e.g. if it is an anaphoric pronoun, // it's that that I can't under**stand** / /, or if it is the wh-item of an interrogative, // *what is it you **want*** // (Halliday 1967a: 231).

In our analysis of the spoken cleft data, we thus sought to answer the following research questions:
i) which constituent(s) of *it*-clefts bear prosodically-coded information focus?
ii) if multiple foci are present in *it*-clefts, can a hierarchy between them be established?

We identified all tonics and inventoried their number and location. The three positions we distinguished between are value, variable, copula. We then compared the relative prominence of the different information foci of clefts bearing multiple foci. For this, we carried out an instrumental analysis of the acoustic correlate of pitch, F0, and took into consideration direction of tone movement and pitch height. In doing so, we established the following hierarchy between information foci: is high fall > mid fall > low fall > high rise > mid rise > low rise (Esser 1988; Van Praet 2019). In this hierarchy, three height levels were compared, namely high, mid and low. Step ups between the different heights were typically of 0.05 logHertz or more. Falling tones are considered higher in the ranking order than rising tones, irrespective of their pitch height. Complex tones such as fall-rises and rise-falls are assimilated to their final movement, i.e. rise and fall respectively. For values and/or variables realised with multiple tone units, only the highest-ranked tone movement was examined.

5 Focus assignment in clefts

In this section, we present our corpus study of focus assignment in clefts. We first give the quantitative results in section 5.1. In Section 5.2, we then seek to derive generalisations from these empirical findings in terms of Halliday's (1967a, 1994) distinction between marked and unmarked information structures.

5.1 Results

We start with the results of our analysis of the number and location of information foci, shown in Table 2.

Table 2: Distribution of foci in *it*-clefts.

	Full clefts	Reduced clefts	Total
Focal + non-focal	12 (8.4%)	—	12 (5.1%)
Focal + focal	91 (63.6%)	—	91 (38.2%)
Non-focal + focal	34 (23.8%)	—	34 (14.3%)
Non-focal + focal + focal copula	6 (4.2%)	—	6 (2.5%)
Focal + 0	—	89 (93.7%)	89 (37.4%)
Focal + 0 + focal copula	—	1 (1%)	1 (0.4%)
Non-focal + 0 + focal copula	—	5 (5.3%)	5 (2.1%)
Total	143	95	238

Each prosodic pattern is by default presented according to the value and the variable carrying foci. The status of the copula is only added when it is focal. A distinction is made between full and reduced clefts. For reduced clefts, the absence of a cleft-relative clause is indicated by 0 under variable.

In the most frequent pattern in full clefts, focal + focal exemplified in (18), both the value and the variable bear one or more tonic accents. In the second most frequent pattern, non-focal + focal as in (19), the cleft is realised as a single tone unit and only the variable carries one or more tonics. In the third attested pattern, only the value carries a tonic accent as in (20). Finally, a small fraction are clefts whose value is part of either the pre- or post-tonic segment while both their copula and the variable bear foci, as in (21) and (22).

(18) oh it's the **gu\ests** // who say ah well can we help you with the washing-up **n\ow** // (LLC)

(19) A: did you meet Fuller
B: y/es // it was he who inv\ited me // (LLC)

(20) it's just one **qu\esti**on that they have to do // /**isn't** it // (LLC)

(21) and within about ten or fifteen years // people are going to be asking // why on earth it **w/\as** // that Britain was allowed to get beh\ind# (LLC)

(22) he it **w\/as** // who built Saint Paul's **Ch\urch** // in Stoke **R/oad** // hims/elf // at his own exp\ense // (LLC)

As far as reduced clefts are concerned, the vast majority of occurrences in the LLC exhibit the focal + 0 pattern in which the value is the sole bearer of one or more information foci, e.g. (23). Along with this pattern, we also found a small number of reduced clefts in which only the copula is focal, e.g. (24), and one example in which value and copula are focal, e.g. (25).

(23) yes cos all sorts of things go into port don't they // I mean it's not just **w\ine** // (LLC)

(24) some publisher or other last year about a year ago asked me what I thought about a series publishing early grammarians
B: oh Perrins perhaps
A: because I forget who it **w/as#** (LLC)

(25) and I so they sent me down for an interview and all that he asked me at the interview // I think it **w/\as** // CP **Sn/ow** // (LLC)

In Section 5.2., we will interpret the patterns involving foci on the value and/or variable of both full and reduced clefts in terms of the information structures set out in Section 2.2. Here we briefly discuss the patterns with focus on the copula. Examples (21) and (24) are interrogative clefts, in which the value, realised by a *wh*-interrogative item, is not focal, but the copular verb in information-unit final position is focal. In (22) the anaphoric value *he* is fronted, which results in the copula occurring in final focal position in the information unit. In the reduced cleft in (25), the copula carries a marked focus whose rise-fall expresses reservation (Halliday and Greaves 2008) about the speaker's certainty.

For the full clefts with foci on both value and variable, which form the majority (63.6%), we give the results of our analysis of the relative prominence between the foci in Table 3 below. Is there a hierarchy of foci (in the sense explained in Section 4), and if so, which is higher, the value or the variable?

The overall results show that three types of hierarchical order exist in full clefts. In 61.5 %, the most prominent focus is on the value, outranking that on the variable, in 22% we observe the opposite order with the most prominent focus being on an element of the variable, and in 13.2 % the foci on value and variable have a comparable level of prominence.

Table 3: Distribution of prosodic hierarchies.

Hierarchy observed	Tone movement in value	Tone movement in variable	Full clefts	Total
Value is higher	fall	fall	38 (41.7%)	56 (61.5%)
	rise	rise	1 (1.1%)	
	fall	rise	17 (18.7%)	

Table 3 (continued)

Hierarchy observed	Tone movement in value	Tone movement in variable	Full clefts	Total
Variable is higher	fall	fall	4 (4.4%)	20 (22%)
	rise	fall	16 (17.6%)	
Value and variable are similar	fall	fall	11 (12.1%)	12 (13.2%)
	rise	rise	1 (1.1%)	
Unclear	-	-	3 (3.3%)	3 (3.3%)[8]
Total			91	

5.2 Discussion of results

In this section we address the question if we can derive generalisations from the distribution of foci (Table 2) and relative prominence of multiple foci (Table 3) in terms of the distinction set out in Section 2.2 between
(i) unmarked information structure with presenting focus
(ii) marked information structure with contrastive focus relating to presupposed information.

The most frequent information structure, if we add up full and reduced clefts, is the *marked* information structure with *contrastive information focus* relating to a presupposed message block (n = 101, 60%).

In our data, full clefts of this type number 12 only, or 5% of the dataset. Example (20), reproduced with more context as (26), illustrates contrastive information focus on the value NP *one question* (contrasting with two or more questions) which relates to the presupposition *that they have to do*.

(26) B: well you give them the lot you see, that's the point, and make sure that there's something fairly closely related to what they've studied
A: // it's just one **qu\est**ion that they have to do // /**isn**'t it // (LLC)

Lambrecht (2001) claims that this prosodic pattern is the prototypical one for clefts, which is a corollary of his claim that cleft syntax codes the information structural

---

[8] Of the 91 full clefts exhibiting the focal + focal pattern, 3 could not be instrumentally analysed due to technical issues such as corrupted file or overlap in conversations and have therefore been labelled unclear.

relation between argument focus and presupposition. The low relative frequency of this type in our data does not support this prototypicality claim, and, as we will see in Section 6, the possibility of selective focus, as in (27), argues against viewing contrastive focus as inherently argument focus.

(27)　because there's not the same pressure on the material // it's the **p\op** material that counts // (LLC)

We argue that reduced clefts with focal value (n=89, 55%) also instantiate the information structure of contrastive focus–presupposition. For instance, in (23), repeated as (28), there is a contrastive focus on *wine* (as a member of the set *all sorts of things*). There is no overt presupposition, but Halliday (1967a: 206) pointed out that information can be recoverable "anaphorically, by reference, substitution or *ellipsis* [italics ours]". As we saw in Section 4, reduced clefts express as such identifying-specificational semantics, which instruct the hearer to infer the variable from the preceding discourse. Hence, we can view the presupposition in clefts like (28) to be anaphorically recoverable by ellipsis, and to be part of the information structure.

(28)　yes cos all sorts of things go into port don't they // I mean it's not just **w\ine** // (LLC)

These *it*-clefts are chosen when the speaker wants to combine the exhaustive specification relation conveyed by the grammatical organisation with the prosodically coded information structure of a contrastive focus relating to a presupposition, which is the unmarked information structure choice within a cleft environment. Reduced *it*-clefts are the most typical realisation of this type.

The other type that is a clear instantiation of a specific information structure is the minority of *it*-clefts (n=34, 14%) that manifest the *unmarked* information structure in which recoverable information precedes a *presenting focus* associated with the final lexical item. This is the case in (22), repeated as (29).

(29)　A:　did you meet Fuller
　　　　B:　y/es // it was he who inv\ited me // (LLC)

In the tradition that views cleft syntax as coding the focus–presupposition relation, this type has been said to have an "informative-presupposition", which "mark[s] a piece of information as fact, known to some people although not yet known to the intended hearer" (Prince 1978: 899). On our analysis, the matrix identifies the value, *he*, that fills the gap in the variable, triggering an exhaustiveness implicature that only *he* invited me. Onto this specification relation, an unmarked information structure is mapped, which starts with the recoverable information of the value and has presenting focus on the last lexical item *invited* of the variable. In this context it is very clear that there is no way in which there is even a hint of presupposition about the information in the CRC, in which the very *un*predictability of the fact that Fuller actually *invited* the speaker motivates the focus on the CRC. Discursively, these *it*-clefts are chosen when the speaker wants to combine the exhaustive specification relation conveyed by the grammatical constituents with presenting focus on the open proposition. Whereas presenting focus is the unmarked option in spoken English at large, it is the marked information structure choice within a cleft environment.

How can we then analyse the full clefts with information foci on both value and variable, which form the second largest portion of the whole dataset (n=91, 38%) and the prototypical information structure of *full clefts* (63.6%)?

In the literature, some authors, e.g. Declerck (1984), have suggested that two subtypes have to be distinguished which are prosodically and information structurally distinct (for discussion, see Bourgoin 2022). The first subtype is claimed to feature a stronger accent on the value and a weaker one on the variable to code a contrastive value relating to an 'old presupposition' in the CRC. The second subtype is claimed to feature strong accents on both value and variable, conveying a contrastive value and a 'new proposition' in the CRC. To investigate this hypothesis, we investigated the hierarchy of foci. The results in Table 3 confirm the prosodic side of the hypothesis: a subset of 61.5% of these clefts have a more prominent focus on the value, as in (30), 22% have a more prominent focus on the variable (32), while in 13% the foci on value and variable are equally prominent (33). However, as we will argue, we do not think that this prosodic difference conveys the different information structures predicted by these authors. In all of these subtypes, subject *it* + *be* is pre-tonic and there is a narrow, contrastive focus on the value NP, which conveys that the speaker chooses (contrasts or adds) an entity or person from a contextually given set of options, as in (30), (32) and (33). This *contrastive focus* on the *value* is combined with a *typically unmarked presenting focus* on the open proposition in the variable, marked by a tonic on the final lexical element. Of the 91 tokens, only 9, or 10 %, have a marked contrastive focus on an element of the variable, as in (32).

The pattern with a more prominent focus on the value is illustrated in (30). The pitch change on *James* in Figure 2 has a larger peak amplitude than the one on *gets*. Sports commentators have been observed to frequently use clefts, with ones like (30) allowing them to give prominence to the changing identity of the player in possession of the ball (Nelson 1997: 346), while also putting presenting focus on the specific actions described in the CRC.

(30) Hemsley chipping the ball into the centre onto the head of Scullion // from the head of Scullion it's J\ames // that g\ets it // but only as far as Hockey (LLC)

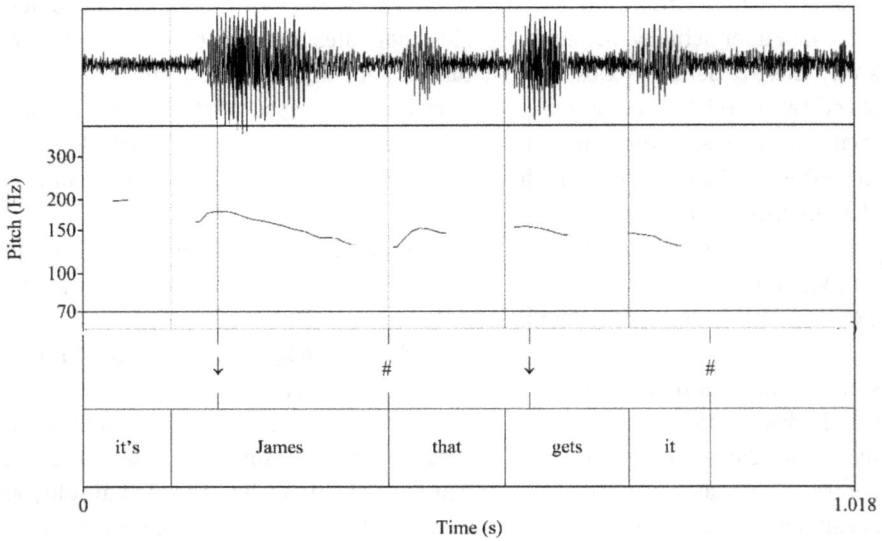

Figure 2: Praat image of (30).

Contra Prince (1978) and Patten (2012), we do not think that the relatively weaker prominence on *gets* in (30) marks the CRC as an information structural 'presupposition', which would entail that this information structure is a sort of subtype of the 'marked' information structure illustrated in (26) and (28). Rather, like the cleft in (31), taken from the same sports commentary, the open proposition in (30) features presenting focus and thus injects new 'communicative dynamism' (Firbas 1992) into the discourse.

(31) that's Tony Dunn // Dunn // down the line now // aiming for Best // or Aston // missed them both // and it's ^Derby that take up the c\ount // (LLC)

In 22% of tokens, we can observe the opposite order in which the highest pitch variation is found on a constituent of the CRC while the focus on the value is realised by a less prominent nucleus. For instance, the fall on *salads* in (32) has a smaller peak amplitude than the fall on *do*, as displayed in Figure 3. A and B are engaged in a humorous conversation about potty-training infants in summer. The cleft is A's answer to the speaker's own earlier probe *why* 'being regular' changes in summer, with contrastively focal *salads* providing the reason. The CRC uses the substitute verb *do*, which relates anaphorically to 'alter one's sort of regular habits in summer' (Halliday 1994: 316–323) and hence provides material that would lend itself well to being wrapped as the presupposition part of an information unit. Yet, it is an information unit in its own right and one with marked contrastive focus on a closed system choice, i.e. the positive polarity form *d\o*. In this example, the higher pitch variation on *d\o* is probably due to this being one of the – rare – examples of contrastive focus in the open proposition.

(32)   A: why does one's sort of regular habits alter in summer
       B: no no but you just
       A: and
       B: wear less clothing so that's it's easier to take the nappies off
       A: maybe
       B: and stick them onto a potty (laughs)
       A: maybe it's **s\al**ads // that **d\o** it // (LLC)

Finally, in 13.2% of full clefts with multiple foci, the value and variable bear foci with a similar level of prominence. This is illustrated with the cleft in (33) whose value *the guests* and final adverb *now* in the open proposition are uttered with a pitch variation of a similar range with a 0.035 logHz difference corresponding to 10Hz in the scale of the Praat image in Figure 4. As in (30) and (32), the information structure combines contrastive focus on the value *the guests* (rather than the hosts) with presenting focus on the open proposition pushing the discourse forward with 'fresh' information.

(33)   oh it's the **gu\ests** // who say ah well can we help you with the washing-up **n\ow** // and we say my God no // (LLC)

In conclusion to Section 5.2, we note that the unmarked–marked distribution of information structures posited by Halliday (1967a, 1994) for spoken English at large is *reversed* in clefts. Their most frequent pattern is the marked information structure with a contrastive focus on the value, which defines the variable as presupposed information. This information structure is found in both full and – most commonly – reduced clefts, in which the variable is anaphorically presupposed by ellipsis. In a minority of cases, full clefts manifest the unmarked information structure with a presenting focus occurring on the final lexical element of the open proposition. This pattern has received little attention in the literature so far. Full clefts are used most frequently with contrastive focus on the value and typically presenting focus on the open proposition. This type of cleft thus combines the

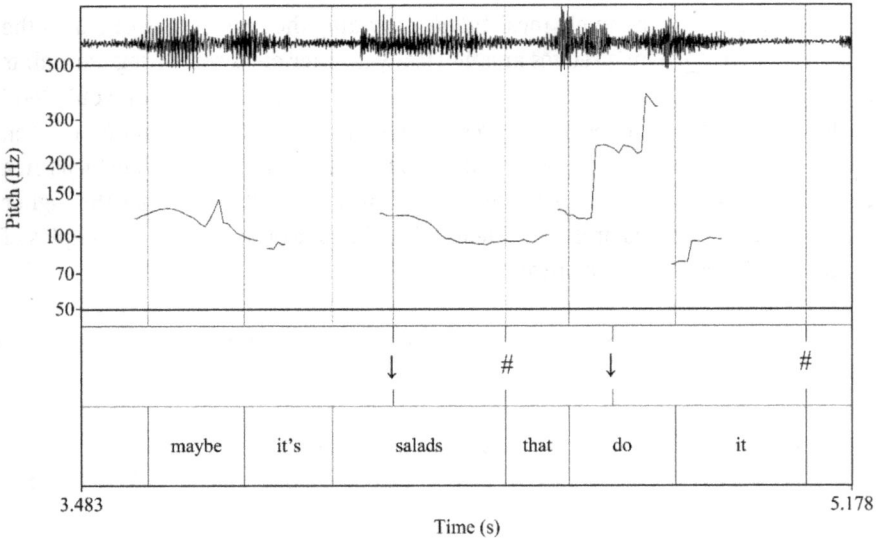

Figure 3: Praat image of (32).

information structural affordances of both the marked and unmarked information structure. Their open proposition is typically not presupposed, which we can capture by describing them as discursively "discontinuous" (Declerck 1984). When studying the use of clefts in discourse, the analyst has to examine how these three information structural patterns are mapped onto the specification relation with its exhaustiveness implicature.

6 Selective focus

Our case for distinguishing the syntactically coded specification relation from prosodically coded information structures is particularly significant for examples with contrastive focus on only a part of the value NP, which we refer to as selective focus.

So far, little substantial study has been devoted to selective focus in *it*-clefts with the exception of Velleman et al. (2012), even though Jespersen (1984: 75) had already noted that the "emphasis (and stress) is even frequently laid on another word than the one singled out by being made the predicative of *it is*". Collins (2006: 1708) observed with regard to example (34) that focal status of *garden* makes the following noun *space* fall within the post-nuclear tail which is, as a result, presented by the speaker as given information, regardless of its actual informational status.

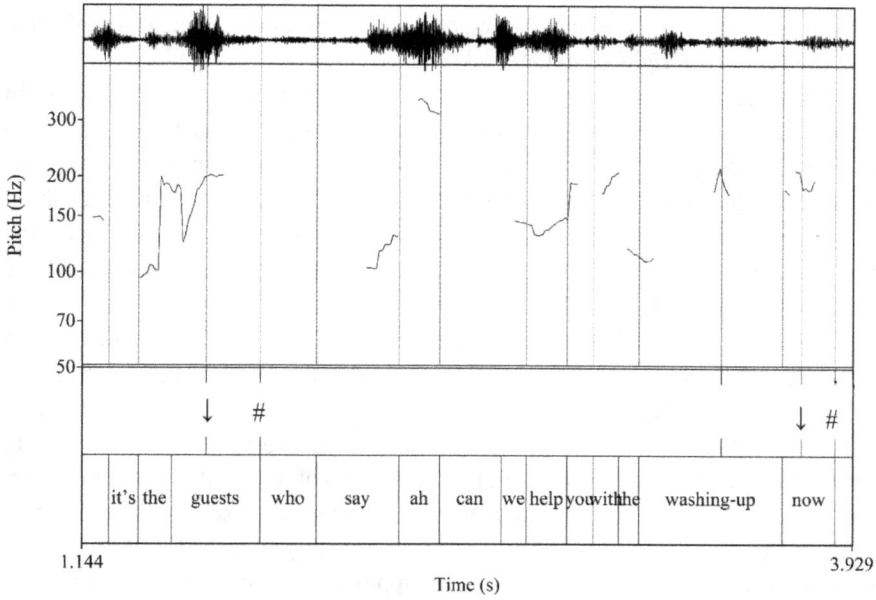

Figure 4: Praat image of (33).

(34) A: I still think that house is perfect until you've got children two children of bout the age of five then it's then then there isn't enough garden probably
B: well the other garden is not much bigger
A: no and it's **g\ar**den space // that is **s\o** // **pr\ecious** // for **k\ids** // not **h\ouse** space // (LLC)

In our dataset, we found 22 tokens of selective focus on the value NP, i.e. 9.2 %, of which 59% are full clefts and 41% reduced clefts, as shown in Table 4 below.

Table 4: Distribution of selective focus.

	Full clefts	Reduced clefts	Total
Raw count (%)	13 (59%)	9 (41%)	22

Besides on defining modifiers of the head noun as in (34) and (35), selective focus was also found to be borne by determiners and quantifiers, e.g. (36) and (37) below. Given that selective focus falls on a lexical item other than the last one, it corresponds to what Halliday describes as contrastive focus while the rest of the information unit is presented as presupposed. Importantly, the extent of this presupposition *differs* depending on whether the variable is represented as presupposed information, as is the case in (35)–(36), or the open proposition forms an information unit in its own right, as in (34) and (37).

If the variable is represented as presupposed information – whether overt in a CRC or anaphorically inferable – then it also includes the presupposed information in the value, and this *whole* extended presupposition is represented as given in, or inferable from, the preceding discourse. Thus, in (35), the presupposition is not just coded by the CRC but also includes the deaccented head noun *material*, yielding *x material that counts*. It is to this presupposition that the selective focus *pop* is related. The speaker is concerned with the tagging of books in libraries and singles out the particular pressure on 'popular' books and CDs (which are in demand with both adults and juniors). As pointed out by Velleman et al. (2012), the selective focus on *p\op (material)* impacts on the exhaustiveness effect of the cleft. The identifying matrix triggers a conversational implicature of exclusiveness to the effect that all other alternatives, i.e. other types of material, do not count. But because it is a conversational implicature, the exhaustive/exclusive effect can be cancelled (cf. Velleman et al. 2012: 443), for instance by adding *there's the cl\assic material that counts too*. In (36), the presupposition includes the anaphorically retrievable variable plus the deaccented head noun *scene*, yielding *x scene(s) that Hamlet is alone with his mother*. The selective focus on *that \one scene* also contextualises as exclusive focus, excluding the existence of 'more' scenes in which Hamlet is alone with his mother. But in this example, the implicature triggered by the identifying main clause is also *asserted* by the exclusive focus particle *just* (Velleman et al. 2012: 443). As pointed out by De Cesare and Garassino (2015), the use of exclusive focus particles like *just* and *only* modifies the pragmatic mechanism of the conversational implicature of clefts.

(35) but it it's the... p\op is the area // where adult and junior mainly overl\ap //
[...]
there's not the same pressure on the material // it's the **p\op** material that counts // (LLC)

(36) A: something of Gertrude's character is thrown up in that scene
B: how many times is Hamlet alone with his mother as he is in the closet can you remember
A: I think it's just that **one** scene // (LLC)

In full clefts with selective focus, the CRC is more frequently uttered on information units of its own, as in (34) and (37). This type of cleft has not only a different internal information structure but it also relates differently to the preceding discourse.

(37) but I understand that we've been honoured by the visit of several distinguished pro-Market editors for this debate with those editors here // it is **th\eir** credibility // that's in **qu/est**ion // (LLC)

We start by considering the relation of these clefts to the preceding discourse. Firstly, the selective focus defines *only* the deaccented head noun as presupposed. In (34), the notion of *space* is indeed given in the preceding discourse, but in (37), *credibility* is arguably less strongly predictable from the preceding discourse so that the information structure chosen by the speaker makes the hearer 'accommodate' the presupposition that credibility is at issue (Schwenter and Waltereit 2010). Secondly, the contrastive selective focus itself activates an anaphoric link with the preceding text, signalling "contrast with what has been said before or what might be expected" (Halliday 1967a: 206). In (34) the selective focus on *g\arden space* positions that *type* of space as the element from the preceding discourse to be attended to while in (37) the selective focus on ***th\eir** credibility* turns the tables against the Pro-Market editors (to whom *their* refers).

In their internal information structure, these clefts first feature a selective focus–presupposition structure within the field of the matrix, typically followed by an unmarked information structure with initial recoverable information (the relative anaphor) followed by presenting foci. In (34), the CRC features three presenting foci with emphatic rhetorical effect. The speaker presents her view that garden space is **s\o**^{9} // **pr\ec**ious // for **k\ids** // as fresh information the hearer has to attend to. In this sense, this example clearly illustrates why ascribing the information structural notion of 'presupposition' to the CRC-constituent does not work. As we have argued throughout this chapter, it is the identifying matrix that triggers the exclusiveness implicature applying to the specificational relation between the value and the variable. As a conversational implicature it can in principle be cancelled, unless the exclusiveness is asserted by another element, like *just* in (36). This is also the case in (34), where the selective focus associates the exclusiveness implicature with *g\arden space* being so precious for kids, but then adds explicitly that the only (binary) contrasting element in this context, *h\ouse space*, is not precious for kids. Thus it is contextually not possible to cancel the exclusiveness implicature by adding another option. In (34) the selective focus triggers the exclusiveness implicature for *their*, and not anyone else's, credibility being called into question.

---

9 Halliday (1967a: 208) notes that intensives like *so* "should perhaps be regarded as a special case of unmarked focus".

Example (38) illustrates the infrequent pattern with a selective focus on an element of the value and a contrastive focus on an element of the variable. The selective focus on *this* is motivated by the exophoric pinpointing of *which chair*, and not just *what*, was offered to Barry by the speaker. In the CRC, there is a non-final marked focus on *offering*, which, as becomes clear in the following information unit, entails potential retraction of the offer to Barry, as the speaker asks another person whether he wants the chair.

(38) A: now you see the disadvantage of these damned ch\airs Barry //
B: yeah holding both his sides
A&B: (2 to 3 seconds untranscribable)
A: it was **th\is** one // I was **off**ering Barry // do you w\ant it // (LLC)

We conclude that the information structural patterns of clefts proposed in Section 5 can also account for selective focus on an element of the value. In case the information pattern is of the focus–presupposition type, then the selective focus relates to a presupposition that includes both the head of the value NP and the variable.

7 Conclusion

In this chapter, we have made a case against the account of *it*-clefts that ascribes the information structural roles of presupposition and focus to the grammatical constituents of the cleft relative clause (CRC) and its antecedent, and links predictions and interpretations of prosodic prominence to this alleged 'grammaticalisation' of information structure in clefts (Lehmann 2008). Grounding our case in close contextual study of the prosody of text examples of full and reduced *it*-clefts, we have shown that for the majority of full *it*-clefts, the interpretation of the CRC as intrinsically presupposed cannot be maintained. The occurrence of selective focus on only a part of the antecedent NP likewise argues against assigning focal meaning to this whole NP.

The alternative account we have proposed to address these problems assumes the theoretical tenet that all grammatical constructions, also clefts, convey different layers of functional meaning, which are all coded naturally by their grammar and prosody (Halliday 1967a, 1994, McGregor 1997, 2021).

We argued that a plausible semantic analysis of *it*-clefts can be developed through analysis of (i) the identifying matrix and (ii) the relation between the CRC, with its distinctive features, and its antecedent. *It*-clefts are specificational constructions, whose relative clause and antecedent represent an open proposition and its filler, i.e. the variable and value, related to each other by the identifying matrix, which triggers an implicature of exhaustiveness.

Onto this identifying-specificational relation, a great variety of prosodically coded information structures can be mapped. We classified and interpreted these information structural patterns in terms of Halliday's (1967a) "neglected distinction", which yet has "been present in the literature for a long time" (Kiss 1998: 249) between (i) unmarked information structures with presenting focus and (ii) marked information structures with contrastive focus relating to presupposed information. We found, firstly, that the latter information structure is the most common in *it*-clefts, but only if we take full and reduced clefts together. Secondly, in a significant minority of cases, full *it*-clefts manifest the unmarked information structure in which recoverable information precedes a presenting focus. Thirdly, the majority of *it*-clefts involve a combination of the contrastive focus pattern on the matrix and presenting foci on the cleft relative clause. For these two latter types, we argued that the information structural notion of presupposition has to be given up – even in the form of the so-called 'informative-presupposition' – as these CRCs present new information that pushes the communication forward. We showed that information structural patterns (i) and (iii) can also account for selective focus on an element of the value, and discussed how this interacts with the implicature of exhaustive specification.

References

Akmajian, Adrian. 1979 [1973]. *Aspects of the grammar of focus in English*. Cambridge, MA: MIT PhD dissertation.
Boersma, Paul. 2001. Praat, a system for doing phonetics by computer. *Glot International* 5(9/10). 341–345.
Bolinger, Dwight. 1977. *Meaning and form*. London/New York: Longman.
Bolinger, Dwight. 1985. The inherent iconism of intonation. In John Haiman (ed.), *Iconicity in syntax*, 97–108. Amsterdam: Benjamins.
Bourgoin, Charlotte. 2022. Towards a new typology of the referential information structure of specificational *it*-clefts. *Text & Talk* 2022. 1–23. https://doi.org/10.1515/text-2021-0081
Bourgoin, Charlotte, Gerard O'Grady & Kristin Davidse. 2021. Managing information flow through prosody in it-clefts. *English Language and Linguistics* 25(3). 485–511.
Chomsky, Noam. 1971. Deep structure, surface structure, and semantic interpretation. In Danny D. Steinberg & Leon A. Jacobovits (eds.), *Semantics*, 183–216. Cambridge: Cambridge University Press.
Clark, Herbert H. & Susan E Haviland. 1977. Comprehension and the given-new contract. In Roy Freedle (eds.), *Discourse production and comprehension*, 1–40. Norwood: Ablex.
Collins, Peter. 1991. *Cleft and pseudo-cleft constructions in English*. London: Routledge.

Collins, Peter. 2006. *It*-clefts and *wh*-clefts: Prosody and pragmatics. *Journal of Pragmatics* 38(10). 1706–1720.
Crystal, David. 1969. *Prosodic systems and intonation in English*. Cambridge: CUP.
Davidse, Kristin. 1999. Are there sentences that can be analyzed as there-clefts? In Guy A. J Tops, Betty Devriendt & Steven Geukens (eds.), *Thinking English grammar: To honour Xavier Dekeyser, Professor emeritus*, 177–193. Leuven: Peeters.
Davidse, Kristin. 2000. A constructional approach to clefts. *Linguistics* 38(6). 1101–1131.
Davidse, Kristin & Ditte Kimps. 2016. Specificational there-clefts: Functional structure and information structure. *English Text Construction* 9(1). 115–142.
Davidse, Kristin & Ngum Njende. 2019. Enumerative there-clauses and there-clefts: specification and information structure. *Acta Linguistica Hafniensia* 51(2). 160–191.
De Cesare, Anna-Maria & Davide Garassino. 2015. On the status of exhaustiveness in cleft sentences: An empirical and cross-linguistic study of English *also-/only*-clefts and Italian *anche-/solo*-clefts. *Folia Linguistica* 49(1). 1–56.
Declerck, Renaat. 1984. The pragmatics of it-clefts and wh-clefts. *Lingua* 64. 251–289.
Declerck, Renaat. 1988. *Studies on copular sentences, clefts and pseudo-clefts*. Dordrecht: Foris Publications.
Declerck, Renaat & Shigeki Seki. 1990. Premodified reduced IT-clefts. *Lingua* 82(1). 15–51.
Donnellan, Keith. 1966. Reference and definite descriptions. *Philosophical Review* 75(3). 281–304.
Esser, Jürgen. 1988. *Comparing reading and spoken intonation*. Amsterdam: Rodopi.
Firbas, Jan. 1992. *Functional sentence perspective in written and spoken communication*. Cambridge: CUP.
Givón, Talmy. 2001. *Syntax. Volume* 11. Amsterdam: Benjamins.
Halliday, M. A. K. 1963. The tones of English. *Archivum Linguisticum* 15(1). 1–28.
Halliday, M. A. K. 1967a. Notes on transitivity and theme in English, Part II. *Journal of Linguistics* 3. 199–244.
Halliday, M. A. K. 1967b. *Intonation and grammar in British English*. The Hague: Mouton.
Halliday, M.A.K. 1994. *An introduction to Functional Grammar, 2nd edition*. London: Arnold.
Halliday M.A. K. & William Greaves. 2008. *Intonation in the grammar of English*. London: Equinox.
Hedberg, Nancy. 1990. *Discourse pragmatics and cleft sentences in English*. Minnesota: University of Minnesota PhD thesis.
Hedberg, Nancy. 2000. The referential status of clefts. *Language* 76(4). 891–920.
Hedberg, Nancy. 2013. Multiple focus and cleft sentences. In Katharina Hartmann & Tonjes Veenstra (eds.), *Cleft structures*. 227–250. Amsterdam: Benjamins.
Hengeveld, Kees. 1989. Layers and operators in Functional Grammar. *Journal of Linguistics* 25. 127–157.
Higgins, Francis. R. 1979. *The pseudo-cleft construction in English*. London: Routledge.
Hjelmslev, Louis. [1943] 1961. *Prolegomena to a theory of language* (revised English edn. of original Danish version 1943). Madison: University of Wisconsin Press.
Horn, Laurence R. 1981. Exhaustiveness and the semantics of clefts. *North East Linguistics Society* 11. 125–142.
Huddleston, Rodney. 1984. *Introduction to the grammar of English*. Cambridge: Cambridge University Press.
Huddleston, Rodney & Geoffrey Pullum. 2002. *The Cambridge grammar of the English language*. Cambridge: Cambridge University Press.
Jespersen, Otto. 1984 [1937]. *Analytic syntax*. Chicago: University of Chicago Press.
Kiss, Katalin É. 1998. Identificational focus versus information focus. *Language* 74. 245–273.
Lambrecht, Knud. 1994. *Information structure and sentence form*. Cambridge: Cambridge University Press.
Lambrecht, Knud. 2001. A framework for the analysis of cleft constructions. *Linguistics* 39(3). 463–516.

Langacker, Ronald. 1987. *Foundations of Cognitive Grammar. Vol. 1. Theoretical prerequisites.* Stanford: Stanford University Press.
Langacker, Ronald. 1991. *Foundations of Cognitive Grammar. Vol. II: Descriptive application.* Stanford: Stanford University Press.
Langacker, Ronald. 2021. Functions and assemblies. In Kazuhiro Kodama & Tetsuharu Koyama (eds.) *The forefront of Cognitive Linguistics,* 1–54. Tokyo: Hituzi Syobo.
Lehmann, Christian. 2008. Information structure and grammaticalization. In Elena Seoane & María José López-Couso (eds.) *Theoretical issues in grammaticalization,* 207–229. Amsterdam: Benjamins.
McGregor, William. 1997. *Semiotic Grammar.* Oxford: Clarendon.
McGregor, William. 2021. *Neo-Firthian approaches to linguistic typology.* London: Equinox.
Nelson, Gerald. 1997. Cleft constructions in spoken and written English, *Journal of English Linguistics* 25(4). 340–348.
O'Grady, Gerard. 2013. *Key concepts in phonetics and phonology.* New York: Palgrave MacMillan.
O'Grady, Gerard. 2014. An investigation of how intonation helps signal information structure. In Wendy Bowcher & Bradley A. Smith (eds.), *Systemic phonology: Recent studies in English,* 27–52. London: Equinox.
Patten, Amanda. 2012. *The English it-cleft: A constructional account and a diachronic investigation.* Berlin: De Gruyter Mouton.
Prince, Ellen. 1978. A comparison *of wh*-clefts and *it*-clefts in discourse. *Language* 54. 883–906.
Rochemont, Michael. 1986. *Focus in generative grammar.* Amsterdam: Benjamins.
Schwenter, Scott & Richard Waltereit. 2010. Presupposition accomodation and language change. In Kristin Davidse, Lieven Vandelanotte & Hubert Cuyckens (eds.), *Subjectification, intersubjectification and grammaticalization,* 75–102. Berlin: Mouton de Gruyter.
Svartvik, Jan (eds.). 1990. *The London corpus of spoken English: Description and research.* Lund Studies in English 82. Lund University Press.
Tench, Paul. 1990. *The roles of intonation in English.* Bern: Peter Lang.
Traugott, Elizabeth. 1982. From propositional to textual and expressive meanings: Some semantic-pragmatic aspects of grammaticalization. In Winfred Lehmann & Yakov Malkiel (eds.), *Perspectives on Historical Linguistics,* 245–271. Amsterdam: Benjamins.
Traugott, Elizabeth. 1989. On the rise of epistemic meanings in English: An example of subjectification in semantic change. *Language* 65. 31–55.
Traugott, Elizabeth. 2010. (Inter)subjectivity and (inter)subjectification: A reassessment. In Kristin Davidse, Lieven Vandelanotte & Hubert Cuyckens (eds.), *Subjectification, intersubjectification and grammaticalization,* 29–74. Berlin: Mouton de Gruyter.
Van Praet, Wout. 2019. Focus assignment in English specificational and predicative clauses: Intonation as a cue to information structure? *Acta Linguistica Hafniensia* 51(2). 222–241.
Velleman, Dan, David Beaver, Emilie Destruel, Dylan Bumford, Edgar Onea & Liz Coopock. 2012. *It-*clefts are IT (inquiry terminating) constructions. *Proceedings of SALT* 22. 441–460.
Verstraete, Jean-Christophe. 2007. *Rethinking the coordinate-subordinate dichotomy. Interpersonal grammar and the analysis of adverbial clauses in English.* Berlin: Mouton de Gruyter.

Karen Lahousse and Morgane Jourdain
5 The emergence and early development of *c'est* 'it is' clefts in French L1

Abstract: This article describes the developmental path of *c'est* 'it is' clefts in French, on the basis of a dataset consisting of over 300 clefts from spontaneous and semi-naturalistic corpora of speech production by very young children (ages 1–3). Our data indicate that syntax rapidly develops from adult-like 'reduced clefts' to non-adult-like 'cleft attempts' and to adult-like 'full clefts'. Since all these formal types of clefts have adult-like information structure articulations, we conclude that children are sensitive to the discourse pragmatics of this syntactic construction before adult-like syntax is acquired. We also provide some evidence confirming the hypothesis according to which reduced clefts are elided full clefts (Belletti 2013) and the 'low analysis' of adult clefts (Haegeman et al. 2013; Belletti 2013).

Keywords: Cleft sentences, French, syntax, information structure, first langauge acquisition

1 Introduction and background

This article is about the interaction between syntax and Information Structure (henceforth IS) in the emergence and development of cleft sentences introduced by *c'est* 'it is' in French first language acquisition (L1).

The linguistic literature on *c'est* clefts in adult French (1) is very rich; both the syntax and IS of these constructions have been extensively analyzed (see Lambrecht 2001 for an overview; Doetjes, Rebuschi, and Rialland 2004; Destruel 2012; Lahousse and Borremans 2014; Karssenberg and Lahousse 2018).

(1) – *Qui   a   mangé   le   gâteau ?*
        Who has   eaten   the   cake
        'Who ate the cake ?'

Note: This is a slightly revised version of the paper by Lahousse and Jourdain (2020). Many thanks to Katerina Palasis for her very helpful comments on an earlier version of this paper.

Karen Lahousse, KU Leuven, e-mail: karen.lahousse@kuleuven.be
Morgane Jourdain, University of Leuven, e-mail: morgane.jourdain@kuleuven.be

https://doi.org/10.1515/9783110734140-006

- *C'est Jean qui l'a fait.*
  It-is Jean who it-has done
  'It's Jean who did it.'

However, almost nothing is known on the *emergence* of clefts in French L1, be it *full clefts* (2), *reduced clefts* (3) or *cleft attempts* (4).

(2) *C'est toi qui m(e) fait les tortues.*
    It-is you who me does the turtles
    'It's you who does the turtles to me.'
    (Marie, 2;9, corpus of Lyon[1])

(3) *C'est Maya.*
    It-is Maya
    'It's Maya.'
    (Héloïse, 2;10.5, corpus TCOF)

(4) *Non ! C'est moi mets.*
    No It-is me put
    'No! It's me who puts.'
    (Anaïs, 2;5.25, corpus of Lyon)

It has been observed that *c'est* clefts in French L1 appear around age 2 (Labelle 1990; De Cat 2002, 2007; Belletti 2005; Canut 2014; Soares-Jesel and Lobo 2019), which confirms research on the acquisition of clefts in other languages (Santos 2006; Lobo, Santos, and Soares-Jesel 2016; Pivi, Del Puppo, and Cardinaletti 2016).

On the basis of an elicited production experiment, Hupet and Tilmant (1989) show that French-speaking children from ages 4 and older correctly produce contrastive clefts, and that subject clefts are more frequent than object clefts. The results of Soares-Jesel and Lobo's (2019) and Soares-Jesel, Lobo, and Santos' (2022) elicited production experiment – with children from age 3;3 and older – confirm that subject clefts are more frequent than object clefts. Moreover, these authors show that the production of full clefts (*standard clefts* in their terminology) increases significantly with age, whereas the proportion of reduced clefts, which are more frequent than full clefts at age 3;7, decreases as from age 4. Jourdain (2022), who studies the acquisition of the semantics and discourse uses of *c'est* clefts in the same

---

[1] For a description of the corpora we used, see section 2 below.

dataset as the one we use in this article (see section 6.2. below for more details), also shows that most early *c'est* clefts in French are subject clefts.

Since the existing production experiments[2] on the acquisition of clefts in French L1 are with children of ages 3 and more, the most important years to describe the emergence and early development of clefts are "missed". Hence, there is almost no data of the syntactic development and the discourse, i.e. information-structural (IS) properties of clefts in early L1 of French (ages 1–3).[3]

The main goals of this article are (i) to analyze the formal development of the main clause (*c'est* 'it is') and the cleft relative clause; (ii) to determine if clefts produced by children and by adults have the same IS and (iii) whether these IS-functions are present from the onset of language production or gradually emerge as syntax develops.

In what follows, we first present our methodology (section 2) and provide an overview of the syntactic development of clefts in our French L1 corpora (section 3). In sections 4 and 5 we use child data to test some specific hypotheses about the structural analysis of clefts. Section 6 analyzes the information structure (IS) of early clefts, and argues in favor of the hypothesis that IS is acquired *before* (rather than *with* or *after*) syntax.

2 Methodology

2.1 Introduction

We conducted a corpus analysis rather than an experiment for the following reasons. First, in order to study the emergence of clefts, data is needed from the onset of language production, i.e. from very young children of ages 1 and 2. At this age, it may be quite difficult to elicit clefts via a controlled production experiment. Second, with respect to syntax, we want to describe the full developmental path of clefts, at different moments, from the onset of language production. This is harder

---

2 Comprehension experiments on child clefts across languages mainly concern subject-object asymmetries, e.g. Aravind, Hackl, and Wexler (2018) on English; Lobo, Santos, and Soares-Jesel (2016), Lobo et al. (2019) on Portuguese, Soares-Jesel, Lobo, and Santos (2022) on French, often in a featural intervention account (see a.o. Rizzi 1990, 2004; Friedmann, Belletti, and Rizzi 2009; Rizzi 2018; Belletti et al. 2012 and Durrleman and Bentea 2021). On feature intervention in adult *c'est* clefts, see e.g. Lahousse, Laenzlinger, and Soare (2014).
3 The semantics of the clefted element and the discourse use of the full cleft in the same data set as the one we use in this article has been studied in a usage-based account by Jourdain (2022). See section 6.2. below for some details on the connection between semantic and IS properties.

to achieve by experiments, unless several follow-up experiments are planned. Thirdly, we consider corpus research as a heuristic: in corpus research, one often finds constructions (see section 5 below) and information-structural articulations of constructions (see section 6) which would probably not have been incorporated in the setup of an experiment. Nevertheless, we are convinced that our analysis of spontaneously produced clefts by very young children can serve as input for further experimental research: if it is determined in which precise contexts children spontaneously produce clefts, these "natural" discourse conditions will be more easily integrated in an ecologically valid experiment.

2.2 Corpora

Given that our goal is to study the emergence of clefts, and that children as from age 4 produce adult-like clefts, we restricted our analysis to children no older than 3. Our analysis is based on data from two corpora: (i) part of the seminaturalistic[4] cross-sectional TCOF corpus (subcorpus of ATILF 2018, www.ortolang.fr/market/corpora/tcof, see André and Canut 2010) and (ii) the spontaneous longitudinal Lyon corpus (Demuth and Tremblay 2008), freely available on the CHILDES database (MacWhinney and Snow 1990), the details of which can be found in Table 1.

Table 1: Description of the corpora.

	Type of file	Type of corpus	Type of interaction	Age	Nb. Children	Nb. recordings	Corpus size
TCOF	sound files, recorded between 2005–2018	cross-sectional	spontaneous conversation with the researcher	2–3	39	39 (5–45 minutes)	4596 speech turns
Lyon	video and sound files, recorded between 2002–2005	longitudinal (fortnightly recordings)	spontaneous conversation with a parent	1,5–3	3 (Anaïs, Marie, Nathan)	120 (one hour each)	12893 utterances

---

4 Thanks to Katerina Palasis (p.c.) for highlighting that the TCOF corpus is a seminaturalistic rather than a spontaneous corpus (following the terminology of Eisenbeiss 2010), because "the children interact with a researcher, not a usual person".

2.3 Data extraction and selection

We first extracted all sentences containing *c'est* 'it is' from the two corpora. We then made a manual section excluding all examples with referential *c'*, i.e. which refers to an entity given in the discourse context (5), e.g. when the child is using *c'est* clauses to describe something that is present in the context, to comment on the image of a book, or to point at something in the room. We also excluded all examples in which *c'* resumes a dislocated constituent, and, hence, is referential (6). In a second step, we removed all examples in which the relative clause is clearly restrictive, such as (7). Both cases, i.e. *c'est* clauses with referential *c'* and *c'est* clauses with a restrictive relative clause, cannot be considered as clefts (see Karssenberg 2018 for an overview of ways to distinguish clefts from cleft-lookalikes).

(5) Father: *C'est qui là ?*
 It-is who there
 'Who is it there?'
 Child: ***C'est Amtaro.***
 It-is Amtaro
 'It's Amtaro.'
 (Anaïs, 2;9.29, corpus of Lyon)

(6) [Context: the child is giving a toy to the adult]
 Ça c'est pour toi.
 That it-is for you
 'That's for you.'
 (Anaïs, 2;8, corpus Lyon)

(7) Adult: *C'est quoi ?*
 It-is what
 'What's that?'
 Child: ***C'est un bouchon qui est très énervé.***
 It-is a cork which is very angry
 'It's a cork which is very angry.'
 (Marie, 3;2.8, corpus of Lyon)

Table 2 gives an overview of our final dataset, which consists of 303 spontaneously produced clefts, which is a rather large dataset for spontaneous speech production by very young children (ages 1–3).

Table 2: Overview of the data.

	Reduced clefts	Cleft attempts	Full clefts	Total
TCOF	21	14	8	43
Lyon	127	80	53	260
	148	94	61	**303**

3 Development of syntax: General view

An analysis of the syntactic form of the clefts in our dataset reveals the following developmental path of the syntax of clefts, with only some months between the first occurrence of each type:[5]

I. The first attestations of REFERENTIAL C'EST X CLAUSES (with referential c') (5–6) appear between age 1;8 and 1;10 in our corpora.
II. Adult-like REDUCED CLEFTS consisting of non-referential c'+est+X (8) are first attested in our corpora between age 2;0 and 2;5.[6]

(8)   Adult: *Mais oui c'est très bien tu l'as coupé en deux.*
               But yes it-is very good you it-have cut in two
               'Yes it's very good you cut it in two.'
        Adult: *Et après on va remettre par-dessus.*
               And then we go to-put-back above
               'And then, we will put it on top of it.'
        Child: *Non, **c'est Nathan !***
               No it-is Nathan
               'No, it's Nathan!'
    (Nathan, 2;5.1, corpus of Lyon)

---

[5] We follow Hamann and Tuller (2014: 52) in taking the "order of acquisition in spontaneous language production to be manifestations of the effect of syntactic complexity".
[6] Soares-Jesel and Lobo (2019) even mention that reduced clefts are already produced by children at age 1;10.

III. Non adult-like CLEFT ATTEMPTS (with cleft prosody)[7] show up between ages 2;0 and 2;7.[8] These combine *c'est X* and an isolated word (NP, infinitive, adjective, participle) (9), and later a VP with inflected verb (sometimes followed by a complement) (10).[9] As far as we can tell, the production of cleft attempts in child language has only been reported for Portuguese L1 by Lobo, Santos, and Soares-Jesel (2016), who call them *proto-clefts*.

(9) *C'est Marie avoir.*
It-is Marie to-have
'It's Marie have.'
(Marie, 2;0.28, corpus of Lyon)

(10) Adult: *Voilà faut les enlever comp, enlever*
There need-to them to-remove comp... to-remove
complètement là l'velcro.
completely there the-velcro
'There, you need to remove comp... to completely remove the velcro.'
Child: *Non velcro. Maman fais !*
No Velcro mommy does
'No velcro. Mommy does!'
Adult: *Voilà.*
There
'There it is.'
Child: ***C'est moi fais.***
It-is me do
'It's me who does it.'
(Marie, 2;5.1, corpus of Lyon)

---

7 Prosody was only used to check whether these utterances form one intonation unit, rather than two, which could indicate that the child is actually cutting the current sentence to start over another one. We did not check whether the pitch contour matched one of those identified in adult French.

8 Note that all examples mentioned here come from the Lyon corpus. The children of the TCOF corpus are older and produce no cleft attempts with isolated words. In addition, this corpus contains only one example with a VP. All the other examples are instances of adult-like (full or reduced) clefts.

9 These attempts of cleft relative clauses are inherently predicative, which confirms that cleft relative clauses are pseudo-relative clauses (see Casalicchio (2016) for an overview). For reasons of space, we cannot go deeper into this issue here.

IV. Clefts of the form *C'EST* X + JUXTAPOSED SENTENCE (with cleft prosody but without complementizer), such as (11), appear between ages 2;5 and 2;9. In these cases, the clefted element can (11a-b) but does not have to be (11c) coreferential with the subject of the juxtaposed sentence. As far as we can tell, the existence of this type of clefts in child language has not been reported before. Interestingly, native speakers moreover confirm that this type of cleft appears in very informal adult French.[10]

(11) a. *C'est ça   c'est vert.*
       It-is that it-is green
       'It's that it's green.'
       (Anaïs, 2;5.11, corpus of Lyon)
   b. *C'est Tigrou il   est pas content.*
       It-is Tiger   he   is   not happy
       'It's Tiger he is not happy.'
       (Nathan, 2;9.7, corpus of Lyon)
   c. *C'est ça   on   montre.*
       It-is that we   show
       'It's that we show.'
       (Marie, 2;5.16, corpus of Lyon)

V. Adult-like FULL CLEFTS with a complete cleft relative clause (*c'est X qui/que* 'it's X who/that' + clause) appear between ages 2;6 and 2;9 in our dataset (12).

---

10 In the literature on *c'est* clefts in adult French, we did not find any mention of such complementizerless clefts introduced by *c'est*. However, the existence of such clefts introduced by *il y a* 'there is' has been reported by Willems and Meulleman (2010):

(i) *Il y a des gens ils viennent acheter de l'aspirine pour faire de l'eau gazeuse.*
    'There are people they come to buy aspirin to make fizzy water.'

(12) Child: *veux faire avec j(e) faire j(e) veux pas*
Want to-do with I to-do I want not
faire les tortues c'est compliqué.
to-do the turtles it-is complicated
'Want do with I do I don't want to do the turtles it's complicated.'
Adult: *Oui c'est un petit peu compliqué mais*
Yes it-is a little bit complicated But
qu'est-ce qu'on peut faire d'autre?
what-we can to-do else
'Yes it's a bit complicated but what else can we do?'
Child: ***C'est toi qui m(e) fais les tortues.***
It-is you who me does the turtles
'It's you who does the turtles for me.'
(Marie, 2;9.1, corpus of Lyon)

In this section, we have analyzed, on the basis of corpus analysis, the acquisition trajectory of different (adult-like and non-adult-like) types of *c'est* clefts in French L1 acquisition.

In the next two sections we will provide some more specific data and "accidental" findings in our corpora. These will allow us to zoom in on two existing claims and hypotheses on adult clefts, concerning the acquisition and syntactic analysis of reduced clefts vs full clefts (section 4), and the structural position of the clefted element (section 5). The background question here is: given that children master clefts so early, do child data offer extra arguments for specific claims on the syntactic analysis of (adult) clefts?

4 The acquisition and syntactic analysis of reduced vs full clefts

The following figures (1–4) show that, in the Lyon corpus, at age 2, reduced clefts (II) are first much more frequent than other types of clefts (III, IV, V), but that the difference between the frequency of both types of clefts reduces between age 2 and age 3 (the child Marie, who is in general ahead of the other children in the corpora, is an exception).

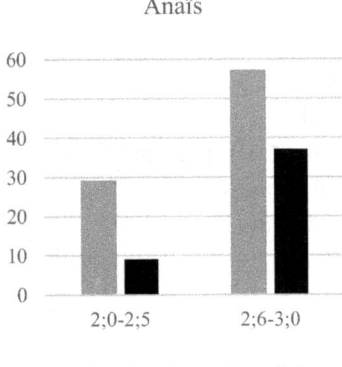

Figure 1: Absolute frequency of clefts and reduced clefts in the data of Anaïs (corpus of Lyon).

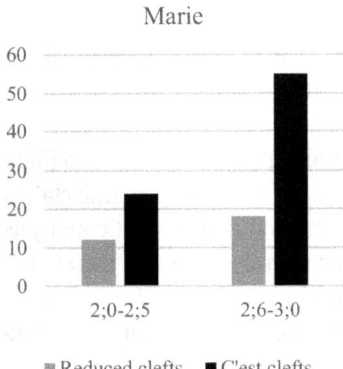

Figure 2: Absolute frequency of clefts and reduced clefts in the data of Marie (corpus of Lyon).

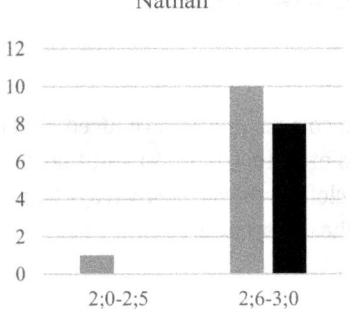

Figure 3: Absolute frequency of clefts and reduced clefts in the data of Nathan (corpus of Lyon).

In the TCOF corpus, the proportion of reduced and other types of cleft is reversed between ages 2 and 3:

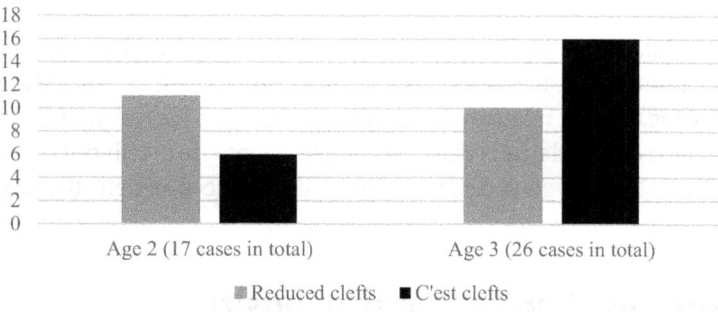

Figure 4: Absolute frequency of clefts and reduced clefts in the corpus TCOF.

There are two theoretically possible ways to explain how children acquire full and reduced clefts:

OPTION 1: Children either acquire full clefts (type V: *c'est X qui/que* 'it's X who/ that' + clause) from the onset of acquisition. The production of reduced clefts (type II) is then a by-product of complexity and/or processing if children cannot immediately produce a full cleft relative clause.

OPTION 2: Children acquire clefts in a compositional way, by combining a non-referential *c'est* main clause (i.e. a reduced cleft, type II) and a relative clause.

Option 2 predicts that relative clauses (outside clefts) in L1 appear *before* clefts with a full cleft relative clause. This prediction is however not borne out in our corpus data: in the Lyon corpus, the first relative clause *outside* the cleft construction appears at age 2;8 (13a). This is slightly later than the first cleft relative clause, which is produced at 2;6 (13b).

(13) a. First relative clause outside cleft
          Mais mais à   la   fille qui fait   bubu.
          But   but   to the girl   who does   bubu
          'But but to the girl who does bubu.'
          (Marie, 2;8.14, corpus of Lyon)
      b. First cleft relative clause
          C'est moi qu'est   fatiguée toute seule.
          It-is   me   who-is   tired   all   alone
          'It's me who is tired all alone.'
          (Marie, 2;6.2, corpus of Lyon)

This is independently confirmed by previous literature according to which all first embedded finite clauses appear inside the cleft construction (De Cat 2002 and Labelle 1990 on French; see also Diessel 2004 and Diessel and Tomasello 2005 on English).

Hence, these data argue in favour of option 1 above: children immediately acquire full clefts but are, at the onset of their language production, not always capable of producing the cleft relative clause. By hypothesis, it is for reasons of processing that the cleft relative clause is either (i) omitted, giving rise to reduced clefts, as argued by Belletti (2013) for adult clefts or (ii) partially produced, in cleft attempts.

5 The "high" vs "low" structural position of the clefted element

With respect to the structural analysis of clefts, two cartographic analyses have been proposed (see Haegeman, Meinunger, and Vercauteren 2013 for a detailed overview of both).[11]

In the "high" or "monoclausal" analysis (Kiss 1998; Meinunger 1998; Sleeman 2012; Frascarelli and Ramaglia 2013), the clefted element (CE) is in the FocP position in the clausal left periphery, which is also supposed to host preposed foci and the fronted *wh*-phrase in root questions (Benincà 1988: 144; Rizzi 1997, 2001):

(14)   [$_{Ground/TopP}$ it is [$_{FocP}$ **the dog** [$_{TopP}$ that Mary saw [$_{TP}$ ..]]]]
             CE

In the "low" analysis proposed by Belletti (2013), the CE is in the vP periphery or the periphery of the cleft relative clause, depending on its interpretation:

(15)   a.   CE = narrow contrastive focus (focus-background cleft)
             [$_{vP}$ be [$_{CP/FocPcorr/contr}$ **Gianni** [$_{FinP}$ che [$_{TP}$ t$_{Gianni}$ ha parlato]]]]
       b.   CE = narrow new information focus (focus-background cleft)
             [$_{FocP/NewInfo}$ **Gianni** [$_{vP}$ be [$_{CP}$ [$_{FinP}$ che [$_{TP}$ t$_{Gianni}$ ha parlato]]]]]
       c.   CE = discourse-given (given-new clefts)
             [$_{TopP}$ **Gianni** [$_{vP}$ be [$_{CP}$ [$_{FinP}$ che [$_{TP}$ t$_{Gianni}$ ha parlato]]]]]
             (adapted from Belletti, 2013, details omitted)

---

11 See Reeve (2012) for an alternative analysis. For reasons of space, we do not present other syntactic analyses of clefts than the cartographic analysis.

Note that Belletti's (2013) derivation of clefts in (15) relies on a cartographic approach of the clause-external periphery (as in Rizzi (1997) and much subsequent work) and of the clause-internal periphery, in line with Belletti (2005). If we assume that this very complex structure also holds for child clefts, this raises the issue of learnability. On the other hand, it makes interesting predictions.

Haegeman, Meinunger, and Vercauteren (2013) provide an extensive series of arguments against the high analysis and, hence, in favour of the low analysis, without however specifying in which precise low position the clefted element would be. In our view, the most important counter-argument given by these authors is the following.

According to the authors, the grammaticality of examples in which a CE has undergone further *wh*-movement (16) or focus-movement (17) is unexpected (i) if the clausal left periphery contains only one focal position (Rizzi 2001) and (ii) if SpecFocP in the clausal left periphery (in the high analysis in (14)) hosts clefted elements (CEs), preposed foci and the *wh*-moved phrase in root questions (cf. supra).

(16) a. *What* was it __ that you saw?
 b. *Who* was it __ that you were going to invite?
 (Haegeman, Meinunger, and Vercauteren 2013: 13)

(17) a. Was it Sue who polished off the cookies?
 No, *Pat* it was __ who ate them.
 (Ward, Birner, and Huddleston 2002: 1420)
 b. What was it __ that you saw?
 JOHN it was __ that Mary saw. (Reeve 2011: 94a)
 (Haegeman, Meinunger, and Vercauteren 2013: 16)

Our corpora also contain spontaneously produced clefts in which the CE is *wh*-moved:[12]

(18) a. *Qui c'est __ a mis scotch ?*
 Who it-is has put sellotape
 'Who is it that put sellotape?'
 (Marie, 2;2.17, corpus of Lyon)

---

[12] Note that focus-preposing in general is very rare in French and limited to very specific registers and contexts (Lahousse 2015).

b. *Qui   c'est _ a   mis   chocolat ?*
   Who   it-is   has put   chocolate
   'Who is it that put chocolate?'
   (Marie, 2;2.17, corpus of Lyon)

The examples in (18), just as those in (16) and (17), are incompatible with a view in which the focus position in the clausal left periphery hosts CEs and *wh*-words in roots, and in which the clausal left periphery contains only one focus position. Hence, they are arguments against a high structural analysis for clefts such as (14).

6 The acquisition of syntax & IS

Our corpus data shed new light on three competing hypotheses with respect to the acquisition order of syntax and information structure (IS).

HYPOTHESIS 1: THE ACQUISITION OF SYNTAX PRECEDES THAT OF IS: "Children may first acquire the syntax of cleft sentences, initially not being fully sensitive to the pragmatic conditions on their use" (Aravind, Hackl, and Wexler 2018: 284). This hypothesis predicts occurrences in child speech production of syntactically adult-like clefts which do *not* have an adult-like IS.

HYPOTHESIS 2: SYNTAX & IS ARE ACQUIRED SIMULTANEOUSLY. The prediction is that children produce clefts with an adult-like IS immediately when adult-like syntax of the construction is acquired.

HYPOTHESIS 3: IS IS ACQUIRED BEFORE ADULT-LIKE SYNTAX: this hypothesis is in line with the cognitive hypothesis put forward by Lambrecht (1994) and psycholinguists such as Levelt (1989), according to whom IS is absolutely fundamental in language production and prior to – rather than simultaneous with – purely linguistic processes concerning form and meaning. If IS is at the basis of syntax and *prior* to linguistic processes, rather than being computed *together with* or *after* linguistic processing, then children should "show sensitivity to pragmatic aspects of clefts before they can build an adultlike syntax for these sentences" (Aravind, Hackl, and Wexler 2018: 284). Hence, this hypothesis predicts that children, as soon as they start to produce (even non-adult-like) clefts do so with an adult-like IS.

Although it might be hard to distinguish between hypotheses 2 and 3, especially because the non target-like form of clefts could be due to processing (cf. supra), we believe that cleft attempts may be an ideal test case, to the extent that they have non-adult-like syntax.

C'est clefts in adult French can have a wide range of IS-articulations (for an overview, see Dufter 2009; Lahousse and Borremans 2014; Karssenberg and Lahousse 2018). They prototypically have (i) a focus-background IS-articulation in which the clefted element is a (contrastive, corrective or a new information) focus, or, less prototypically, (ii) a topic-comment articulation ("cohesive clefts"),[13] in which the CE functions as an aboutness-topic "what the sentence is about" (Reinhart 1981) or a stage topic (Chafe 1976; Erteschik-Shir 1986). In addition, they can (iii) display a double contrast and (iv) in very specific registers and discourse contexts (e.g. in jokes), even an all-focus interpretation.

In our corpora, all children's early *c'est* clefts display the prototypical discourse interpretations of adult clefts in which the clefted element is a focus, in clefts with all syntactic types of cleft relative clauses. For instance, in the reduced clefts in (19–21) below, the clefted element is a new information focus (19), a contrastive focus (20) or a corrective focus (21).

(19)   Adult: *Oui   et   qui est-ce qui   te   l'a   offert ?*
                  Yes   and   who   you   it-has   offered
                  'Who offered it to you?'
       Child: *Euh   c'est   Maya.*
                  Erm   it-is   Maya
                  'It's Maya.'
       (Héloïse, 2;10.5, corpus TCOF)

---

13 In our corpora, cohesive clefts such as (i) show up at age 4. This relatively late appearance could however be due to the fact that such clefts are typical of narrative contexts, which are not that frequent in the interactions in our corpora:

(i)   Enfant: *en fait il aime pas trop Tic Tic et Tac et euh hum et voilà il veut leur faire du mal il est méchant.*
      'Child: in reality he does't like too much Tic Tic and Tak and euh and he wants to harm them he is naughty.'
     C'est   pour   ça   qu'il   crie   très   méchamment.
     It-is   for   that   that-he   shouts   very   nastily
     (Laureen, 4;10.2, corpus TCOF)

(20) Adult: *C'est qui qui fait une maison ?*
It-is who who makes a house
C'est moi ou c'est toi ?
It-is me or it-is you
'It's who who makes a house? It's you or it's me?'
Child: ***C'est toi.***
It-is you
'It's you.'
(Mélanie, 3;9.19, corpus TCOF)

(21) Adult: *C'est toi qui l'as acheté ?*
It-is you who it-has bought
'It's you who bought it?'
Child: *Non,* ***c'est maman.***
No it-is mommy
'No, it's mommy.'
(Clara, 3;1.5, corpus TCOF)

Similarly, in the cleft attempts in (22) and (23), the clefted element is a corrective focus (22) or a new information focus (23):[14]

(22) Child: *J'arrive pas à ouvrir. J'arrive pas yyy.*
I-manage not to to-open I-manage not yyy
'I can't open it. I can't yyy.'
Mother: *Fais voir !*
Make to-look
'Let me have a look!'
Child: *<Non,>* ***c'est moi réparer.***
No it-is me to-repare
'No it's me who repares.'
(Anaïs, 2;5.2, corpus of Lyon)

(23) Father: *Ah ouais je l'ai abîmé.*
Ah yes I it-have damaged
'Ah yes, I damaged it.'

---

14 In this example, the function of the interrogative cleft is to reconfirm the previous statement. Hence, the clefted element can be considered new information focus.

Child:	Ici.	*C'est*	*toi*	*a*	*cassé ?*
	Here	it-is	you	has	broken

'Here. It's you who broke?'
(Anaïs, 2;9.16, corpus of Lyon)

The next example is a cleft with a juxtaposed clause, in which the clefted element has a contrastive interpretation:

(24) Child: *Moi je veux.*
Me I want
'I want.'
Adult: *Tu veux les deux ?*
You want the two
'You want both of them?'
Child: *ouais*
'yeah'
Adult: *et puis Geoffrey on lui prend quoi ?*
and then Geoffrey we for-him take what
'And then Geoffrey, what do we take for him?'
Child: ***c'est Jéré- c'est Jérémy il veut avoir celle-ci***
It-is Jéré- it-is Jérémy he wants to-have this-one
'It's Jéré- it's Jérémy who wants to have this one'
(Jordan, 2;8.25, corpus TCOF)

Hence, as soon as children produce clefts in French, whether the cleft relative clause is target-like or not, they do so with an adult-like focus interpretation of the clefted element. A previous semantic analysis carried out on the same corpus (Jourdain 2022) suggests that children might make use of some semantic categories to help form the focus category. Jourdain (2022) shows that not only are clefted elements mostly subjects, but they are also overwhelmingly referring to human agents. This is particularly striking, because studies on early dislocation in child French, a construction which mostly affects subjects, especially in early child speech, show that children initially produce inanimate non-agentive entities as dislocated subjects (Jourdain, Canut, and Lahousse 2020a, 2020b). While it is not entirely clear how this semantic distinction relates to the IS properties of *topic* and *focus*, it seems that agents could possibly be more easily categorized by children as foci. Several eye-tracking studies reveal that participants tend to look at agents before patients or other aspects of an event, showing how important agents are for event perception (Sauppe and Flecken 2021; Cohn and Paczynski

2013). Further research is however necessary to determine exactly the association between human agents and focus in child French.

Hence, in all the examples of early clefts in our corpus the construction has an adult-like IS-articulation. This shows that IS is present at the onset of language production, which goes against HYPOTHESIS 1 ("The acquisition of syntax precedes that of IS") and which also runs against approaches in which IS is only computed at LF. Furthermore, the fact that cleft attempts (22–23), which *do not* have adult-like syntax, *do* have adult-like IS seems to be an argument in favour of HYPOTHESIS 3 ("IS is acquired before adult-like syntax") rather than HYPOTHESIS 2 ("Syntax & IS are acquired simultaneously"). Of course, with respect to this, more research needs to be done on the precise influence of processing on the syntax of cleft attempts.

7 Conclusion

The main aims of this article were (i) to analyze the formal development of the main clause and the cleft relative clause; (ii) to determine if clefts produced by children and by adults have the same IS and (iii) if these IS-functions gradually emerge and develop. The main findings are the following.

The developmental path of the syntax of clefts is (with only some months between the 1st occurrence of each type): I. *c'est X* clauses with referential *c'*; II. *reduced clefts* of the type *c'est X*; III. *cleft attempts*: *c'est X* + an isolated word (infinitive, adjective, participle) and later a VP (with inflected verb, without complementizer) (see Lobo, Santos, and Soares-Jesel 2016 on proto-clefts in Portuguese L1); IV. clefts of the form *c'est* X + juxtaposed sentence (without complementizer); V. full clefts with a complete cleft relative clause (*c'est X qui/que* + clause).

At age 2, reduced clefts are more frequent than cleft attempts and full clefts, but their proportion decreases between age 2 and 4. It is inside the cleft construction that the first relative clauses are produced in the corpus, which confirms that relative clauses emerge in contexts with a "light" main verb (Diessel and Tomasello 2005). The production of reduced clefts, cleft attempts, full clefts and relative clauses in French L1 acquisition argues in favor of an analysis of reduced clefts in child L1 as full clefts with an elided cleft relative clause (see Belletti 2013 on adult clefts).

Young children perform complex syntactic operations (*wh*-movement) on the clefted element. This indicates that the clefted element is not in the clausal left periphery, but in a low, clause-internal position (see Haegeman et al. 2013; Belletti 2013 on adult clefts).

With respect to Information Structure, we have shown that all prototypical discourse interpretations of adult *c'est* clefts, i.e. focus-background clefts in which the clefted element has a corrective / contrastive / new information interpretation, occur in our French L1 corpora (ages 1,5 – 3), in all syntactic types of clefts. The fact that children seem to have access to all discourse features of adult clefts before full (adult-like) syntax of clefts is acquired, indicates that syntax is not acquired earlier than IS in L1. Put differently, the fact that syntactically non-adult-like cleft attempts do have adult-like IS, suggests that children are sensitive to the pragmatics of this syntactic construction before adult-like syntax is acquired. This confirms cognitive hypotheses put forward by Lambrecht (1994) and psycholinguists such as Levelt (1989). It is also in line with syntactic approaches which integrate IS in syntax (rather than assign it post-syntactically at LF), such as the cartographic approach à la Rizzi (1997 and subsequent work), in which information-structural notions are present in the syntactic structure of the clause, although accounts for clefts in this line could face a learnability problem for clefts (see section 4 above). One solution might be to integrate IS-features in a Featural Relativized Minimality (Friedmann, Belletti, and Rizzi 2009) approach to the syntax of clefts, as has been proposed by, among others, Lahousse, Laenzlinger, and Soare (2014). This might lead to a simpler derivation, and reduce the learnability problem. We leave this for further research.

References

André, Virginie & Emmanuelle Canut. 2010. Mise à disposition de corpus oraux interactifs : le projet TCOF (Traitement de Corpus Oraux en Français). *Pratiques linguistique, littérature, didactique* 147. 35–51.
Aravind, Athulya, Martin Hackl & Kenneth Wexler. 2018. Syntactic and pragmatic factors in children's comprehension of cleft constructions. *Language Acquisition* 25(3). 284–314.
Belletti, Adriana. 2005. Answering with a "cleft": The role of the null subject parameter and the VP periphery. In Laura Brugè, Giuliana Giusti, Nicola Munaro, Walter Schweikert & Giuseppina Turano (eds.), *Proceedings of the Thirtieth "Incontro di Grammatica Generativa"*, 63–82. Venice: Cafoscarina.
Belletti, Adriana. 2013. The focus map of clefts: Extraposition and prediction. In Ur Shlonsky (ed.), *Where do we go from here? Chapters in syntactic cartography*, 42–59. Oxford: Oxford University Press.
Belletti, Adriana, Naama Friedmann, Brunato Dominique & Luigi Rizzi. 2012. Does gender make a difference? Comparing the effect of gender on children's comprehension of relative clauses in Hebrew and Italian. *Lingua* 122. 1053–1069.
Benincà, Paola. 1988. L'ordine degli elementi della frase e le costruzioni marcate. In Lorenzo Renzi, Giampaolo Salvi & Anna Cardinaletti (eds.), *Grande grammatica italiana di consultazione*, 115–195. Bologna: il Mulino.
Canut, Emmanuelle. 2014. Acquisition des constructions syntaxiques complexes chez l'enfant français entre 2 et 6 ans. *Congrès mondial de linguistique française*. 1437–1452.
Casalicchio, Jan. 2016. Pseudo-relatives and their left-periphery. In Ernestina Carrilho, Alexandra Fiéis, Maria Lobo & Sandra Pereira (eds.), *RomancelLanguages and Linguistic theory. Selected papers from 'Going Romance' 28, Lisbon*, 23–42. Amsterdam: John Benjamins.

Chafe, Wallace. 1976. Givenness, contrastiveness, definiteness, subjects, topics and point of view. In Charles Li (ed.), *Subject and topic*, 25–55. New York: Academic Press, INC.

Cohn, Neil & Martin Paczynski. 2013. Prediction, events, and the advantage of agents: The processing of semantic roles in visual narrative. *Cognitive Psychology* 67(3). 73–97.

De Cat, Cécile. 2002. French dislocation. York: University of York PhD thesis.

De Cat, Cécile. 2007. *French dislocation, interpretation, syntax, acquisition*. Oxford: Oxford University Press.

Demuth, Katherine & Annie Tremblay. 2008. Prosodically-conditioned variability in children's production of French determiners. *Journal of Child Language* 35(1). 99–127.

Destruel, Emilie. 2012. The French *c'est*-cleft: An empirical study on its meaning and use. In Christopher Piñón (ed.), *Empirical Issues in Syntax and Semantics* 9. 95–112.

Diessel, Holger. 2004. *The acquisition of complex sentences*. Cambridge: Cambridge University Press.

Diessel, Holger & Michael Tomasello. 2005. New look at the acquisition of relative clauses. *Language* 81. 882–906.

Doetjes, Jenny, Georges Rebuschi & Annie Rialland. 2004. Cleft sentences. In Francis Corblin & Henriëtte De Swart (eds.), *Handbook of French semantics*, 529–552. Stanford: CSLI Publications.

Dufter, Andreas. 2009. Clefting and discourse organization: Comparing Germanic and Romance. In Andreas Dufter & Daniel Jacob (eds.), *Focus and background in Romance languages*, 83–121. Amsterdam/Philadelphia: John Benjamins.

Durrleman, Stephanie & Anamiara Bentea. 2021. Locality in the acquisition of object A'-dependencies: Insights from French. *Glossa: A Journal of General Linguistics* 6(1). 1–27.

Eisenbeiss, Sonja. 2010. Production methods in language acquisition research. In Elma Blom & Sharon Unsworth (eds.), *Experimental methods in language acquisition research*, 11–34. Amsterdam: John Benjamins.

Erteschik-Shir, Nomi. 1986. Wh-questions and focus. *Linguistics and Philosophy* 9. 117–149.

Frascarelli, Mara & Francesca Ramaglia. 2013. (Pseudo)clefts at the syntax-prosody-discourse interface. In Tonjes Veenstra & Katharina Hartmann (eds.), *Cleft structures*, 97–138. Amsterdam: John Benjamins.

Friedmann, Naama, Adriana Belletti & Luigi Rizzi. 2009. Relativized relatives: Types of intervention in the acquisition of A-bar dependencies. *Lingua* 119. 67–88.

Haegeman, Liliane, André Meinunger & Aleksandra Vercauteren. 2013. The architecture of it-clefts. *Journal of Linguistics* 50(2). 269–296.

Hamann, Cornelia & Laurice Tuller. 2014. Genuine versus superficial relatives in French: The depth of embedding factor. *Revisita di grammatica generativa* 36. 146–181.

Hupet, Michel & Brigitte Tilmant. 1989. How to make young children produce cleft sentences. *Journal of Child Language* 16(02). 251–261.

Jourdain, Morgane. 2022. The emergence of information structure in child speech: The acquisition of *c'est*-clefts in French. *Cognitive Linguistics* 33(1). 121–154.

Jourdain, Morgane, Emmanuelle Canut & Karen Lahousse. 2020a. Item-based acquisition of dislocation in early child French. *Journal of Monolingual and Bilingual Speech* 2(1). 44–72.

Jourdain, Morgane, Emmanuelle Canut & Karen Lahousse. 2020b. The L1 acquisition of dislocation in French: A usage-based analysis of information structure. In Megan M. Brown & Alexandra Kohut (eds.), *Proceedings of the 44th Annual Boston University Conference on Language Development*. Vol. 1, 238–251. Somerville MA: Cascadilla.

Karssenberg, Lena. 2018. *Non-prototypical clefts in French: A corpus analysis of French il y a clefts*. Berlin: De Gruyter Mouton.

Karssenberg, Lena & Karen Lahousse. 2018. The information structure of French *il y a* clefts and *c'est* clefts: A corpus-based analysis. *Linguistics* 56(3). 513–548.

Kiss, Kátalin É. 1998. Identificational focus versus information focus. *Languages* 74(2). 245–273.
Labelle, Marie. 1990. Predication, wh-movement, and the development of relative clauses. *Language Acquisition* 1. 95–119.
Lahousse, Karen. 2015. A case of focal adverb preposing in French. In Elisa Di Domenico, Cornelia Hamann & Simona Matteini (eds.), *Structures, strategies and beyond: Studies in honour of Adriana Belletti*. Amsterdam: John Benjamins.
Lahousse, Karen & Marijke Borremans. 2014. The distribution of functional-pragmatic types of clefts in adverbial clauses. *Linguistics* 52(3). 793–836.
Lahousse, Karen & Morgane Jourdain. 2020. The emergence of full and reduced clefts in French L1. In Megan M. Brown & Alexandra Kohut (eds.), *Proceedings of the 44th Annual Boston University Conference on Language Development*. Vol. 1, 266–279. Somerville MA: Cascadilla.
Lahousse, Karen, Christopher Laenzlinger & Gabriela Soare. 2014. Contrast and intervention at the periphery. *Lingua* 143. 56–85.
Lambrecht, Knud. 1994. *Information structure and sentence form: Topic, focus, and the mental representation of discourse referents*. Cambridge: Cambridge University Press.
Lambrecht, Knud. 2001. A framework for the analysis of cleft constructions. *Linguistics* 39(3). 463–516.
Levelt, Willem J.M. 1989. *Speaking: from intention to articulation*. Cambridge, MA: Massachusetts Institute of Technology Press.
Lobo, Maria, Ana Lúcia Santos & Carla Soares-Jesel. 2016. Syntactic structure and information structure: The acquisition of Portuguese clefts and Be-fragments. *Language Acquisition* 23(2). 1–33.
Lobo, Maria, Ana Lúcia Santos, Carla Soares-Jesel & Stéphanie Vaz. 2019. Effects of syntactic structure on the comprehension of clefts. *Glossa: A Journal of General Linguistics* 4(1). 1–23.
MacWhinney, Brian & Catherine E. Snow. 1990. The child language data exchange system: An update. *Journal of Child Language* 17. 457–472.
Meinunger, André. 1998. A monoclausal approach to cleft and pseudo-cleft sentences. *ZAS Papers in Linguistics* 10. 89–105.
Pivi, Margherita, Giorgia Del Puppo & Anna Cardinaletti. 2016. The elicited oral production of Italian restrictive relative clauses and cleft sentences in typically developing children and children with developmental dyslexia. In Pedro Guijarro Fuentes, Maria Juan-Garau & Pilar Larrañaga (eds.), *Acquisition of Romance languages*, 231–262. Berlin: De Gruyter Mouton.
Reeve, Matthew. 2011. The syntactic structure of English clefts. *Lingua* 121(2). 142–171.
Reeve, Matthew. 2012. *Clefts and their relatives*. Amsterdam: John Benjamins.
Reinhart, Tanya. 1981. Pragmatics and linguistics: An analysis of sentence topics. *Philosophica* 27(1). 53–94.
Rizzi, Luigi. 1990. *Relativized minimality*. Cambridge, Mass.: MIT Press.
Rizzi, Luigi. 1997. The fine structure of the left periphery. In Liliane Haegeman (ed.), *Elements of grammar. A handbook of generative syntax*, 281–337. Dordrecht: Kluwer.
Rizzi, Luigi. 2001. On the position of Int(errogative) in the left periphery of the clause. In Guglielmo Cinque & Giampolo Salvi (eds.), *Current studies in Italian syntax: Essays offered to Lorenzo Renzi*, 286–296. Amsterdam: North-Holland.
Rizzi, Luigi. 2004. Locality and the left periphery. In Adriana Belletti (ed.), *Structures and beyond: The cartography of syntactic structures*, 223–251. Oxford/New York: Oxford University Press.
Rizzi, Luigi. 2018. Intervention effects in grammar and language acquisition. *Probus* 30(2). 339–367.
Santos, Ana Lúcia. 2006. *Minimal answers. Ellipsis, syntax and discourse in the acquisition of European Portuguese*. Lisbon: University of Lisbon.

Sauppe, Sebastian & Monique Flecken. 2021. Speaking for seeing: Sentence structure guides visual event apprehension. *Cognition* 206. Article 104516.

Sleeman, Petra. 2012. Quantifier preposing in French and Italian as a root phenomenon: A syntactic or a pragmatic approach? *Bucharest Working Papers in Linguistics* 14(1). 5–22.

Soares-Jesel, Carla & Maria Lobo. 2019. The acquisition of clefts: Syntax and information structure, International workshop on the L1 and L2 acquisition of information structure. Leuven, Belgium.

Soares-Jesel, Carla, Maria Lobo & Ana Lúcia Santos. 2022. The problem of pseudoclefts in French: intersection configurations and intervention in language acquisition. *Isogloss* 8(5). https://doi.org/10.5565/rev/isogloss.227

Ward, Gregory, Betty J. Birner & Rodney Huddleston. 2002. Information packaging. In Rodney Huddleston & Geoffrey K. Pullum (eds.), *The Cambridge grammar of the English language*, 1363–1447. Cambridge, UK: Cambridge University Press.

Willems, Dominique & Machteld Meulleman. 2010. *Il y a des gens ils viennent acheter des aspirines pour faire de l'eau gazeuse*. Sur les raisons d'être des structures parataxiques en *il y a*. In Marie-José Béguelin, Mathieu Avanzi & Gilles Corminboeuf (eds.), *La parataxe. Tome 2. Structures, marquages et exploitations discursives*, 167–184. Bern: Peter Lang.

Giuseppe Samo and Paola Merlo
6 Distributed computational models of intervention effects: A study on cleft structures in French

Abstract: Object *it*-cleft constructions are complex structures which also occur rarely in corpora. When present, it has been demonstrated that there is a cross-linguistic tendency to disfavour matching configurations in terms of intervention effects triggered by morpho-syntactic features between the fronted clefted element and the intervening subject. If the investigation in large scale-corpora suggest that similarity between the clefted fronted object and the intervening subject is avoided, we expect that computational models sensitive to the statistics might show a dispreference for matching and a preference for mismatching configurations as predicted from a theory of locality. In this paper, we carry out two studies on artificial neural network models, which represent powerful domain-general learning mechanisms with weak learning biases, trained in French. What we observe is that the representations of neural network models are sensitive to morpho-syntactic features (type/number/person and number/gender), since we observe gradation of effects that vary with the number of matching features.

Keywords: object clefts, large language models, intervention effects, French

1 Introduction

A wealth of literature has investigated the syntactic nature and the complexity of computation of cleft structures (Prince 1978; Meinunger 1998; Roggia 2008; Dufter 2009; Reeve 2012; Frascarelli and Ramaglia 2013; Stark 2014; Haegeman et al. 2015; Belletti 2015; Karssenberg and Lahousse 2018; De Cesare and Garassino 2018).

In this paper, we investigate *it*-cleft structures. In these structures, it is widely assumed that the clefted element has been extracted from a lower structure (Kiss 1998), via A'-movement (but see Doetjes et al. 2004 for discussion). Clefts, thus, belong to the set of structures involving a long-distance dependency relation,

---

Giuseppe Samo, Beijing Language and Culture University / University of Geneva,
e-mails: samo@blcu.edu.cn / giuseppe.samo@unige.ch
Paola Merlo, University of Geneva, e-mail: paola.merlo@unige.ch

https://doi.org/10.1515/9783110734140-007

whose availability and acceptability has been accounted for by different factors, both across languages and within individual languages. Experimental studies have shown that subject clefts are easier to parse than object clefts (Bever 1974; Dick et al. 2004; Lobo et al. 2019; Chesi and Canal 2019 and references therein; see also Aravind et al. 2018). But even object clefts are not all equally difficult to parse. The movement of the object to a higher position is subject to locality effects (Rizzi 1990, 2004; Starke 2001; Belletti 2018). The dissimilarity between the fronted object and the intervening subject, in clefts, but also other long-distance dependencies, has been proven to have ameliorative parsing effects in different populations of speakers, such as adults, children and speakers affected by language pathologies (Grillo 2008; Friedmann et al. 2009; Belletti et al. 2012; Martini et al. 2020; Lobo et al. 2019; Chesi and Canal 2019), while the similarity has the opposite effect of creating less acceptability for the long distance dependency. Let us take, as an initial reference, the French examples in (1).

(1) a. *C'est la présidente que le ministre recontre < la présidente >*
It is the president that the minister meets
'It is the president that the minister meets'.
b. *C'est la présidente que nous reconcontrons < la présidente >*
It is the president that we meet
'It is the president that we meet'

In both (1a) and (1b), the DP object *la présidente* 'the president' moves from its base argumental position, marked in angled brackets, to a higher position, so that it is ultimately interpreted as a clefted element. In (1a), the DP object crosses another DP, the subject *le ministre* 'the minister'; while in (1b) the clefted object crosses the subject *nous* 'we', which is a pronoun (not a DP), but also plural (not singular) and it bears first person (not third person) features. It is usually assumed that (1a) is less acceptable than (1b) (Chesi and Canal 2019 and reference therein).

We study here the predictions of an intervention theory of locality (Rizzi 1990, 2004; Krapova and Cinque 2008), by exploring the effect of the similarity or dissimilarity between the fronted element in cleft structures and the intervener on word-by-word predictions of a neural network processing model. Inspired by Merlo (2016) and related works, we use computational measures in the spirit of the *computational quantitative syntax* framework: differentials in computational effects might be the expression of underlying grammatical properties.

The notion of similarity (or dissimilarity) is defined in terms of matching or mismatching features. Matching configurations in cleft structures are disfavoured in large-scale corpora crosslinguistically (not only in French, but also Italian and English). This conclusion is reached by comparing expected counts based on the prediction of the linguistic theory to actually observed counts. Frequencies in object clefts are lower than *a priori* expected (on the basis of the distribu- tion of features in canonical orders) (Samo and Merlo 2021). This contrasts with feature matching configurations in subject clefts, where no intervention is at play. These configurations are roughly as frequent as expected. Moreover, Samo and Merlo (2021) also found that the size of the intervention effect is proportional to the number of matching configurations.

If large-scale corpora suggest that similarity between the fronted object and the intervening subject is avoided, we expect that computational models sensitive to the statistics in the corpus might show a dispreference for matching and a preference for mismatching configurations. While corpus-based investigations, such as the one presented in Samo and Merlo (2021), are an important first step in defining the quantitative properties of a theory, they do not provide mechanistic models of how the theory and its quantitative aspects might be implemented in the language processing system. In this paper, we test whether the predictions of the theory and the quantitative results observed in corpora give rise to a word-by-word behaviour in computational architectures that corresponds to an intervention effect in the time-course of processing the sentence. Like much recent literature on computational modelling of long-distance structural properties, we choose current artificial neural network models for our investigation, models that have recently been shown to perform complex linguistic tasks without explicit instruction (Gulordava et al., 2018; Wilcox et al., 2018; Linzen and Leonard, 2018; Chowdhury and Zamparelli, 2018; Futrell et al., 2019; Linzen et al., 2019; Chaves, 2020; Warstadt et al., 2020; Linzen and Baroni, 2021). These models were chosen because they are powerful domain-general learning mechanisms with weak learning biases not specific to learning cleft construction or even long-distance dependencies.[1]

We study French, a language where cleft structures naturally occur with a higher frequency and higher productivity than in other languages (Dufter 2009; Belletti 2010). We mainly concentrate on three morpho-syntactic features: *type* (maximal projection vs. head), *number* (singular vs. plural) and *person* (1st vs. 3rd),

---

[1] Currrent artificial neural network architectures are trained to optimise the very generic task of assigning a probability to the input corpus. This is achieved by predicting the probability of each sentence, which is in turn achieved by using these networks as 'language models'. A *language model* is an algorithm that assigns a probability to a sentence by breaking it down into its constituent words and assigning the probability of a word given the preceding words in the sentence. Training networks to achieve this task can be done without any annotation to the input text, as each word provides the right answer to its own prediction, and is therefore scalable to extremely large corpora.

but we also investigate the status of the morphosyntactic feature *gender* (masculine vs. feminine).

We organise the paper as follows. In section 2, we present theoretical considerations on locality in experimental studies (human and computational) and we focus on the intervention effects in cleft structures. In section 3, we introduce our model and our hypotheses drawn from the previous literature. Section 4 presents the materials and methods of the study, while sections 5 and 6 discuss the results in light of the defining properties of the models, and draw conclusions.

2 Modelling locality

2.1 Representational models of locality: Featural relativized minimality

The theory of locality is a major component in generative grammar. We investigate here intervention effects in terms of featural Relativized Minimality (henceforth fRM, an intervention theory of blocking effects observed for long-distance relations Rizzi 1990, 2004; Starke 2001; Rizzi 2013b).

A local relation is disrupted by the intervention of an element with certain properties which makes the intervener a potential participant in that local relation. Let us observe, for example, the difference between a grammatical structure in (2a) and an ungrammatical configuration in (2b).

(2) a. ***When*** *do you think John left <**when**>?*
 b. ****When*** *do you wonder who left <**when**>?*
      (Rizzi 2013a: 172,11)

In structures like (2b), fRM (Rizzi 1990, 2004; Starke 2001) predicts that the generation site of *when* and the landing site cannot be related since *who* qualifies as an intervener of the "same structural type", being an interrogative element, contrary to the nominal element *John* in (2a). "Being of the same structural type" is understood as sharing features of the same class, where features represent (morpho-) syntactic or scope-discourse properties (see an early typology discussed in Rizzi 2004: 243; 61). In a nutshell, according to the theory of intervention in terms of fRM, the crucial property is not the amount of material that can be considered as intervener, but rather its quality.

It is therefore an integral part of the theory and its empirical confirmation to study the features that give rise to intervention effects. The results of extensive experimental studies show that the dissimilarity in values of only a selected set of features help (or hinder) adult grammars in parsing grammatical sentences and improve (or disrupt) comprehension in child grammars and in specific populations, such as atypical development or in language pathology (Friedmann et al. 2009; Belletti et al. 2012; Bentea 2015; Durrleman et al. 2015; Belletti 2015; Franck et al. 2015; Villata et al. 2016; Belletti 2018; Martini et al. 2018; Chesi and Canal 2019; Martini et al. 2020).

Features Which features provide ameliorative effects in locality? An early property can be traced back to the core formulation of intervention locality theory (Rizzi 1990) and whose ameliorative effects are confirmed by early studies on locality in acquisition (Friedmann et al., 2009), namely the dissimilarity in *type* between the intervener and the moved element. This feature might have different values: an element can be a maximal projection (we adopt the label XP; e.g., *le ministre* 'the minister' or *la présidente* 'the president'), or a HEAD like pronominal elements (e.g. *elle* 'she'), or can be null, as it is the case in null-subject languages (Rizzi 1982; Frascarelli 2007). Adopting an English example as a reference point, intervention locality predicts that a sentence such as *'It is the president$_{XP}$ that she$_{Pron}$ meets'* should be easier to parse than *'It is the president$_{XP}$ that the translator$_{XP}$ meets'* since the values of the feature *type* do not match.

The feature of number (e.g., singular, plural) has also been investigated and provides information related to the richness of the verbal system beyond the mere nature of the clefted element and the intervener (Friedmann et al., 2009; Adani, 2012; Bentea, 2015). For example, locality predicts that the sentence *'It is the president$_{Sing}$ that the translators$_{Plur}$ meet'* is easier than a sentence of the type *'It is the president$_{Sing}$ that the translator$_{Sing}$ meets'*, since we observe mismatching values with respect to the feature *number* between the fronted element and the subject. Moreover, agreement with the subject is signalled on the inflection of the verbal element.

Finally, another feature providing ameliorative effects is the *person* feature (1st, 2nd, 3rd), which was early considered as a mitigator in parsing difficult structures in long-distance dependencies (Bever, 1974) and proven to be active in cleft structures (Chesi and Canal, 2019). Locality predicts that the sentence *'It is the president$_{3rd}$ that I$_{1st}$ met.* should be easier than a sentence of the type *'It is the president$_{3rd}$ that he$_{3rd}$ met'*.[2]

---

[2] As noted by an anonymous reviewer, referential ambiguity might be involved in those cases in which the clefted element and the subject share the same person and number features. See Thornton et al. (2018) for a detailed discussion. At the same time, it is important to remark that coreference is not marked in the input on which the model of type transformer BERT (see section 4) was pre-trained.

Finally, the *gender* feature has shown clear asymmetries in acquisition studies. In languages where gender is morpho-syntactically realized on the verb, such as Hebrew, ameliorative effects are observed, whereas in those languages where gender is not morpho-syntactically active in inflection, such as Italian (but also French, the language investigated in this study) no effects have been empirically detected by Belletti et al. (2012).

Other features either do not show any effects or mixed results are to be found within the literature. For example, case mismatch does not result in any ameliorative effect (Friedmann et al., 2017). The status of features like animacy in ameliorating processing in long-distance dependencies in child grammar still remains unclear: some results show an ameliorative effect (Brandt et al. 2009), while other studies do not find any effect (Adani 2012; Martini 2019).

Therefore, a general, but non-trivial, conclusion is that mismatching in syntactic features encode ameliorative effects if these features are syntactically relevant in a given language (e.g., for movement/agreement; see Belletti et al. 2012).

2.2 Processing models of locality

The intervention-based account we follow here is centred on representational theories of locality. In this respect, it is closely related to, but different from, other theories of locality that concentrate on processing effects.

Memory-based accounts explain the asymmetry between subjects and objects in long-distance dependencies (clefts, as well as relative clauses) as deriving from a different amount of material stored in memory (Gibson, 1998; Gordon et al., 2001; Lewis and Vasishth, 2005). For example, subject clefts, where only one element is stored (the subject), are easier to parse and yield lower processing complexity than object-oriented clefts, since two elements (subjects and objects) are stored when the verb and its dependencies need to be parsed. Similarity-based processing accounts argue that a limitation for memory is due to similarity-based interference (Gordon et al. 2001, 2002, 2004, 2006). The account only partially overlaps with syntactic locality (Rizzi 1990; Friedmann et al. 2009). Similarity-based processing approaches are defined on (morpho-)syntactic features (type, person, number, gender, case), but, unlike grammatical accounts, also on extrasyntactic features, for example, animacy, and assume that all features equally contribute to memory interference. For example, a sentence of the type *'it is the window that the wind shut'* should be harder to parse than a sentence of the type *'it is the book that the student read'*, because in the former subject and relativised object match in (lack of) animacy, while in the latter the subject is animate. However, as mentioned above, the status of features like animacy in ameliorating processing in long-distance dependencies in child grammar still remains unclear: some results show an ameliorative effect (Brandt et al., 2009), while other studies do not find any effect (Adani 2012; Martini 2019).

Other memory-load accounts do not take into account the similarity of the two elements stored in memory (as it is the case of object clefts), but rather the joint costs of integrating them within the parsing structure being built (Gibson 1998; Gibson and Warren 2004; Warren and Gibson 2002). The structural integration costs are based on an accessibility scale of referentiality (Ariel, 1990). Elements such as deictic pronouns (e.g., *I, we, you*) are more accessible and elements such as indefinite descriptions (e.g., *a linguist*) are less accessible. For example, sentences of the type '*it is the book/a book/books that a student/the student/she reads*' would have different structural integration costs depending on the actual elements being combined.

Finally, theories such as the Adaptive Control of Thought-Rational (ACT-R), also focus on memory effects and specifically on the distance of the dependency (Lewis and Vasishth 2005). The calculation of the integration cost of the constituent depends also on the distance from the re/attachment point/generation locus. The longer the dependency, the harder the retrieval.

While these theories are appealing and have shown good empirical coverage, they also present some practical difficulties for our kind of work and do not fit into our conceptual aims. Empirically, results by Villata et al. (2016) show that similarity yields difficulty at retrieval, but facilitation at storage, thereby indicating that the relationship between intervention, similarity, and processing is not yet entirely clear, and if it is related to memory effects, it requires more complex models than referentiality or distance. Moreover, referentiality cannot be quantified in a simple way. We would need a model to quantify the values of the pronouns in the languages under investigation (Cardinaletti and Starke 1999) and to quantify indefiniteness (Cardinaletti and Giusti 2020) or discourse linking (Pesetsky 1987).

2.3 Computational models of locality

In this paper, we use neural networks as a language model (Linzen and Baroni 2021 for an overview), in which the network, after observing words in a sentence, assigns a probability to the words that would follow. This probability is the output of a training derived from exposure to large amounts of raw, non-annotated, texts. Many papers have recently investigated the grammatical abilities of these networks, in particular investigating if such generic models can learn structural properties of language and long-distance relations. Studies adopting different architectures

(Linzen et al. 2016; Bernardy and Lappin 2017) have reported that neural networks are able to perform complex tasks on subject-verb agreement (mainly on English) with the presence of linearly intervening subjects (e.g. *the parents of the student *is/are*). In particular, Gulordava et al. (2018) showed that recursive NNs perform well in grammatical well-formed, but non-sensical sentences (in English, Russian, Hebrew and Italian) and whose accuracy is comparable with a control group of human speakers. Other syntactic structures have been explored, such as filler-gap dependencies, auxiliary fronting or other island effects, with mixed results (Wilcox et al. 2018; Linzen and Leonard 2018; Chowdhury and Zamparelli 2018; Marvin and Linzen 2018; Futrell et al. 2019; Linzen et al. 2019; Chaves 2020; McCoy et al. 2020; Warstadt et al. 2020; Merlo and Ackermann 2018; Merlo, 2019).

3 Quantifying the hypotheses

In this work, we will use generic computational models as the explanatory mechanism of intervention locality. To be able to do so, we must be able to formulate our hypotheses quantitatively. To quantify our hypotheses, we use the notion of similarity, feature match and intervention defined in Samo and Merlo (2021) and repeated here for convenience.

FEATURES The clefted element and the intervening subject are represented as sets of movement relevant *features*. Features are *(type:value)* pairs, such as (number: plural).

SIMILARITY The head of the cleft and the intervener are *similar* if their features match.

FEATURE MATCH A *feature match*, $match_f(C,I)$, is true iff, for a given feature f, the head of the cleft C and the intervener I are instantiated and have the same value. If one of the two elements being compared, the head of the cleft C and the intervener I or both are not instantiated then $match_f(C,I)$ is false.

Feature values To establish the contribution of the nature of the intervener to the strength of the intervention effect in object cleft structures, we investigate the morpho-syntactic features of *type, number, person*, which have been discussed as having an ameliorative effect in locality (Friedmann et al. 2009; Chesi and Canal 2019), and contrast it to the feature *gender* which is described as non-ameliorative (Belletti et al. 2012). The values of *type* are XP (nouns, proper nouns) and HEADS (pronouns); for the feature *person* we selected two values out of three: 1st

and 3rd person.[3] The feature *number* has two values: SINGULAR and PLURAL. Finally, the feature *gender* distinguishes between two values, FEMININE and MASCULINE. In Figure 1, we show two examples of object cleft with these features in the full matching and full mismatching configurations.

CONFIGURATION	COPULA	CLEFTED ELEMENT	COMP	Subject	Verb
FULL MATCHING	C'est	la présidente XP, 3rd, Sing, (Fem)	que	la traductrice XP, 3rd, Sing, (Fem)	rencontre rencontrons
FULL MISMATCHING	C'est	la présidente XP, 3rd, Sing	que	nous H, 1st, Plur	

Figure 1: Examples of object cleft clauses in two featural configurations. A condition in which all the values of the feature match (full matching) and a condition in which none of the values match (full mismatching) between the fronted object clefted element and the intervening subject (XP = maximal projection, 3rd = 3rd person, Sing = singular, Fem = feminine).

Metrics Different metrics can be adopted to evaluate whether and how the learning algorithm performs the linguistic task. As explained above, the neural network architecture we adopt is trained to predict the next word, so at each step it produces a probability distribution of all the words that could possibly follow the current word. Then, the most natural measure of this behaviour is the conditional probability given the surrounding context of predicting the word that is given in the input at the current position. The actual measure that is commonly used is *surprisal*, the logarithm of the reciprocal of this probability (Hale 2001, 2016; Levy 2008, 2011; Wilcox et al. 2018). The less predicted the word is at a given position given the context, the higher its surprisal value. Not only is surprisal well-defined for the task at hand, but also it is an incremental complexity metrics that has been found to be strongly correlated with processing complexity (Hale 2001; Levy 2008).

Hypotheses on representations of intervention Several scenarios are logically possible given the computational architecture that we test and the fact that it is trained for the simple sequential unstructured task of predicting the next word. This architecture and this training regime do not introduce any *a priori* bias that will lead to avoiding feature matches. So it is not a priori clear that it will learn to

---

[3] We have decided to not investigate the 2nd person since these data might in future studies be compared with an analysis on, for example English, in which the pronoun *you* is undetermined for number.

avoid feature matches, nor why. The neural network might learn to avoid intervention, but it might also not learn this constraint, either because it is too weak, and it is not sensitive to the corpus frequencies that show that feature matches are infrequent (we know that corpus counts have this information (Samo and Merlo 2021), or because it too strong, and it can learn not to be 'fooled' by an intervening element.

H_1: If the neural network learns to avoid intervention, then we should see a difference in surprisal between the matching and the non-matching configurations.

Moreover, if H_1 is confirmed, there are several representational options that might underlie the sensitivity to intervention: the network representation of the cleft element and the subject might be distributed and feature-based, or might be holistic. If the network encodes intervention in a feature-based distributed fashion, we should see a surprisal effect proportional to how many features are matching (and an ameliorative effect proportional to how many are mismatching), giving rise to hypothesis H_2; if its representations are holistic then H_2' should be verified.

H_2: If the network encodes intervention in a feature-based distributed fashion, then when the number of mismatching morpho-syntactic features increases, the measure of surprisal on the intervening subject decreases.

H_2': If the morpho-syntactic features are encoded holistically and in an entangled way, then the measure of surprisal on the intervening subject is not correlated to the numerosity of the (mis)matching features.

Hypotheses on the time-course of intervention It is harder to predict *where* in the course of the processing of the sentence we should see these effects, as it is hard to predict whether the network will learn specific parameters for avoiding matching features, or will learn feature representations and exhibit an intervention effect as an indirect emergent effect derived from a limitation in the capacity of learning more than one value of each feature. Intuitively, if feature-based intervention effects are confirmed, that is H_1 and H_2 are confirmed, the simplest expectation is that an increase in surprisal for matching features (and a corresponding decrease in surprisal for mismatching features) should occur on encountering the intervener.

4 Materials & methods

Our methodology investigates linguistic phenomena through the lens of the mechanistic model provided by neural networks. It uses the neural network like a blackbox that needs to be studied by experimental methods. We define here the materials and methods of this experimentation.

Experimental stimuli The experimental items are based on Renaud's (2020) studies on relative clauses, which tested materials from Franck et al. (2015). We selected 8 out of 24 Renaud's (2020) lexical entries for the object relatives and transform the relative clauses into cleft structures. We only use those constructions in which both the object and the subject were animate (e.g. *C'est la candidate que la jurée attend fermement après l'audition* 'it is the candidate that the jury member resolutely waits for after the audition'), balancing the relevant feature distributions.

Syntactic regions Every sentence is then split into eight syntactic regions, as exemplified in Figure 2. The first and the second region, common to every sentence and every condition, host the *c'* 'it' element and an inflected copula *est* 'to be'. The third region involves the fronted clefted object, whose surprisal is investigated in H_2. The fourth region is dedicated to the complementizer. The locus of investigation for both H_1 and H_2, namely the subject of the embedded clause which acts as the local intervener for the A'-movement, can be detected in the fifth region. Finally, the last three regions host the inflected verb, an adverbial element and an oblique (circumstantial) complement.

				Regions			
It	be	clefted	comp	subject	verb	Adverbial	Complement
C'	est	l'actrice	que	la spectatrice	applaudit	frénétiquement	à chaque représentation
it	is	the actress	that	the audience.member	applauded	frantically	at each performance

Figure 2: Syntactic Regions and one example of an experimental stimulus.

Conditions We create 8 conditions. Figure 3 shows an example for the stimuli for each condition.

Repetitions Every condition is tested on four repetitions, to avoid possible bias with pronominal forms, which are more frequent than lexical entries of specific *n*-grams. Figure 4 offers an example for the stimuli for one item and repetitions.[4]

---

[4] The relevant .csv files of the experimental sentences has been processed by python (Python Core Team 2019). All the scripts and experimental items, as well the results output, are available all the following link: https://github.com/samo-g/clefts-french. All the processed output has been analyzed with R (R Core Team 2017) for statistical analysis.

#M	T_M	N_M	P_M	It+be	Clefted$_f$	Comp	Subject$_f$
3	1	1	1	C'est	l'actrice$_{XP,Sing,3rd}$	que	la spectatrice$_{XP,Sing,3rd}$
2	1	1	0	C'est	moi$_{H,Sing,1st}$	que	elle$_{H,Sing,3rd}$
2	1	0	1	C'est	l'actrice$_{XP,Sing,3rd}$	que	les spectatrices$_{XP,Plur,3rd}$
2	0	1	1	C'est	l'actrice$_{XP,Sing,3rd}$	que	elle$_{H,Sing,3rd}$
1	1	0	0	C'est	moi$_{H,Sing,1st}$	que	ils$_{H,Plur,3rd}$
1	0	1	0	C'est	moi$_{H,Sing,1st}$	que	la spectatrice$_{XP,Sing,3rd}$
1	0	0	1	C'est	elle$_{H,Sing3rd}$	que	les spectatrices$_{XP,Plur,3rd}$
0	0	0	0	C'est	nous$_{H,Plur,1st}$	que	la spectatrice$_{XP,Sing,3rd}$

Figure 3: Number of matching features, matching feature and experimental stimuli per condition (M=match, T = type, N = number, P = person, XP = maximal projection, H = head, 3rd = 3rd person, Sing=singular, Plur=plural).

It	be	Clefted	Comp	Subject	Verb
C'	est	l'actrice XP, Sing, 3rd	que	la spectatrice XP, Sing, 3rd	applaudit
C'	est	les actrices XP, Plur, 3rd	que	les spectatrices XP, Plur, 3rd	applaudissent
C'	est	elle H, Plur, 3rd	que	elle H, Sing 3rd	applaudit
C'	est	elles H, Plur, 3rd	que	elles H, Plur, 3rd	applaudissent

Figure 4: Example of an experimental setting 'It is the actress that the spectator has been applauding frantically after each show' in four experimental items (H = head, XP = maximal projection, Sing = singular, Plur = plural, 1st = first person, 3rd = third person, Fem = feminine).

Methods We test the BERT architectures (Devlin et al. 2019), a pre-trained transformer language model, in its version for French, FlauBERT (Flaubert-cased; Le et al. 2020).[5] The experimental stimuli are input to the transformer.[6] The probability distribution for possible predicted continuation at each input word gives a measure of surprisal, then aggregated for each region.

BERT is a bidirectional transformer trained as a masked language model (Devlin et al. 2019). This choice of architecture is based on its several desirable properties for our analysis. First of all, it is an architecture trained as a generic language model,

---

[5] This is a pretrained model, whose training data is described in detail in Le et al. (2020). Briefly, the uncompressed 270 GB of French text corpus consists of 24 sub-corpora gathered from different sources, (e.g. Wikipedia and books, random text crawled from the Internet (e.g. Common Crawl).
[6] We use the code discussed in Renaud (2020), available at the following address: https://github.com/celinerenaud/Memoire (last accessed 08/2021).

without specific biases for the particular structures we are studying.[7] In fact, transformers have been used in many non-linguistic domains, such as vision, so the architecture is not specific even for language (Khan et al. 2021). Moreover, they have shown very good performances, and are, as such, a good model of human-like levels of performance on some linguistic tasks. More importantly, a transformer makes use of a mechanism called attention, which allows it to encode relations among elements that are distant in the sentence, encoding what is considered a sort of memory (Vaswani et al. 2017). Most important is the way this memory is encoded: attention is encoded as a mechanism based on (query, key, value) triples. Relations of entities in the representation are not stored, but calculated on the fly. Entities in the latent representations have certain values, and their relations are calculated on demand if a query triggers a search for a certain key-value pair of features. So the model can be considered a reasonably accurate, and certainly extremely successful, representation of generic memory mechanisms and its distributed nature makes it a plausible candidate for representations of neural encoding in humans.

4.1 Control groups

It has been argued that neural networks can learn structural information as an emergent property, without explicit structural objective functions at training. Their ability to learn long-distance agreement and filler-gap dependencies, without interference of linear attractors, has been brought as evidence for this claim (Linzen et al. 2016; Gulordava et al. 2018; Wilcox et al. 2018). Another result, perhaps under an even more stringent test, would be to show that neural networks can exhibit effects of intervention only with structural interveners. Specifically, it has been shown that intervention is not a linear effect by showing that interveners that do not c-command the trace do not have a blocking effect in human acceptability judgements (Rizzi 1990, 2004).

This test enables us to tease apart several alternative explanations on the behaviour of these computational models. First, these controls allow us to distinguish whether these effects of locality are a real structural intervention effect or if they simply apply to any intervener, as simply the network cannot represent NPs with the same traits, for example because they have only one way of representing

---

[7] Strictly speaking, since it is bidirectional, it is trained as a masked language model, that is, it is trained to predict a masked word, so that the predicted word can have both preceding and following context.

plural, only one way of representing singular, but no way to represent different entities with these attributes. Second, we also introduce a control for different length of distance between the cleft element and the intervener. Examples are given in Figure 5 and Figure 6.

#M	N_M	G_M	Sentence
0	0	0	*C'est les étudiants que la voix de l'orateur endort sérieusement depuis le début* It is the student$_{Plur,Masc}$ that the voice$_{Sing,Fem}$ of the speaker makes sleep seriously since the start.
1	1	0	*C'est l'étudiant que la voix de l'orateur endort sérieusement depuis le début* It is the student$_{Sing,Masc}$ that the voice$_{Sing,Fem}$ of the speaker makes sleep seriously since the start.
1	0	1	*C'est les étudiants que le bruit de l'orateur endort sérieusement depuis le début* It is the student$_{Plur,Masc}$ that the noise$_{Sing,Masc}$ of the speaker makes sleep seriously since the start.
2	1	1	*C'est l'étudiant que le bruit de l'orateur endort sérieusement depuis le début* It is the student$_{Sing,Masc}$ that the voice$_{Sing,Masc}$ of the speaker makes sleep seriously since the start.

Figure 5: Sentences with calculations of matches between cleft noun and c-commanding head noun. Number of matching feature, features match and an experimental stimulus per condition (M=match, N = number, G = gender, Sing=singular, Plur=plural, Masc = masculine, F = feminine).

#M	N_M	G_M	Sentence
0	0	0	*C'est les étudiants que la voix de la présentatrice endort sérieusement depuis le début* It is the student$_{Plur,Masc}$ that the voice of the speaker$_{Sing,Fem}$ makes sleep seriously since the start.
1	1	0	*C'est l'étudiant que la voix de la présentatrice endort sérieusement depuis le début* It is the student$_{Sing,Masc}$ that the voice of the speaker$_{Sing,Fem}$ makes sleep seriously since the start.
1	0	1	*C'est les étudiants que la voix de l'orateur endort sérieusement depuis le début* It is the student$_{Plur,Masc}$ that the noise of the speaker$_{Sing,Masc}$ makes sleep seriously since the start.
2	1	1	*C'est l'étudiant que la voix de l'orateur endort sérieusement depuis le début* It is the student$_{Sing,Masc}$ that the voice of the speaker$_{Sing,Masc}$ makes sleep seriously since the start.

Figure 6: Sentences with calculations of matches between cleft noun and embedded non-ccommanded noun. Number of matching feature, features match and an experimental stimulus per condition (M= match, N = number, G = gender, Sing = singular, Plur = plural, Masc = masculine, F = feminine).

5 Results and discussion

5.1 Hypotheses 1 and 2

The results for H_1 are shown in Figure 7 and can be compared to the patterns of surprisal for subject clefts in Figure 8. The pattern of surprisal for object clefts is fully compatible with intervention expectations. All types of clefts exhibit an increase in surprisal at the region indicating the beginning of a cleft, region 3. The surprisal at region 5 (intervening subject) in object clefts is as expected: the feature matching configurations show sustained surprisal, while feature mismatches show low surprisal, in a pattern that is fully consistent with a different gradation depending on the number of (mis)matching features. Spearman's rank correlation was computed to assess the relationship between number of matching features and surprisal for region 5. There was a positive correlation between the matches and surprisal (the higher the number of matching features, the higher the surprisal), $r(254) = .20, p = .001$. A one-way ANOVA revealed that there was a statistically significant difference in surprisal in the regions of subjects and objects between groups of matching configurations for object clefts, ($F(3,252) = [4.151], p < .01 = [0.0128]$), but not for subject clefts ($p = [0.143]$). A post hoc Tukey test showed that the full matching and full mismatching configurations groups differed significantly at $p < .05$.

Compare the object clefts results to the subject clefts results. Recall that subject clefts do not cause any intervention effects and were found not to have any lower-than-expected frequencies in corpora (Samo and Merlo, 2021). The subject cleft clearly does not show the differential surprisal of object clefts in the corresponding region 6 (object). While full mismatches do show a decrease in surprisal, the other conditions are not consistent with a feature-based intervention effect, as predicted.

5.2 Controls of hypotheses 1 and 2

Controls aimed at measuring if neural networks can exhibit effects of intervention only with structural interveners, and thereby tease apart several alternative explanations on the behaviour of these computational models. These controls allow us to distinguish whether these effects of locality are a real structural intervention effects or if they simply apply to any intervener, as simply the network cannot represent NPs with the same traits. The network could be representing each attribute globally, and have only one way of representing each attribute or even each value for each attribute, but no way to represent different entities with these attributes.

Results are shown in Figure 9. They clearly show that there is a small effect when the intervener is a c-commanding head (which shows up in the intermediate position between the cleft element and the intervening head, probably due to the bidirectional nature of the architecture), while there is no correspondence to the sharing of features of the embedded non-c-commanding noun. In our sample, a c-commanding intervening noun shows differences in surprisal among conditions in region 3 (surprisal for the clefted element) compared to the intervening non-commanding, embedded, noun ($t(510) = 2.3337, p = .0198$).

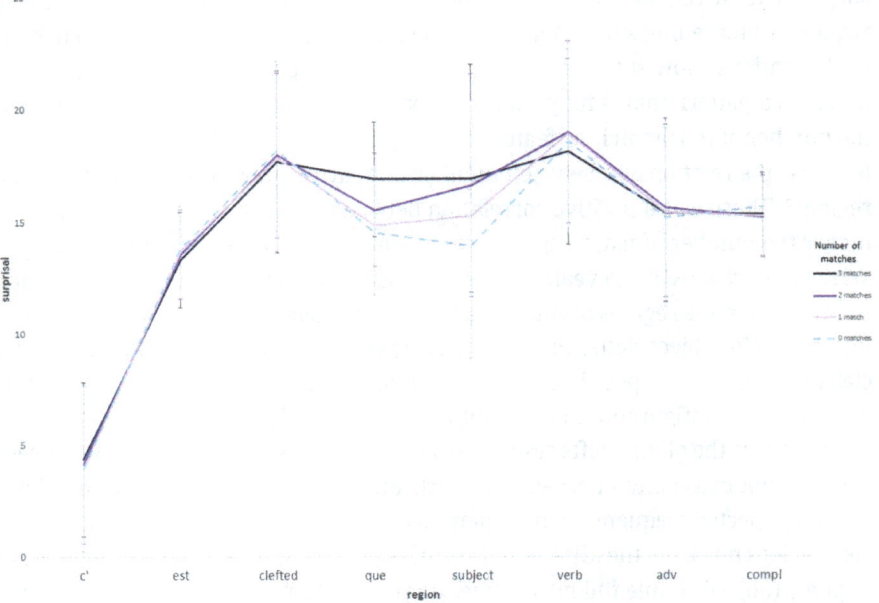

Figure 7: Mean surprisal and syntactic regions for the features *type*, *number* and *person* in object clefts.

5.3 Discussion

The investigation reported here provides a new contribution to the debate about the role of features in intervention effects in long-distance dependency structures, in the spirit of previous papers on quantitative and computational modelling of intervention (Merlo and Ackermann 2018; Merlo 2019; Samo and Merlo 2019, 2021). Our results provide a more articulate characterisation of the quantitative properties and computational mechanisms that underlie intervention locality.

First, they show that the investigated mechanisms develop representations and computations that are sensitive to the features and the entities to which they are attributed, as we see gradation of effects that vary with the number of matching

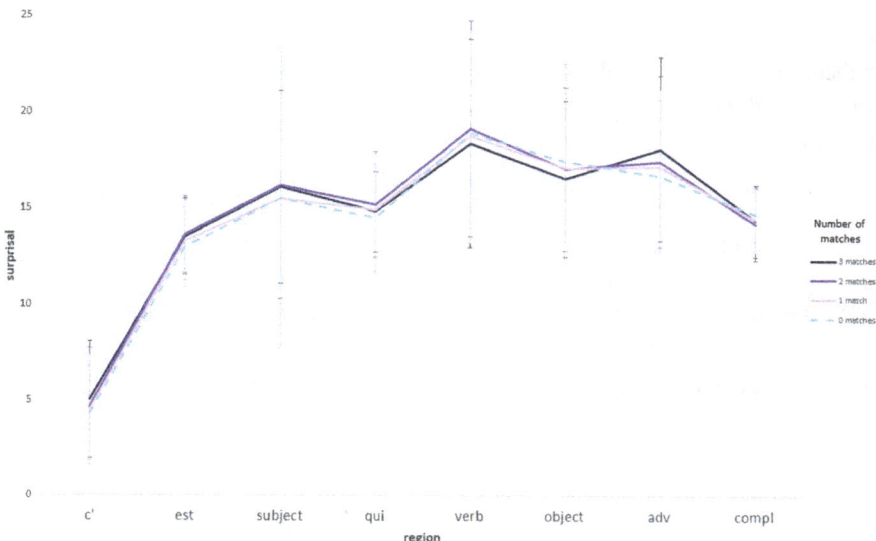

Figure 8: Mean surprisal and syntactic regions for the features *type, number* and *person* in subject clefts. (Example sentence *C'est la spectatrice qui applaudit l'actrice frénétiquement après le spectacle.* 'It is the audience member that applauds the actress frantically after the show').

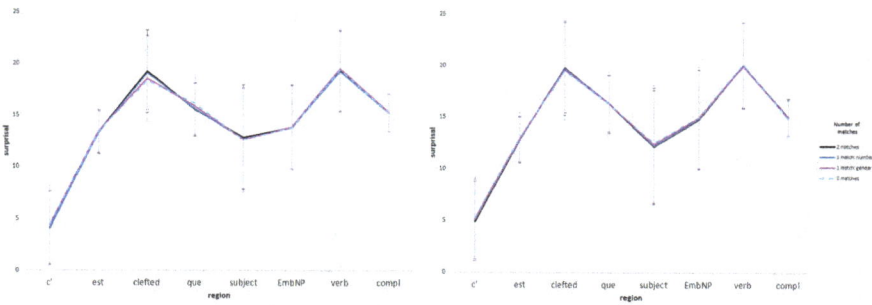

Figure 9: Mean surprisal and syntactic regions for the features *number* and *gender* in object clefts with complex subject, matches calculated at the head (left panel) and at the embedded noun (right panel).

features. These effects clarify that features are associated to entities and not holistically. In this respect, our results join the family of results begin recently developed on neural language models, that have found that number and gender features in long-distance agreement effects in Italian have a sparse representation, that also shows effects of embedding, congruence of subjects in multiple agreement configurations and very sparse representations (Lakretz et al. 2021).

Secondly, our results show that the encoding of intervention and the actual locality relation can be conceived as a (query,key,value) mechanism, the mechanism provided by attention in transformers. This is a memory-on-demand mechanism, that constructs relations if queries are made to match a key with a given value, but the relation is not there unless the attention mechanism pays attention to them.

Thirdly, the fact that the mechanism is generic provides us with information about the richness or poverty of the stimulus. Feature-based locality effects arise because they are present in the input, despite the constructions being very rare and the effect quite small in the input (Samo and Merlo 2021). This result clearly indicates that the input is sufficiently rich and that mechanistic biases are not specifically grammatical, but that the architecture is constructed to be sensitive to grammatical features that shape the distribution of the input.

6 Conclusions

Like many other areas of cognitive science, truly understanding locality requires moving from formalisms and functional or logical specifications of the observed properties to constructing models of the architectures and mechanisms that generate these observed properties. Mechanistic explanations provide precise contributions to cast light on the algorithmic and neural bases of locality. The models we study here are anchored in vectorial, distributed representations of the meaning of the input words, and of syntactic combinatoriality. While the theory of feature-based intervention locality is itself a theory based on vectorial representations, it assumes a small set of features and an atomic representation of these morpho-syntactic properties. The mechanisms we have used, by contrast, do not make any such assumptions and yet they exhibit the predicted behaviour. In this sense, they provide a causal explanation for intervention locality effects, as they show how the observed grammatical effects arise as an interaction of representation and computation. Future research should involve a bigger set of languages and a comparative dimension. These data also needs to be further compared with results from the study of other long-distance dependencies, such as relative clauses or topicalization/focalization (Rizzi 1997).

References

Adani, Flavia. 2012. Some notes on the acquisition of relative clauses: New data and open questions. In Valentina Bianchi & Cristano Chesi (eds.), *Enjoy Linguistics! Papers Offered to Luigi Rizzi on the Occasion of his 60th Birthday*, 6–13. Siena: CISCL Press.

Aravind, Athulya, Martin Hackl & Ken Wexler. 2018. Syntactic and pragmatic factors in children's comprehension of cleft constructions. *Language Acquisition* 25(3). 284–314.
Ariel, Mira. 1990. *Accessing Noun-Phrase Antecedents*. London: Routledge.
Belletti, Adriana. 2010. *Structures and Strategies*. New York: Routledge.
Belletti, Adriana 2015. The focus map of clefts: Extraposition and Predication. In Ur Shlonsky (ed.), *Beyond Functional Sequence*, 42–60. Oxford/New York: Oxford University Press.
Belletti, Adriana. 2018. Locality in syntax. In *Oxford Research Encyclopedia of Linguistics*. New York/Oxford: Oxford Universtiy Press. https://doi.org/10.1093/acrefore/9780199384655.013.318
Belletti, Adriana, Naama Friedmann, Dominique Brunato & Luigi Rizzi 2012. Does gender make a difference? Comparing the effect of gender on children's comprehension of relative clauses in Hebrew and Italian. *Lingua* 122(10). 1053–1069.
Bentea, Anamaria J. 2015. *Intervention Effects in Language Acquisition: The Comprehension of A-bar Dependencies in French and Romanian*. Geneva: University of Geneva dissertation.
Bernardy, Jean-Phillipe & Shalom Lappin. 2017. Using deep neural networks to learn syntactic agreement. *Linguistic Issues in Language Technology* 15(2). 1–15.
Bever, Thomas G. 1974. The ascent of the specious, or there's a lot we don't know about mirrors. In David Cohen (ed.), *Explaining Linguistic Phenomena*, 173–200. Washington: Halsted Press.
Brandt, Silke, Evan Kidd, Elena Lieven & Michael Tomasello 2009. The discourse bases of relativization: An investigation of young German and English-speaking children's comprehension of relative clauses. *Cognitive Linguistics* 20(3). 539–570.
Cardinaletti, Anna & Giuliana Giusti 2020. Indefinite determiners in informal Italian: A preliminary analysis. *Linguistics* 58(3). 679–712.
Cardinaletti, Anna & Michal Starke 1999. The typology of structural deficiency: A case study of the three classes of pronouns. In Henk van Riemsdijk (ed.), *Empirical Approaches to Language Typology*, 145–233. New York: Mouton de Gruyter.
Chaves, Rui. 2020. What don't RNN language models learn about filler-gap dependencies? In *Proceedings of the Society for Computation in Linguistics 2020*, 1–11. New York: Association for Computational Linguistics.
Chesi, Cristiano & Paolo Canal. 2019. Person features and lexical restrictions in Italian clefts. *Frontiers in Psychology* 10. 2105.
Shammur Absar Chowdhury & Roberto Zamparelli. 2018. RNN simulations of grammaticality judgments on long-distance dependencies. In *Proceedings of the 27th International Conference on Computational Linguistics*, 133–144. Santa Fe, New Mexico, USA: Association for Computational Linguistics.
De Cesare, Anna-Maria & Davide Garassino. 2018. Adverbial cleft sentences in Italian, French and English. In Marco G. García & Melanie Uth (eds.), *Focus Realization in Romance and Beyond*, 201–255. Amsterdam & New York: John Benjamins Publishing Company.
Devlin, Jacobm, Ming-Wei Chang, Kenton Lee & Kristina Toutanova. 2019. BERT: Pre-training of deep bidirectional transformers for language understanding. In *Proceedings of the 2019 Conference of the North American Chapter of the Association for Computational Linguistics: Human Language Technologies, Volume 1 (Long and Short Papers)*, 4171– 4186. Minneapolis, Minnesota: Association for Computational Linguistics.
Dick, Frederic Beverly Wulfeck, Magda Krupa-Kwiatkowski & Elizabeth Bates. 2004. The development of complex sentence interpretation in typically developing children compared with children with specific language impairments or early unilateral focal lesions. *Developmental Science* 7(3). 360–377.

Doetjes, Jenny, Georges Rebuschi & Annie Rialland. 2004. Cleft sentences. In Francis Corblin & Henriëtte de Swart (eds.), *Handbook of French semantics*, 529–552. Stanford, CA: CSLI Publications.

Dufter, Andreas. 2009. Clefting and discourse organization: Comparing Germanic and Romance. In Andreas Dufter & Daniel Jacob (eds.), *Focus and Background in Romance languages*, 83–122. Amsterdam & Philadelphia: John Benjamins.

Durrleman, Stephanie, Loyse Hippolyte, Sandrine Zufferey, Katia Iglesias & Nouchine Hadjikhani 2015. Complex syntax in autism spectrum disorders: A study of relative clauses. *International Journal of Language & Communication Disorders* 50(2). 260–267.

Franck, Julie, Saveria Colonna & Luigi Rizzi. 2015. Task-dependency and structure-dependency in number interference effects in sentence comprehension. *Frontiers in Psychology* 6. 349.

Frascarelli, Mara. 2007. Subjects, topics and the interpretation of referential pro. *Natural Language & Linguistic Theory* 25(4). 691–734.

Frascarelli, Mara & Francesca Ramaglia. 2013. (Pseudo) clefts at the syntax-prosody-discourse interface. In Katharina Hartmann & Tonjes Veenstra (eds.), *Cleft Structures*, 97–138. Amsterdam: John Benjamins.

Friedmann, Naama, Adriana Belletti & Luigi Rizzi. 2009. Relativized relatives: Types of intervention in the acquisition of A-bar dependencies. *Lingua* 119(1). 67–88.

Friedmann, Naama, Luigi Rizzi & Adriana Belletti. 2017. No case for case in locality: Case does not help interpretation when intervention blocks A-bar chains. *Glossa: A Journal of General Linguistics* 2(1).

Futrell, Richard, Ethan Wilcox, Takashi Morita, Peng Qian, Miguel Ballesteros & Roger Levy. 2019. Neural language models as psycholinguistic subjects: Representations of syntactic state. In *Proceedings of the 2019 Conference of the North American Chapter of the Association for Computational Linguistics: Human Language Technologies, Volume 1 (Long and Short Papers)*, 32–42. Minneapolis, Minnesota: Association for Computational Linguistics.

Gibson, Edward. 1998. Linguistic complexity: Locality of syntactic dependencies. *Cognition* 68(1). 1–76.

Gibson, Edward & Tessa Warren. 2004. Reading-time evidence for intermediate linguistic structure in long-distance dependencies. *Syntax* 7(1). 55–78.

Gordon, Peter C., Randall Hendrick & Marcus Johnson. 2001. Memory interference during language processing. *Journal of Experimental Psychology: Learning, Memory, and Cognition* 27(6). 1411.

Gordon, Peter C., Randall Hendrick & Marcus Johnson. 2004. Effects of noun phrase type on sentence complexity. *Journal of Memory and Language* 51(1). 97–114.

Gordon, Peter C., Randall Hendrick, Marcus Johnson & Yoonhyoung Lee. 2006. Similarity-based interference during language comprehension: Evidence from eye tracking during reading. *Journal of Experimental Psychology: Learning, Memory, and Cognition* 32(6). 1304.

Gordon, Peter C., Randall Hendrick & William H. Levine. 2002. Memory-load interference in syntactic processing. *Psychological Science* 13(5). 425–430.

Grillo, Nino. 2008. *Generalized Minimality*. Utrecht: University of Utrecht dissertation.

Gulordava, Kristina, Piotr Bojanowski, Edouard Grave, Tal Linzen & Marco Baroni. 2018. Colorless green recurrent networks dream hierarchically. In *Proceedings of the 2018 Conference of the North American Chapter of the Association for Computational Linguistics: Human Language Technologies, Volume 1 (Long Papers)*, 1195–1205. Association for Computational Linguistics.

Haegeman, Liliane, André Meinunger & Aleksandra Vercauteren. 2015. The syntax of it-clefts and the left periphery of the clause. In Ur Shlonsky (ed.), *Beyond Functional Sequence*, 73–90. Oxford/New York: Oxford University Press.

Hale, John. 2001. A probabilistic Earley parser as a psycholinguistic model. In *Second Meeting of the North American Chapter of the Association for Computational Linguistics*. 1–8. Morristown, NJ, USA: Association for Computational Linguistics

Hale, John. 2016. Information-theoretical complexity metrics. *Lang. Linguistics Compass* 10. 397– 412.
Karssenberg, Lena & Karen Lahousse. 2018. The information structure of French *il y a* clefts and *c'est* clefts: A corpus-based analysis. *Linguistics* 56(3). 513–548.
Khan, Salman, Muzammal Naseer, Munawar Hayat, Syed Waqas Zamir, Fahad Shahbaz Khan, Mubarak Shah. 2021. Transformers in vision: A survey. arXiv:2101.01169.
Kiss, Katalin E. 1998. Identificational focus versus information focus. *Language* 74(2). 245–273.
Krapova, Iliyana & Guglielmo Cinque. 2008. On the order of wh-phrases in Bulgarian multiple wh-fronting. In Gerhild Zybatow, Luka Szucsich, Uwe Junghanns & Roland Meyer (eds.), *Formal Description of Slavic Languages: The Fifth Conference (FDSL5), Leipzig 2003*, 318–336. Frankfurt am Main: Peter Lang.
Lakretz, Yair, Dieuwke Hupkes, Alessandra Vergallito, Marco Marelli, Marco Baroni & Stanislas Dehaene. 2021. Mechanisms for handling nested dependencies in neural-network language models and humans. *Cognition* 213. 104699.
Le, Hang, Loïc Vial, Jibril Frej, Vincent Segonne, Maximin Coavoux, Benjamin Lecouteux, Alexandre Allauzen, Benoit Crabbé, Laurent Besacier & Didier Schwab. 2020. Flaubert: Unsupervised language model pre-training for French. In *Proceedings of The 12th Language Resources and Evaluation Conference*, 2479–2490. Marseilles: European Language Resources Association.
Levy, Roger. 2008. Expectation-based syntactic comprehension. *Cognition* 106(3). 1126–1177.
Levy, Roger. 2011. Integrating surprisal and uncertain-input models in online sentence comprehension: Formal techniques and empirical results. In *Proceedings of the 49th Annual Meeting of the Association for Computational Linguistics: Human Language Technologies*, 1055–1065. Portland, Oregon, USA: Association for Computational Linguistics.
Lewis, Richard L. & Shravan Vasishth. 2005. An activation-based model of sentence processing as skilled memory retrieval. *Cognitive science* 29(3). 375–419.
Linzen, Tal & Marco Baroni. 2021. Syntactic structure from deep learning. *Annual Review of Linguistics* 7. 195–212.
Linzen, Tal, Grzegorz Chrupała, Yonatan Belinkov & Dieuwke Hupkes (eds.). 2019. *Proceedings of the 2019 ACL Workshop BlackboxNLP: Analyzing and Interpreting Neural Networks for NLP*. Florence: Association for Computational Linguistics.
Linzen, Tal, Emmanuel Dupoux & Yoav Goldberg. 2016. Assessing the ability of LSTMs to learn syntaxsensitive dependencies. *Transactions of the Association of Computational Linguistics* 4(1). 521–535.
Linzen, Tal & Brian Leonard. 2018. Distinct patterns of syntactic agreement errors in recurrent networks and humans. In *Proceedings of the 40th Annual Conference of the Cognitive Science Society*, 692–697. Austin, Texas: Cogn. Sci. Soc.
Lobo, Maria Lobo, Ana L. Santos, Carla Soares-Jesel & Stéphanie Vaz1. 2019. Effects of syntactic structure on the comprehension of clefts. *Glossa* 4. 1–23.
Martini, Karen. 2019. Animacy does not help French-speaking children in the repetition of object relatives. In Pedro Guijarro-Fuentes & Cristina Suárez-Gómez (eds.), *Language Acquisition and Development. Proceedings of GALA 2017*, 221–240. Durham: Cambridge Scholars Publishing.
Martini, Karen, Adriana Belletti, Santi Centorrino & Maria Garraffa. 2020. Syntactic complexity in the presence of an intervener: The case of an Italian speaker with anomia. *Aphasiology* 34(8). 1016–1042.
Martini, Karen, Adriana Belletti, Carla Contemori & Luigi Rizzi. 2018. On the role of lexical restriction and intervention in production: A new angle on the subject-object relatives asymmetry. *Generative Grammar in Geneva* 11. 120–135.

Marvin, Rebecca & Tal Linzen. 2018. Targeted syntactic evaluation of language models. In *Proceedings of the 2018 Conference on Empirical Methods in Natural Language Processing*, 1192–1202. Brussels: Association for Computational Linguistics.

McCoy, R. Thomas, Robert Frank & Tal Linzen. 2020. Does syntax need to grow on trees? Sources of hierarchical inductive bias in sequence-to-sequence networks. *Transactions of the Association for Computational Linguistics* 8. 125–140.

Meinunger, André. 1998. The structure of cleft and pseudo-cleft sentences. *Texas Linguistic Forum* 38. 235–246.

Merlo, Paola. 2016. Quantitative computational syntax: Some initial results. *Italian Journal of Computational Linguistics* 2(1). 11–30.

Merlo, Paola. 2019. Probing word and sentence embeddings for long-distance dependencies effects in French and English. In *Proceedings of the 2019 ACL Workshop Blackbox NLP: Analyzing and Interpreting Neural Networks for NLP*, 158–172. Florence: Association for Computational Linguistics.

Merlo, Paola & Francesco Ackermann. 2018. Vectorial semantic spaces do not encode human judgments of intervention similarity. In *Proceedings of the 22nd Conference on Computational Natural Language Learning*, 392–401. Brussels: Association for Computational Linguistics.

Pesetsky, David. 1987. Wh-in-situ: movement and unselective binding. In Eric Reuland & Alice Ter Meulen (eds.), *The Representation of (In)definiteness*, 98–129. Cambridge, MA: MIT Press.

Prince, Ellen F. 1978. A comparison of wh-clefts and it-clefts in discourse. *Language* 54(4). 883–906.

Python Core Team 2019. *Python: A Dynamic, Open Source Programming Language*. Python Software Foundation. Python version 3.7.

R Core Team. 2017. *R: A Language and Environment for Statistical Computing*. Vienna: R Foundation for Statistical Computing.

Reeve, Matthew 2012. *Clefts and their Relatives*. Amsterdam / New York: John Benjamins.

Renaud, Céline. 2020. Traitement des relations longue distance par les reseaux de neurones en anglais, français et italien. Geneva: University of Geneva MA thesis.

Rizzi, Luigi. 1982. *Issues in Italian Syntax*. Dordrecht: Foris.

Rizzi, Luigi. 1990. *Relativized Minimality*. Cambridge MA: The MIT Press.

Rizzi, Luigi. 1997. The fine structure of the left periphery. In Liliane Haegeman (ed.), *Elements of Grammar*, 281–337. Dordrecht: Kluwer Academic publisher.

Rizzi, Luigi. 2004. Locality and left periphery. In Adriana Belletti (ed.), *Structures and Beyond*, 223–251. Oxford / New York: Oxford University Press Oxford.

Rizzi, Luigi. 2013a. Locality. *Lingua* 130. 169–186.

Rizzi, Luigi. 2013b. Notes on cartography and further explanation. *Probus* 25(1). 197–226.

Roggia, Carlo E. 2008. Frasi scisse in italiano e francese orale: evidenze dal C-ORAL-ROM. *Cuadernos de filología italiana* 15. 9–29.

Samo, Giuseppe & Paola Merlo. 2019. Intervention effects in object relatives in English and Italian: A study in quantitative computational syntax. In *Proceedings of the First Workshop on Quantitative Syntax (Quasy, SyntaxFest 2019)*, 46–56. Paris: Association for Computational Linguistics.

Samo, Giuseppe & Paola Merlo. 2021. Intervention effects in clefts: A study in quantitative computational syntax. *Glossa: A Journal of General Linguistics* 6(1):1–39.

Stark, Elizabeth. 2014. Frequency, form and function of cleft constructions in the Swiss SMS corpus. In Anna-Maria De Cesare (ed.), *Frequency, Forms and Functions of Cleft Constructions in Romance and Germanic: Contrastive, Corpus-Based Studies*, 325–344. Berlin, Munich & Boston: Mouton de Gruyter.

Starke, Michal. 2001. *Move Dissolves into Merge: A Theory of Locality*. Geneva: University of Geneva dissertation.

Thornton, Rosalind, Hirohisa Kiguchi & Elena D'Onofrio. 2018. Cleft sentences and reconstruction in child language. *Language* 94(2). 405–431.
Vaswani, Ashish, Noam Shazeer, Niki Parmar, Jakob Uszkoreit, Llion Jones, Aidan N. Gomez, Łukasz Kaiser & Illia Polosukhin. 2017. Attention is all you need. In Isabelle Guyon, Ulrike Von Luxburg, Samy Bengio, Hanna M. Wallach, Rob Fergus, S.V.N. Vishwanathan & Roman Garnett (eds.), *Advances in Neural Information Processing Systems*, Volume 30. Curran Associates, Inc.
Villata, Sandra, Luigi Rizzi & Julie Franck. 2016. Intervention effects and relativized minimality: New experimental evidence from graded judgments. *Lingua* 179. 76–96.
Warren, Tessa & Edward Gibson. 2002. The influence of referential processing on sentence complexity. *Cognition* 85(1). 79–112.
Warstadt, Alex, Alicia Parrish, Haokun Liu, Anhad Mohananey, Wei Peng, Sheng-Fu Wang & Samuel R. Bowman. 2020. BLiMP: The benchmark of linguistic minimal pairs for English. *Transactions of the Association for Computational Linguistics* 8. 377–392.
Wilcox, Ethan, Roger Levy, Takashi Morita & Richard Futrell. 2018. What do RNN language models learn about filler–gap dependencies? In *Proceedings of the 2018 EMNLP Workshop BlackboxNLP: Analyzing and Interpreting Neural Networks for NLP*, 211–221. Brussels, Belgium: Association for Computational Linguistics.

Alina McLellan
7 *It*-cleft constructions in Réunion Creole

Abstract: Adducing primary data from corpora and native speaker judgements, this article provides the first detailed description of the structure of *sé*-clefts in Réunion Creole, a French-lexified creole language. There are two variants of the *sé*-cleft construction, the difference being the presence or absence of a relative marker in the cleft relative clause. I analyse *sé* as a copular verb, and therefore propose that both constructions with and without a relative marker are variants of one biclausal cleft construction, comparable to the well-studied English *it*-cleft. What distinguishes Réunion Creole not only from its lexifier French, but also from the other French-lexified creoles, is that in subject clefts (those in which the clefted constituent functions as a subject in the cleft relative clause), the relative marker is preferably omitted. The article contributes to our wider understanding of Réunion Creole grammar – the distribution of two copulas (*sé* and *lé*), and relative marking in the language. It also begins to address the syntax of focus in Réunion Creole, considering the cleft construction against other available focalising strategies in the language. I claim that Réunion Creole is freer than French in regard to its word order and possible positions of focus in the sentence, yet clefts appear relatively frequently in the corpus.

Keywords: Réunion Creole, *it*-clefts, copulas, relative clause marking, focalisation strategies

1 Introduction

Réunion Creole is a French-lexified creole language spoken by the majority of the population on Réunion Island, a French overseas department in the Indian Ocean

---

Note: I gratefully acknowledge the Arts and Humanities Research Council (AHRC) for funding the research project from which this article reports results. I would like to thank Delia Bentley and Eva Schultze-Berndt for our numerous discussions of this data, and for providing valuable comments on several versions of this work. Thanks also go to an anonymous reviewer, to Julio Villa-García and to audiences at *Manchester Forum in Linguistics (mFiL) 2021*, *Groupe de Recherche Grammaires Créoles (GRGC)* and the 2021 Summer Conference of the *Society for Pidgin and Creole Linguistics*, for their insightful comments and questions on versions of this work. I am most grateful to the native speakers who participated in questionnaires and interviews, providing their judgements, and to Emmanuelle for recording sentences to be used in those interviews. All errors and shortcomings are my own.

Alina McLellan, The University of Manchester, e-mail: alina.mclellan@manchester.ac.uk

https://doi.org/10.1515/9783110734140-008

(Bollée 2013).¹ A creole language is defined here in a socio-historic sense: it is a language which has developed in the context of European colonisation beginning around the 17th century (DeGraff 2004). From the beginning, there has been close, sustained contact between this creole language and its lexifier – more so than in other French creole settings. As a result, Réunion Creole is often said to be structurally more similar to French than most other French-based creoles (e.g. Holm 1989: 393, Corne 1999: 70). It is distinct from the neighbouring French creoles in the Indian Ocean (those of Seychelles, Mauritius and Rodrigues), which are often grouped together, without Réunion Creole, as one variety (e.g. Corne 1999; Syea 2017).

Réunion Creole has a cleft construction ((1)–(2)) which is comparable to the well-studied English *it*-cleft and French *c'est*-cleft but has important properties not shared by the English and French clefts. Notably, there is no pronominal expletive subject, and the cleft relative clause is more often not introduced by a relative marker (2).² When it is introduced by a marker, that marker is *ke*, which I argue is invariant.

(1) Sé   la   mashine k'i   konvien pa³
    HL   the   machine REL-FIN   work   NEG
    'It's the machine that doesn't work.'   (Blog)

(2) Sé   lo   sistèm   lé   mal   roganizé
    HL   the   system   COP   badly   organised
    'It's the system which is badly organised.'   (Newspaper)

I argue that the Réunion Creole structures illustrated in (1) and (2) are variants of one cleft construction, which I will call a *sé*-cleft. I understand the term cleft construction, in the sense of Lambrecht (2001), to be a biclausal focus construction which expresses a single proposition and has a monoclausal counterpart. The construction is biclausal because it has two finite verbs, one of which is a finite

---

1 For a map of the island, see https://habiter-la-reunion.re/cartes-de-la-reunion/.
2 *Sé* could be analysed as containing an expletive subject, but I provide arguments against this analysis in section 4.1. Some authors (e.g. Collins 1991: 52) point out that it is possible for English subject clefts to be zero-marked. However, in English, zero-marking is not a widespread tendency, but rather a possibility in some varieties. In Réunion Creole, on the other hand, zero-marking in subject clefts is preferred over marking.
3 Except where indicated, examples presented in this article come from the author's corpus or are constructed by the author and judged by native speakers (cf. section 3). In the former case, the textual type of the source is indicated. The Leipzig abbreviations are used in the glosses (https://www.eva.mpg.de/lingua/pdf/Glossing-Rules.pdf), with the following additions: ANT = anterior; FIN = finite; HL = highlighter.

copular verb. The difference between the constructions in (1) and (2) is that the cleft relative clause in (1) is introduced by a relative marker *ke*, while that in (2) contains no relative marker. According to a previous analysis by Bollée (2013), only the construction in (1) is considered a cleft; (2) is instead considered to be a case of focus fronting. Bollée (2013) follows Maurer and the APiCS Consortium's (2013) classification of cleft constructions. In their classification, a cleft construction is introduced by a highlighter, which may be either a copula or a focus particle. If the cleft construction does not contain a relative marker introducing the cleft relative clause, then the highlighter must be a copula for the construction to be considered a cleft. In other words, to be classified as a cleft in their terms, the construction must have either a copula, or a marked cleft relative clause, or both. Bollée (2013) analyses the highlighter *sé* as a focus particle rather than a copula, and therefore does not classify (2) as a cleft construction. I argue that *sé* is in fact a copula, so, even in Maurer and the APiCS Consortium's (2013) terms, the construction in (2) is a cleft construction. The two variants of the *sé*-cleft construction, illustrated in (1) and (2), are equivalent in Réunion Creole, and I assume that they have the same syntactic structure, aside from the presence or absence of the relative marker.

It is often remarked that a higher frequency of clefts is found in French than in other languages such as English, Spanish and Italian (e.g. Lambrecht 2001; Dufter 2009; Lahousse and Lamiroy 2012). Some authors offer an explanation for this in terms of the rigid word order and constraints on focus structure of French, which the cleft construction allows it to satisfy (e.g. Lambrecht 2001), though others have criticised this view, arguing that the increased frequency of clefts found in French cannot be explained only with respect to the (un)availability of alternative focalising strategies in that language compared to other languages (e.g. Dufter 2009). There are gaps in our knowledge of the grammar of Réunion Creole, including the syntax of focus in the language. This article constitutes the first study dedicated to cleft constructions in Réunion Creole.[4] Of interest is not only how the Réunion Creole cleft construction differs structurally from that of French, but also how the properties of this construction might interact with other characteristics of the language, such as the freedom it exhibits in regards to word order and focus structure, and in relation to that, its other strategies for realising focus structure articulations

---

[4] Other cited references, such as Bollée (2013), form part of broader studies of the language, which only briefly discuss constructions with *sé*. Corne (1995) discusses the apparent optionality of relative marker *ke*, noting that it is generally preferred in focus constructions with *sé*. In section 4.3, I point out that this is not the case in my corpus, and I unveil patterns regarding the distribution of *ke* in these constructions.

which deviate from the canonical predicate focus.[5] I will argue that Réunion Creole is freer than French regarding both its word order and its focus structure, yet clefts appear relatively frequently in the corpus.

The article is organised as follows: in section 2, I provide socio-historic background of the Réunion Creole language and describe some core aspects of its grammar, which will become relevant to the discussion of the *sé*-cleft construction. In section 3, I describe the data used for the study. I then introduce the data for *sé*-clefts (section 4): I first present evidence for analysing *sé* as a copula and therefore classifying both *sé*-constructions in (1) and (2) as clefts. I then discuss the distribution of this copula and another copula, *lé*. In 4.2, I describe the types of constituent that can be clefted in Réunion Creole, and in 4.3, I discuss the cleft relative clause. I uncover patterns of relative marking in cleft relative clauses, arguing that they are preferably zero-marked, but this is particularly the case in clefts in which the clefted constituent functions as a subject or object in the cleft relative clause. In section 5, I consider the broader picture, discussing the place of the *sé*-cleft construction as a focalisation strategy in Réunion Creole. I summarise and draw my conclusions in section 6. Throughout the discussion, I draw comparisons with French and other French-based creoles where possible and appropriate.

2 Réunion Creole

Réunion Creole is an officially recognised regional language, spoken by the majority of Réunion's population alongside French, the national language (Bollée 2013).[6] The sociolinguistic context is traditionally described as diglossic, French being the "higher" prestige language and Réunion Creole being the "lower" prestige language, though attitudes towards the latter are increasingly positive, and its use is no longer confined to private spheres. Nevertheless, French remains the primary language of education and administration. Réunion Creole has undergone no standardisation; there is no agreed-upon orthography, though several have been proposed. For the examples given in this article, I use the orthography of the authors in the case

---

5 Lambrecht (1994) distinguishes three focus structure articulations: predicate focus, argument focus and sentence focus. In a canonical subject-predicate sentence, the focus is on the predicate, and this focus structure articulation is named predicate focus. It is said to be the unmarked focus structure, meaning that it is the most frequent focus structure articulation, with the greatest distributional freedom (Lambrecht 1994: 17).
6 In 2018, the population of Reunion was 855, 961 (INSEE 2021: 192).

of written texts; for oral materials, I use the phonetic-based orthographic system known as *Lékritir 83/KWZ*.[7]

Like many creole languages, Réunion Creole exhibits a high degree of variation. In describing variation in speech found on Réunion Island, authors refer to a linguistic continuum spanning from standard French, on the one end, to Réunion French (a regional variety of French), acrolectal Réunion Creole, and basilectal Réunion Creole, on the other end (Chaudenson 1974; Corne 1999; Bollée 2013 and others). 'Acrolectal' is the term used in the creole literature to describe the variety that is closest to the lexifier – in this case, French. It contrasts with 'basilectal', which describes the variety furthest from the lexifier (de Rooij 1994: 53). Traditionally, authors have distinguished two distinct lects of Réunion Creole along these lines: *Créole des Hauts* is the acrolectal variety typically spoken in the highlands of the island, and *Créole des Bas* is the basilectal variety of the island's lowlands. The two varieties are no longer necessarily confined to these areas, though – both varieties are found all over the island (Gaze 2019: 33), and the idiolect of an individual may include features of both varieties (Albers 2019: 32). I will next outline some features of the grammar of Réunion Creole, focusing on those which will be particularly relevant for the subsequent discussion of the cleft data.

Réunion Creole is an SVO language. Unlike French, Réunion Creole does not have clitic pronouns, and pronominal objects occupy the same position as non-pronominal objects would (Watbled 2018). The difference between the two languages in this regard is illustrated by examples (3a) and (3b).

(3) a. *Ou   la   apèl   amwin*   Réunion Creole
       2SG   PRF   call   1SG
    b. *Tu   m'   a   appelé*   French
       2SG   1SG.OBJ   have.3SG   call.PST.PTCP
       'You called me.'

The verbal system of Réunion Creole distinguishes it clearly from other French-based creoles, where tense, modality and aspect are marked via pre-verbal markers known as TMA markers, and verb forms are usually invariant.[8] Réunion Creole has a complex verbal system, which involves preverbal TMA markers, but also verbal inflection. For example, the imperfect may be formed either with the

---

7 For an overview of the systems that have been proposed, including details of the *Lékritir 83/KWZ* system, see https://lofislalangkreollarenyon.re/lekritir-nout-kreol/4-manier-ekrir-jordi/.
8 Though some verbs of many of the French creoles display an alternation between a long and short form, cf. Syea (2017: 213).

preverbal marker *té*, as illustrated in (4a) or with an inflectional suffix *-é*, as illustrated in (4b).

(4) a. zot té (i) manz
    3PL IPFV FIN⁹ eat
   b. zot i manzé
    3PL FIN eat.IPFV
    'They were eating/They used to eat.'

The formation with preverbal *té* is generally more characteristic of basilectal varieties of Réunion Creole, while inflection is often considered acrolectal. In Réunion Creole, verbs do not mark gender or number agreement as do French verbs, so the imperfect form *manzé* is the same across all persons.

As can be observed in examples (4a) and (4b), Réunion Creole has a particle *i*. The interaction between this particle and the relative marker *ke* will become relevant in our discussion of cleft relative clauses in section 4.3. Many other French creoles also have a particle *i*, though its function and distribution vary between these languages (Wittmann and Fournier 1981). In Réunion Creole, the particle is analysed as a preverbal marker of finiteness (e.g. Corne 1995; Corne 1999; Watbled 2013; Watbled 2015; Gaze 2019).¹⁰ The particle *i*, which occurs with all persons, immediately precedes finite verbs. There are certain contexts where it is optional, and others where it is ungrammatical: *i* is optional before verbs which are marked as imperfect with the pre-verbal marker *té* (cf. (4b)); *i* is ungrammatical with the future tense marker *va* and the perfect auxiliary *la* (Watbled 2015).

Another feature which will be relevant to our discussion of cleft constructions in Réunion Creole is its copula. While the copula *lé* (5a) is recognised in general descriptions of the language, I argue that Réunion Creole has an additional copula, *sé*, which is not often recognised as a copula in descriptions of the language. The copula *sé* occurs not only in cleft constructions (cf. (1) and (2)), but also in other copular constructions, illustrated in (5b).

(5) a. Nou lé an dirèk
    1PL COP in live
    'We are live.' (Radio)

---

9 The particle *i* is the finiteness marker, see below for relevant discussion.
10 Note that for Réunion Creole, some have argued that, rather than having the syntactic function of marking finiteness, *i* has a semantic function (temporal-aspectual or modal). See Watbled (2013; 2015) for arguments against this hypothesis.

b. *Moun- la sé Kozima*
   person DEM COP Kozima
   'That person is Kozima.' (Magazine)

I shed light on the distribution of these two copulas in section 4.1, not only in cleft constructions, but also in other copular constructions, arguing that *sé* is favoured in specifying and identifying constructions, while *lé* is favoured in predicative constructions.

Finally, unlike French, Réunion Creole is a pro-drop language. Subject and object pronouns may be omitted in Réunion Creole, when they are co-referent with an antecedent, as in (6a) and (6b).

(6) a. *Kan zot la giny zot retrét po sat la kontinyé*
       when 3PL PRF gain 3PL.POSS pension for those PRF continue
       travayé bonpé, la artourn dan zot péi mé lé
       work lots PRF return to 3PL.POSS country but COP
       pi lo minm moun kan la kit Larénion
       NEG the same person when PRF leave La Réunion
       'When they got their pension, for those who continued to work a lot, (they) returned to their country but (they) are no longer the same people as when (they) left Réunion Island.' (Newspaper)
    b. *M' a ramas in grin m' a planté la sorti*
       1SG PRF collect a seed 1SG PRF plant PRF grow
       'I collected a seed, I planted (it), (it) grew.' (Albers 2019: 59)

Réunion Creole also allows subject-less sentences in impersonal constructions, illustrated in (7a) and (7b), where (7b) is translated as a generic third-person plural impersonal.

(7) a. *non mi di azot fo swiv*
       no 1SG-FIN say 2PL must follow
       'I'm telling you, you/one must follow.' (Comedy sketch)
    b. *kom i di ke manzé sé inn de promyé*
       as FIN say COMP eat COP one of first
       plizir de monn
       pleasure of world
       'As they say, eating is one of the world's greatest pleasures.' (TV)

In the next section, I describe the data that were gathered and used in the investigation into Réunion Creole *sé*-clefts.

3 Data and methodological considerations

The data for this study come from a corpus composed of primary materials collected by the author, where several genres are represented: magazines, newspapers, short stories, blogs, radio, a TV programme and comedy sketches. These materials are supplemented by the Réunion Creole section of the *Corpus de la Parole* (Baude 2010), and the Réunion Creole component of the *SMS4Science* corpus (Cougnon 2012). The former includes 27 free and semi-structured interview recordings gathered and transcribed between 1970 and 2007. The latter includes 12,000 SMS messages sent by speakers on Réunion Island in 2008.

Many of the sources contain both French and Réunion Creole, which gives rise to a methodological consideration of how to distinguish between the two languages. Examples of the constructions under study were coded along a scale as either Réunion Creole, French, or plausibly belonging to both languages. Examples coded as French were excluded from the study. The criteria used for distinguishing Réunion Creole from French appear in (8).

(8) *Diagnostics for distinguishing between Réunion Creole and French*

i. Agglutinated articles in Réunion Creole nouns, e.g. *le landroi* 'the place'.
ii. Determiners: Réunion Creole plural marker *bann;* no gender marking on nouns that would be feminine in French;[11] bare noun phrases (BNPs) in contexts where they would not be permitted in French (BNPs are more freely permitted in Réunion Creole than in French, see Albers (2019; 2020)).
iii. Lexical items belonging to Réunion Creole but not French, e.g. *kas larmwar* 'to be dressed up to the nines'.
iv. Omission of subordinator *ke* in Réunion Creole complement clauses (Corne 1995; Ledegen 2012).
v. Order of objects in Réunion Creole: indirect and direct objects may come in any order in Réunion Creole when they are not pronouns; their ordering is not subject to the same rules as in French, where the direct object usually must precede the indirect object (Holm 2004: 131).
vi. Prepositions (case markers) are often not required for indirect objects in Réunion Creole (Holm 2004: 131).
vii. Omission of the subject is possible in Réunion Creole (cf. section 2).

---

11 Some varieties of Réunion Creole have retained some gender marking, but of course this can still be used as a diagnostic in cases where it is not found.

viii. Pronominal system. E.g., personal pronouns: *mwin/amwin* (1sg), *ou/aou; twé/ atwé; vou/avou* (2sg), *li/ali* (3sg), *nou/anou* (1pl), *zot/azot* (2pl, 3pl). Long forms (with *a-*) are found in object position unless preceded by a preposition, and in subject position when focalised. The forms *vou* and *nou*, being identical to the French versions, were not used as diagnostics. See Armand (2014) for details of the rest of the pronominal system.

ix. Tense/Aspect system, e.g. Réunion Creole often marks tense and aspect with preverbal markers rather than inflection; verb forms are the same for all persons (cf. section 2).

The corpus data are supplemented with judgements and elicitations from interviews with seven native speakers of Réunion Creole.[12] The informants include four males and three females, with ages ranging from 20 to 66, and diverse backgrounds in terms of occupation and region. All informants speak French alongside Réunion Creole but have different stories of language acquisition: two grew up in entirely Creolophone households and learnt Réunion Creole before learning French at school, while the others learnt the two languages simultaneously. When eliciting acceptability judgements, care was taken to distinguish between rejection of a sentence that the informant would not say themselves, from rejection of a sentence that they would not hear any Réunion Creole speaker utter. This was to help overcome issues of dialectal variation on the island leading to divergent judgements, and to separate what was ungrammatical in the language from what was disliked, or simply not a part of one speaker's idiolect.

In section 4.3, I also refer to grammaticality judgements obtained via an online questionnaire, completed by 50 native speakers of Réunion Creole in April 2021. Participants ranged from 20 to 70 years, and there was a roughly even split of male and female speakers. The majority came from the lowlands of the island and were educated to degree-level. In the next section, I begin discussion of the *sé*-cleft construction, based upon the several strands of data described here.

4 The *sé*-cleft construction

As outlined in section 1, Réunion Creole has two variants of one focus construction introduced by a highlighter, *sé*. I argue here that both variants are cleft constructions, comparable to the English *it*-cleft and French *c'est*-cleft. The *sé*-con-

---

[12] Due to COVID-19, these were conducted via online video conferencing in June and July 2021, in conformity with the recommendations of The University of Manchester's ethics committee.

struction is poorly understood, and until now, a detailed investigation of its structure has not been undertaken. I describe here the structure of the Réunion Creole *sé*-cleft, its copula, the clefted constituent, and the cleft relative clause, on the basis of 224 cleft constructions found in the corpus, and acceptability judgements obtained via the interviews and online questionnaire described in section 3. The discussion contributes to wider understanding of Réunion Creole grammar – the distribution of two copulas and relative marking in the language. I begin with the copula.

4.1 The copula

As noted in the introduction, Bollée (2013) analyses the highlighter *sé* as a focus particle, and, therefore, she considers the two constructions in (1) and (2), repeated here in (9) and (10), to be different focalisation strategies.

(9) *Sé la mashine k'i konvien pa*
    HL the machine REL-FIN work NEG
    'It's the machine that doesn't work.' (Blog)

(10) *Sé lo sistèm lé mal roganizé*
     HL the system COP badly organised
     'It's the system which is badly organised.' (Newspaper)

Since (10) contains neither a copula nor a relative marker, according to Bollée's analysis, it is considered to be focus fronting, rather than a cleft construction. I argue that both constructions with and without a relative marker should be analysed as cleft constructions, as *sé* is in fact a copula. In section 5, I point out that Réunion Creole does permit focus fronting, but this is a separate focalisation strategy not involving *sé*.

I understand a particle to be an invariant form, and a copula to be a verb taking inflection. Evidence for *sé* being analysed as a copula rather than a particle comes firstly from temporal inflection. In cleft constructions in the corpus, I found *sé* in the future tense as *sra*, as illustrated in (11).

(11) zot la pa konpri ke nou lé pi dan zané 60–70, le pep la sanzé, la grandi é la anvi désid par li minm podvré é
'They haven't understood that we're no longer in the 60s–70s, the people have changed, have grown, and want to decide for themselves, and'

sra	pa	in	tribunal	kolonial	ke	va	anbar	anou
COP.FUT	NEG	a	tribunal	colonial	REL	FUT	bar	1PL

va	anpes	anou	arash	nout	liberté
FUT	stop	1PL	snatch	1PL.POSS	freedom

'it will not be a colonial tribunal that will bar us, will stop us from claiming our freedom.' (Newspaper)

This cleft construction featuring the future tense form of *sé* was also found in cleft constructions without a relative marker, as is illustrated in (12).

(12) *Bann marmay CM2 Kréol Français Rivière le Por la met ansanm zanmari baré pou shant dann kabardock. In rankont, in spétak bann marmay lé pa pré oublié.*
'Children from the year 5 French-Creole class at *Francis Rivière* got together with *Zanmari Baré* to sing at the *Kabardock*.[13] It was a meeting, a show the children will not forget.'

somanké	demin	**sra**	zot	va	port	la	mizik	La
surely	tomorrow	COP.FUT	3PL	FUT	carry	the	music	La

Renyon	anlèr.
Réunion	above

'Surely tomorrow it will be them who will carry the music of La Réunion up top.' (Magazine)

In addition, I found *sé* in cleft constructions in the past tense as *sété*, exemplified in (13a) and (13b), where (13a) contains a relative marker *ke*, and (13b) does not.

(13) a.
zot	lété	in	ti	pé	koupab	mé	**sété**	pa
3PL	COP.PST	a	little	bit	guilty	but	COP.PST	NEG

zot	ke	noré	fé	le	krim
3PL	REL	have.COND	do	the	crime

'They were a little bit guilty, but it wasn't them who were alleged to have done the crime.' (Guided conversation)

---

[13] *Zanmari Baré* is a Reunionese maloya band, and the *Kabardock* is a performing arts theatre in Le Port, Réunion Island.

b. **sété** la vyé pèrson vyé pèrson i parté a la
   COP.PST the old person old person FIN leave.IPFV to the
   mézon i parté rogardé
   house FIN leave.IPFV look
   'It was the old person, the old person (who) went to the house,
   went to look.' (Guided conversation)

In the corpus, occurrences of *sété* were infrequent (cf. Table 1 below), and among those examples, there was only one, (13b), whose cleft relative clause did not contain a relative marker. There is a possibility that (13b) is not a cleft construction, but rather two sentences: 'It was the old person. The old person went to the house, they went to look.', in which case, it is not relevant here. However, data from interviews, discussed further below, found that the cleft construction with a past tense copula *sété* and no relative marker was grammatical.

The examples from (11)–(13) suggest that *sé* is not a particle, but rather a copula, as it inflects for tense, occurring in the future tense as *sra* and the past tense as *sété*. That is not to say that this copula does not fulfil a focalising function in the construction under investigation – it does indeed serve to focalise a clefted constituent, but it is a copular verb, which inflects for tense. In turn, this indicates that the construction is biclausal according to the definition in section 1 above.

As noted in section 2, *sé* is not the only copula in Réunion Creole; the other copula is *lé*, which has a past-tense form *lété*.[14] Past-tense forms *lété* and *sété* may be reduced to *té*, which is homophonous with the preverbal imperfect marker *té* (cf. section 2). There is only one future tense form of the copula: *sra*. Table 1, which illustrates the distribution of the two copulas in the corpus, including their tensed forms, adds to current understanding of the distribution of the two copulas.

---

14 Some authors (e.g. Albers 2019, Gaze 2019) note that the present tense copula *lé* may be realised as *la*, particularly when it co-occurs with negation. *La* is also a present-tense form of the verb *nana* 'have' in Réunion Creole, along with two other present-tense forms *na* and *nana*. Réunion Creole has a *na(na)*-cleft construction too, which typically has a presentational function:

(i) Na in nafèr la ariv pou ou
    have a thing PRF arrive for 2SG
    'There's something that's arrived for you.' (SMS)

There were six clefts with *la* in the corpus; however, these were all examples of the type illustrated in (i), with *la* as 'have' rather than a variation of the *lé* 'be' copula, because they are presentational constructions, or ones which negate the existence of something. These examples were not included in the study and will therefore not be discussed further. Clearly, further research is needed on the distribution of *la* as a variant of *lé*.

Table 1: Distribution of copular forms in cleft constructions in the corpus.

	sé	lé		Total
Past forms	sété	lété	té	9
	5	1	3	
Present forms	sé	lé		201
	189	12		
Future forms	sra			14
	14			
Total[15]	194	13		224
	94%	6%		

Table 1 shows that, in the corpus, the presence of *sé* in the cleft construction outweighs that of *lé*, with *sé* being found in its present tense form in the majority of cleft constructions. This pattern of preference for *sé* over *lé* in cleft constructions was supported by native speaker judgements: only two of the seven informants accepted *lé* in all cleft constructions presented to them. The other five rejected it from all cleft constructions presented to them, with the exception of one sentence. Example (14) was accepted by all four speakers to whom it was presented, and two of those informants were ones that had rejected *lé* in other cleft constructions.[16]

(14) *Lé èk Romin (ke) Noémi sava lèrmitaz*
 COP with Romain REL Noémie go Ermitage
 'It's with Romain that Noémie is going to the Ermitage beach.'

Though this requires further research, I suggest that the acceptability of *lé* in cleft constructions could therefore be sensitive to the type of clefted constituent: *lé* may be more acceptable with clefted constituents that are prepositional phrases (14) rather than noun phrases like (15).

(15) ?*Lé Éloiz (k) i sava Lèrmitaz.*
 COP Éloise REL FIN go Ermitage
 'It's Éloise who is going to the Ermitage beach.'

---

15 The totals in the *sé* and *lé* column do not include the future tense form since it is the same for both.
16 Unfortunately, not every sentence was tested with all seven informants, due to differing time constraints and practical considerations.

Note that the sentences in (14) and (15) were accepted by all speakers when *lé* was replaced by *sé*. Although the *s*- form was accepted consistently in the present tense in interviews, this was not the case for the past tense. *Sété* was found to be more frequent than *lété* in the corpus (cf. Table 1), but *lété* received better acceptability judgements from native speakers in interviews than *sété* did, in examples where the cleft relative clause was in the past tense, like (16).

(16) *Lété/sété   an   mars   (ke)   nou   la   fé   sa.*
      COP.PST   in   March   REL   1PL   PRF   do   DEM
      'It was in March that we did that.'

Of six informants asked about the acceptability of *sété* and *lété* in an example identical to (16) or minimally different, all accepted *lété* and three expressed a preference for *lété* over *sété*. No informant preferred *sété* over *lété*, and one rejected it. Reasons offered for this was that *sété* was described as less creole and closer to French.

When the verb in the cleft relative clause is in the past tense, it is also possible to have the present tense copular form *sé*, rather than past-tense forms *sété* or *lété*. In this respect, Réunion Creole follows a general trend: it has been noted that the copula in cleft constructions (and other specificational sentences) can occur in the present tense when the verb of the cleft relative clause is in a different tense, if there is still relevance in the present moment (e.g. Declerck 1988: 82–85 for English specificational sentences; Dufter 2008 for French clefts). This is demonstrated for Réunion Creole in (17a), (17b) and (17c), where there is not agreement in the tenses of the copula and the verb of the cleft relative clause.

(17) a. *sé* + **past**
          sé   zot   la   réaliz   bann   reportaz-la
          COP   3PL   PRF   make   PL   report-DEM
          'It's them who made those reports.'   (Magazine)
      b. *sé* + **imperfect**
          sé   lé   vyé   moun   i   dansé   sa
          COP   the   old   person   FIN   dance.IPFV DEM
          'It's the old people who used to dance that!'   (Guided conversation)
      c. *sé* + **future**
          sé   li   nora   la   responsabilité
          COP   3SG   have.FUT   the   responsibility
          'It's him who will have the responsibility.'   (Newspaper)

The interviews corroborated this finding from the corpus, as indicated by the acceptability of *sé, sété* and *lété* in (18), and *sé* and *sra* in (19).

(18) *Sé/sété/lété   plaz   lèrmitaz   (ke)   Noémi   té   yèr*
      COP/COP.PST   beach   Ermitage   REL   Noémie IPFV   yesterday
      'It is/was Ermitage beach that Noémie was at yesterday (not Boucan Canot beach).'

(19) *Sé/sra   domin   (ke)   Romin   va   alé   Boukan   Kanot*
      COP/COP.FUT tomorrow   REL   Romain   FUT   go   Boucan   Kanot
      'It is/will be tomorrow that Romain will go to Boucan Canot.'

In example (18), the form *lété* was generally preferred by my informants over both *sété* and *sé*, but there was no preference for either form over the other in (19).

The discussion in this section has indicated that *sé* is generally the preferred copula in cleft constructions: it appears more frequently in the corpus and it was consistently accepted by native speakers while *lé* was not. However, *sé* is not only found as a copula in cleft constructions; in fact, further support for the analysis of *sé* as a copula comes from its occurrence in other copular constructions, classified below as identifying, specifying or predicative as in Bentley (2017). Identifying copular constructions are those in which a relation of identity is expressed between a pre-copular referential noun phrase and a post-copular referential noun phrase (Bentley 2017: 336). In Réunion Creole, *sé* is found in identifying copular constructions, illustrated by the corpus examples (20a), (20b) and (20c).

(20) a. *Sé   Yvo   li?*
        COP   Yvo   3SG
        'Is he Yvo?'   (Guided conversation)
     b. *Moun-la   sé   Kozima*
        person-DEM   COP   Kozima
        'That person is Kozima.'   (Magazine)
     c. *Amwin   sé   out   kolèg   Bruno*
        1SG.FOC COP   2PL.POSS colleague   Bruno
        'I'm your colleague Bruno.'   (Radio)

The acceptability judgements indicated that *sé* is the preferred copula in identifying copular constructions: *sé* was preferred by all informants in example (21), where *lé* was ungrammatical for four of the seven informants.

(21) Mwin *lé/sé Alina
    1SG   COP   Alina
    'I am Alina.'

Sé was also preferred over *lé* in the specifying copular construction in (22). Specifying copular constructions are defined, following Bentley (2017: 335) and Huddleston (2002: 266), as those in which a value is specified for a variable, the value being the post-copular noun phrase and the variable being the pre-copular noun phrase.

(22) Alina *le/sé mwin
    Alina COP 1SG
    'Alina is me.'

The main difference between the identifying (21) and specifying (22) copular constructions is that the former has subject-predicate word order, whereas the latter has predicate-subject word order.

Sé can also occur in predicative copular constructions, as illustrated by the corpus examples (23a) and (23b).

(23) a. Amwin   sé   ryin   apré Jacky Lechat
       1SG.FOC COP nothing after Jacky Lechat
       'I'm nothing compared to Jacky Lechat!'   (TV)
    b. Lékol   sé   in   nafèr tro   sèryé
       school COP INDF thing too   serious
       'School is too serious a thing.'   (Blog)

However, in predicative constructions where the post-copular noun phrase is a locative (24a) or an adjective (24b), *sé* is judged as ungrammatical by my informants, and instead, *lé* is required.

(24) a. Mwin lé/*sé marsé   sodron
       1SG   COP   market   chaudron
       'I'm at Chaudron Market.'
    b. Mwin lé/*sé kontan
       1SG   COP   happy
       'I am happy.'

The distribution of these two copulas in Réunion Creole merits further research; however, the data presented here support a hypothesis that *sé* is the preferred copula in identifying and specifying copular constructions and *lé* is favoured in predicative copular constructions. The occurrence of *sé* in predicative constructions is possible but restricted: it is ungrammatical if the post-copular noun phrase is locative or is an adjective. The data presented in Albers (2019) also support this argument: Albers (2019: 57), who does recognise *sé* as a copula in Réunion Creole, found that *sé* is primarily found in identifying constructions in her corpus.

Synchronically, I do not consider the forms *sé* or *lé* to contain a clitic subject pronoun, though they appear to have originated from the combination of the French third person clitic subjects followed by the copula: *c'est* and *il est*. The examples discussed above illustrate that the Réunion Creole copulas *sé* and *lé* occur in the same form in copular constructions which have a subject as they do in cleft constructions, indicating that the copulas found in cleft constructions do not contain a clitic subject. This is illustrated for *sé* in (20a–c), (21), (22) and (23a–b) above, and for *lé* above in (24a–b) and below in (25).

(25) Li   lé   matèr
     3SG   COP   liar
     'He is a liar.'   (Newspaper)

French has structures which look identical to the expressions in (21), (22) and (23b), but in French they would be analysed as a dislocated NP or pronoun, followed by a subject clitic and the copula. Such an analysis is not warranted for Réunion Creole though: the comparison with structures with other verbs reveals that French always requires a subject clitic, regardless of the presence of a nominal or pronominal subject, whereas Réunion Creole does not. This is illustrated with the verb *signe* 'sign' in example (26a) from the corpus. The subject is a dislocated topic, and there is no clitic subject in the Réunion Creole example, but in the French equivalent (my translation) in (26b), a clitic subject is required.

(26) a. Réunion Creole
        An   1674,   Jacob   de   la   Haye,   i   signe   in   "ordonnance"
        in   1674   Jacob   of   the   Haye   FIN   sign   an   ordonnance
     b. French
        En   1674,   Jacob   de   la   Haye,   il   signe   in   "ordonnance"
        in   1674   Jacob   of   the   Haye   3SG   sign   an   ordonnance
        'In 1674, Jacob de la Haye, he signs an ordonnance...'   (Magazine)

Evidence from other contexts, that Réunion Creole sentences do not require a subject, was presented in section 2, and indicates that the presence of an expletive subject in cleft constructions cannot be motivated by a need to satisfy the requirement for a subject in the language.

To summarise, in this section, I have argued that Réunion Creole *sé* is a copula given that it carries temporal inflection and is found in other copular constructions in the language. With the view that *sé* is a copula, I argue that the *sé* focus constructions with and without a relative marker are variants of one cleft construction. The discussion in this section has furthered our understanding of the distribution of the two copulas, finding that *sé* is the preferred copula in cleft constructions and in identifying and specifying copular constructions, whereas *lé* is the preferred copula in predicative copular constructions. In the next section, I discuss the types of constituents that are clefted in Réunion Creole *sé*-clefts.

4.2 The clefted constituent

Bollée's (2013) and Corne's (1995) discussions of cleft constructions in Réunion Creole only deal with the focalisation of noun phrases. In this section, I discuss the range of possible elements that may be clefted. In many of the examples presented thus far, the clefted constituent has been a nominal constituent functioning as the subject of the cleft relative clause. However, clefts in which the clefted constituent is the object or an adjunct adverbial of the cleft relative clause are also found in the corpus, and the adjuncts are realised as adverb phrases (27a), prepositional phrases (27b), and adverbial clauses (27c).

(27) a. c   ri1   ke   hier   mi   sorte   ek   {NAME}[17]
        COP nothing but   yesterday 1SG-FIN go.out   with NAME
        'it's only yesterday that I went out with NAME.'   (SMS)
   b. Sé   èk   lo   MIR   é   Serge Sinamalé ke   nou la   avans
        COP with the   MIR   and Serge Sinamalé REL 1PL PRF advance
        kom i   fo   po   amin   nout   konba   dan bann
        as   FIN   must to   bring 1PL.POSS fight   in   PL
        gran   lasanblé   internasional.
        grand assembly   international
        'It's with the MIR and Serge Sinamalé that we've advanced as we must to bring our fight to the grand international assemblies.'   (Newspaper)

---

17 I preserve the speaker's original spelling in their SMS. The corpus was anonymised by its compilers, so names are removed.

c. *sé kan li la bésé an okipan sa marmit*
   COP when 3SG PRF lower in look.after 3SG.POSS pot
   komsa ke la pas ali in kou dan sa tèt
   like.that REL PRF pass 3SG a blow on 3SG.POSS head
   'It's when he bent down to pick up his pot like that that he was hit on the head.' (Guided conversation)

Regarding the semantic types of adverbial cleft, I found time, manner, place and reason adjuncts in the clefted position, and these adverbial clefts often clefted the anaphoric expressions given in Table 2.

Table 2: Adverbial clefts in the corpus.

Place/time	anaphoric clefted phrase	*là* 'there/then'
	% anaphoric clefted phrase	53 %
	Total place/time clefts	15
Manner	anaphoric clefted phrase	*komsa* 'like that'
	% anaphoric clefted phrase	80 %
	Total manner clefts	10
Reason	anaphoric clefted phrase	*posa* 'for that'
	% anaphoric clefted phrase	85 %
	Total reason clefts	33

Before concluding this section, a note on predicate clefting is appropriate, given that a certain type of predicate clefting has received considerable attention in the creole literature (see, for example, Muysken 1977; Lumsden & Lefebvre 1990; Cozier 2006). The type of predicate cleft construction in question involves the repetition of the clefted predicate (an adjective (28a) or verb (28b)) in its canonical position in the clause, as exemplified in the Haitian examples (28a) and (28b). Small caps are used to indicate the focalised constituent.

(28) a. *Se **malad** Bouki **malad**, li pa mouri.*
    HL sick Bouki sick 3SG NEG dead
    'It is SICK that Bouki is, not dead.' (Haitian)
    (Holm 1988, cited in DeGraff 2007: 113; translation modified from original 'Bouki is *sick*, not dead.')

b. Se **mache** Bouki te **mache**, li pa te kouri.
   HL walk Bouki ANT 3SG   3SG NEG ANT run
   'Bouki had WALKED, not run.'[18]   (Haitian)
   (Holm 1988, cited in DeGraff 2007: 113)

In the creole literature, this type of predicate clefting, involving the doubling of the predicate, is usually discussed in relation to the Caribbean creoles, which had large influence from West African languages. This type of predicate clefting is found in the West African Kwa languages and therefore its presence in the Caribbean creoles is attributed to input from this language group (e.g. Muysken 1977; Seuren 1993). As for Réunion Creole, an Indian Ocean creole with no known input from this language group (Seuren 1993: 57), I found no evidence of this structure in my corpus, and interviews suggested that this type of predicate cleft is not found in the language. The interviews involved an elicitation task followed by acceptability judgements of the constructed examples in (29a) and (29b), where the clefted predicate, a verb in (29a) and an adjective in (29b), also occurs in its canonical position in the clause.

(29) a. *Sé naz (ke) Romin i naz
       COP swim REL Romain FIN swim
       'Romain is SWIMMING/?It's SWIMMING that Romain is doing.'
    b. *Sé kontan (ke) Éloiz lé kontan
       COP happy REL Eloise COP happy
       'Eloise is HAPPY/It's HAPPY that Eloise is.'

---

18 As reflected by the looser translation of (28b), predicate clefting is restricted in English (see, for example, Quirk et al. 1985: 1385). Clefting of verbs in English is ungrammatical without making the verb non-finite and without the addition of a verb like 'do'. For example, the verb *gave* in the canonical sentence (iia) cannot be clefted as in (iib) (examples adapted from Cozier 2006: 656–657).

(ii) a. Tim gave his car to Misha.
     b. *It is/was gave that Tim his car to Misha.

For it to be grammatical, the verb would have to be made non-finite, the complements of the predicate would need to be clefted with the predicate, and the verb 'do' would need to be added, as in (iii).

(iii) It was give his car to Misha that Tim did.

In the predicate cleft construction of the type found in Haitian and other creole languages, the predicate has to occur alone, it cannot be clefted with its complements. The phenomenon of predicate clefting as discussed in the creole literature for languages like Haitian, and illustrated in (28a) and (28b), seems to be different to the approximate equivalents in English (cf. Lumsden & Lefebvre 1990; Cozier 2006).

No participant produced a cleft structure in the elicitation task, and the sentences in (29a) and (29b), with and without *ke*, were categorically rejected by all seven informants.[19] Instead, informants produced sentences with canonical word order and prosodic focus on the predicate. Different languages have different strategies for realising focus. As well as syntactic strategies, there are phonological and phonetic strategies for the prosodic realisation of focus phrases. Focus can change, for example, patterns of stress assignment and prosodic phrasing (see, e.g. Selkirk 1984, 1995; Féry & Ishihara 2009; Büring 2010; Gürer 2020, among others, for the relation between prosody and focus). I give further attention to alternative focalising strategies available in Réunion Creole in section 5; in the next section, I discuss the cleft relative clause.

4.3 The cleft relative clause

So far, I have argued that Réunion Creole has two variants of a *sé*-cleft, which have an equivalent syntactic structure, the only difference between them being whether or not their cleft relative clause is introduced by a relative marker.[20] To understand the structure of cleft relative clauses, and to evaluate the similarities between cleft

---

19 To elicit these structures, participants were presented with an image which showed the character (Romain or Eloise) showing an emotion or doing an action (e.g. happy, swimming). They were then played a sentence recorded by a native speaker (for example, translating to 'Eloise is sad', 'Romain is walking'). If the sentence did not correspond to what the image showed, they were instructed to respond by contesting it. So, for example, an image of Romain swimming was presented to them, and an audio clip translating to 'Romain is walking' was played. The intention was to elicit a sentence translating roughly to 'No, Romain is SWIMMING.', which exhibits contrastive focus on the predicate.

20 I do not assume that the variant of the *sé*-cleft that does not exhibit a relative marker has an underlying empty syntactic position, which is filled by *ke* in the variant that does exhibit the relative marker. In my doctoral thesis (McLellan 2023), I adopt a syntactic framework which does not posit an underlying syntactic structure (Role and Reference Grammar (RRG; Van Valin and LaPolla 1997; Van Valin 2005, 2008 and others)). For RRG, there is only one syntactic structure, which represents a given sentence as it occurs in a language. RRG does not permit syntactic movement, and instead relies on the mapping between syntax, semantics and pragmatics to capture generalizations which other frameworks capture in derivational terms. I thus assume that the cleft constructions with and without the relative marker have identical syntactic representations aside from the presence or absence of *ke*, which is analysed as a clause linkage marker (CLM) (cf. Van Valin and LaPolla 1997: 676–677), and correlates with the syntactic function of the clefted element in the cleft relative clause. An RRG analysis of the syntactic structure of Réunion Creole *sé*-clefts, and the mapping between syntax, semantics and pragmatics in these constructions, is beyond the scope of the present article, but is given in McLellan (2023).

relative clauses and restrictive relative clauses in Réunion Creole, it will be helpful to begin by looking briefly at how the latter are formed in the language.

Restrictive relatives are clauses that modify a noun and narrow down its reference. In Réunion Creole, they are post-nominal but unlike in French, they may be zero-marked, as exemplified by (30).[21]

(30) *in gran mersi bann zanseygnan kréol, bann profeser*
a big thanks PL teacher creole PL teacher
kolej la partisipé
college PRF participate
'A big thank you to all the creole teachers, and college teachers who participated!' (Magazine)

Corne (1995) remarked that Réunion Creole relative clauses contain an "optional" relative marker, but further, detailed investigation had until now not been carried out, neither in the language's cleft relative clauses, nor its restrictive relative clauses. There are likely to be several factors at play regarding the presence of the relative marker in relative constructions. For reasons of space, I will confine this discussion to one factor, which is undoubtedly significant: the syntactic function of the antecedent in the relative clause. The figures in Table 3 clearly indicate that this is a factor governing the distribution of the relative marker in restrictive relative clauses: subject and object relative clauses favour zero-marking but oblique relative clauses are preferably marked.

Table 3: Distribution of relative markers in restrictive relative clauses in the corpus.

	Relative marker	No relative marker	Total
Subject	13%	87%	192
	25	167	
Object	28%	72%	94
	26	68	
Oblique[22]	76%	24%	50
	38	12	
Total	26%	74%	336
	89	247	

---

21 It is noted that in some regional varieties of French a relative marker may be omitted though, e.g. Acadian French (Hill 2017), Ivorian French (Moseng Knutsen 2009).
22 Here I count prepositional complements, locatives and temporals.

The fact that subject restrictive relative clauses strongly disfavour the presence of the relative marker distinguishes Réunion Creole not only from French, but also from many of the other French-based creoles, in which a relative marker is obligatory for subject relative clauses (Syea 2017).[23]

Turning now to the relative clause of *sé*-clefts, Corne (1995) stated that the relative marker actually seemed to be favoured in focus constructions with *sé*. However, this is not the case in my corpus, nor is it supported by the judgements of my informants. Table 4 shows the distribution of the relative marker in *sé*-cleft relative clauses in my corpus, according to the syntactic function of the clefted constituent in the cleft relative clause.

Table 4: Distribution of relative marker in cleft constructions in corpus.

	Relative marker	No relative marker	Total
Subject	33%	67%	132
	44	88	
Object	28%	72%	25
	7	18	
Adverbial	46%	54%	68
	31	37	
Total	36%	64%	225
	82	143	

Looking first at the total number of clefts which do not contain a relative marker, Table 4 shows that it is not simply a case of the relative marker occasionally being omitted; it is the more frequent option in Réunion Creole, counter to Corne's (1995) observation from his corpus. This again shows a difference with French clefts, which do require a relative marker.

Regarding the distribution of the relative marker according to the syntactic function of the clefted constituent in the cleft relative clause, Table 4 indicates that a preference for the relative marker to be omitted holds for cleft constructions in which the clefted constituent functions either as a subject or object in the cleft rel-

---

23 According to Syea (2017), a relative marker is obligatory for subject relatives in Haitian, Martinican, Guadeloupean, St. Lucian, Guyanese and Karipuna. It is optional in the Indian Ocean Creoles of Mauritius, Seychelles and Rodrigues, and in Louisiana Creole and Tayo. Nothing is said about whether those languages simply permit zero-marking in subject relative clauses, or favour it, like Réunion Creole does. The data presented on subject relatives in Michaelis, Haspelmath & the APiCS Consortium (2013) indicate that Réunion Creole is the only French-based creole in which more than 50% subject relative clauses are marked, which I set as a threshold for zero-marking constituting a preferred strategy rather than just a possibility.

ative clause, but less so for adverbials. There are some differences between the patterns found for relative marking in restrictive relative clauses and cleft relative clauses: the preference for zero-marking in cleft relative clauses is stronger in object cleft relative clauses than subject cleft relative clauses (cf. Table 4), but this is the reverse for restrictive relative clauses (cf. Table 3). However, there is a low number of object clefts in the corpus, so it is possibly a reflection of this.

The acceptability judgements gathered in interviews indicated that a preference for zero-marking is the most consistent for subject clefts, being favoured by all seven informants. For all but two informants, zero-marking but was in fact favoured regardless of the syntactic function of the clefted constituent. No informant produced a relative-marked cleft in the elicitation tasks conducted: the five clefts successfully elicited from informants all had zero-marked cleft relative clauses. Following the elicitation task, when presented with two versions of the subject cleft in (31), with and without a relative marker, all seven informants expressed a preference for the zero-marked version.

(31) Sé   Éloiz   (k)   i   sava   Boukan   Kanot
     COP   Éloise REL   FIN   go   Boucan   Canot
     'It's Eloise who is going to Boucan Canot beach.'

A preference for zero-marked cleft relative clauses held for object and adverbial clefts too, for all but two informants, one of which preferred the relative-marked option in object clefts presented to them such as (32).

(32) Sé   li   (ke)   mwin   la   vi
     COP   3SG   REL   1SG   PRF   see
     'It's him that I saw.'

The other participant offered inconsistent judgements regarding the presence or absence of the relative marker, meaning no conclusions could be drawn about their preferences. In discussing the difference between two versions of a cleft construction with and without a relative marker, informants noted that the presence of *ke* depended on the person speaking, and there were occasional comments that the version with a marker was influenced by French or less authentically Réunion Creole. Regardless of the several potential factors at play governing the presence of *ke* in Réunion Creole clefts, the preference for zero-marked cleft relatives in subject and object clefts in particular is clear. This preference for zero-marking in subject clefts constitutes another difference between Réunion Creole and the other French-based creoles. Syea (2017) notes that cleft relative clauses are obligatorily marked when the clefted constituent is a subject, but zero-marked otherwise, with the exception of the Indian Ocean Creoles (IOC), where the relative marker is optional for subjects too.[24]

Réunion Creole patterns similarly to many of the other French-based creoles regarding the type of relative marker that is found in cleft relative clauses, when they are marked by one. In the French-based creoles, this relative marker tends to be invariant, whereas in French, when the clefted constituent is a subject in the cleft relative clause, the relative marker is *qui* 'who', and elsewhere it is *que* 'that' (abstracting away from the case in which the relative marker follows a preposition). At first sight, it may appear that Réunion Creole follows the same pattern as French, with *ki* being used for subjects and *ke* elsewhere (compare (31) and (32) above). This is not the case, though: the form *ki* in Réunion Creole only occurs when *ke* is followed by the preverbal finiteness marker *i* (see Corne 1995; McLellan, 2023). Given that Réunion Creole is an SVO language, the interaction between *ke* and *i* occurs most often in subject relative clauses (33): the subject is the missing argument in the relative clause and as such, there is usually nothing intervening between relative marker *ke* and particle *i*, which immediately precedes finite verbs, like *répon* 'respond' in (33).

(33) *Là   sé   ou   ki   répon   pi   là!*
      there COP   2SG   REL-FIN   respond NEG   there
      'There it's you who stopped responding!'   (SMS)

---

24 However, what Syea (2017) describes as a cleft construction in the IOC does not have a highlighter – neither a focus particle nor a copula:

(iv) *Zan   (ki)   ti   vini.*
      John   COMP   PST   come
      'It was John who came.' (Syea 2017: 448)

If the structure in (iv) had no relative marker (complementizer according to Syea's glossing), I would not consider it a biclausal cleft construction, as it is structurally indistinguishable from the monoclausal declarative sentence *Zan ti vini* 'John came'. The latter can bear prosodic stress on *Zan*, allowing it to exhibit argument focus as does a cleft construction. In such cases, Syea (2017) analyses *Zan* as a clefted constituent, rather than the subject of an unmarked declarative clause, referring to evidence from case forms when the subject is pronominal. As previously mentioned (see note 21), in my doctoral thesis (McLellan 2023), I adopt a syntactic framework which does not allow empty, underlying syntactic elements, so would instead analyse this as a monoclausal sentence with prosodic prominence as a focalisation strategy. The presence or absence of a relative marker in the Réunion Creole cleft constructions, illustrated in (1) and (2), on the other hand, does not change the analysis I propose: the construction is biclausal whether or not *ke* is present, because it contains a copular verb.

However, as noted in section 2, there are contexts, such as the perfect marker *la*, which do not permit the preverbal particle *i*, and such examples exhibit *ke* rather than *ki*, as in (34).

(34) Sé   nou   ke   la   pa   kompri
     COP   1PL   REL   PRF   NEG   understand
     'It's us who didn't understand!'   (Oral guided conversation)

If *ki* were found in all subject clefts as *qui* is in French, we would expect to find it in examples like (34), but instead we find *ke*. Similarly, the form *ki* occurs in non-subject clefts whose cleft relative clause does not have a subject. Réunion Creole allows clauses with no subject in impersonal constructions (cf. section 2). In such examples, there is no subject intervening between the relative marker *ke* and the particle *i*, so we thus find *ki*, as in (35).

(35) sé   sa   k'   i   aplé   fèr   la   rantré?
     COP   DEM   REL   FIN call.IPFV do   the   comeback
     'It's that that one called "make a comeback"?'   (Guided conversation)

For further evidence that *ki* is not a subject relative pronoun, see McLellan (2023). Before concluding this section, I briefly discuss a difference between the relative marker found in locative cleft constructions and locative restrictive relative clauses. In restrictive relative clauses, Réunion Creole has a locative relative marker, *ousa* or *ou* 'where', illustrated in (36a) and (36b) respectively.

(36) a. in   lékonomi   sovaz   ousa   sat   na   plis   mwayin
        an   economy   savage   where   those   have   more   mean
        i   domine
        FIN   dominate
        'A savage economy where those who have more (financial) means dominate.'   (Newspaper)
     b. dan   in   konférans   internasional   ou   li   té
        in   a   conference   international   where   3SG   IPFV
        roprézant   anou
        represent   1PL
        'At an international conference where he was representing us.'
                                                                      (Newspaper)

In locative restrictive relative clauses, the marker *ou(sa)* is preferred over both zero-marking and over *ke*, neither of which occur at all in the 20 examples of locative restrictive relative clauses found in the corpus. The acceptability of *ke* in locative restrictive relative clauses was tested in the online questionnaire and received low acceptability judgements. Three versions of the sentence in (36b), containing three different relative markers – *ke*, *ou* and *ousa* – were presented to participants to be judged. Table 5 reports the results of their judgements, showing that *ke* is disliked in locative restrictive relative clauses.[25]

Table 5: Grammaticality judgements for locative restrictive relative clause with *ke*, *ou* and *ousa*.

	Relative marker	Strong Accept	Weak Accept	Reject	Responses[26]
Example (36b)	ke	8 %	36 %	55 %	47
	ou	43 %	47 %	10 %	49
	ousa	64 %	30 %	6 %	50

While *ke* is at least disliked in locative restrictive relative clauses, it is perfectly acceptable in locative cleft relative clauses: it occurs in locative clefts in the corpus, illustrated in (37), and locative cleft relatives marked with *ke* were judged as acceptable by all seven informants in interviews.

(37) *Sé   là   k   li   sava*
     COP there REL 3SG go
     'It's there that he's going.'   (Guided conversation)

Although *ousa* was not found in locative clefts in the corpus, it was accepted by my informants in examples such as (38), though disfavoured over *ke*.

(38) *Non sé   Boukan Kanot ke/ousa Noémi   sava*
     no   COP Boucan   Canot REL   Noémie go
     'No, it's Boucan Canot beach that/where Noémie is going to.'

Two informants preferred *ke* over *ousa* in locative clefts, commenting that the latter was heavy, though it must be noted that the version with no relative marker was

---

[25] Participants were asked to judge sentences as one of three options: (i) "It's good, I would say something like this"; (ii) "I wouldn't say this, but other Réunion Creole speakers would."; (iii) "It's not good, no Réunion Creole speaker would say this.". I translate option (i) to a participant strongly accepting the sentence, (ii) weakly accepting it, and (iii) as rejecting it.
[26] The total number of responses is not the same for all because it was not obligatory to answer every question in the questionnaire. In some cases, participants signalled the one that they would say and did not judge the others.

preferred over both markers. This indicates some important differences between locative cleft relatives and locative restrictive relatives: the latter prefer a relative marker, which is preferably *ou(sa)* rather than *ke*, while the former, if marked, are preferably marked with *ke* rather than *ousa*.

Overall, in this section I have argued that zero-marking is favoured in *sé*-cleft relative clauses in which the clefted constituent is a subject or object. This is a pattern also exhibited in restrictive relative clauses of the language, and one that distinguishes Réunion Creole from French, which requires a relative marker in both restrictive relative and cleft relative clauses. The other difference between the two languages regards the type of relative marker found: while French requires *qui* for clefts in which the clefted constituent is a subject in the cleft relative clause, and *ke* otherwise, Réunion Creole *ke* does not vary depending on the role of the clefted constituent in the cleft relative clause, but interacts with the finiteness marker *i* to give a surface form *ki*, if *ke* immediately precedes *i*. In the next section, I consider the *sé*-cleft construction in the broader picture of the grammar of Réunion Creole.

5 The *sé*-cleft as a focalisation strategy in Réunion Creole

The aim of this section is to situate the *sé*-cleft more broadly as a construction in the grammar of Réunion Creole and consider future directions concerning research into the syntax of focus in the language. The *sé*-cleft construction discussed in this article, and its comparable cross-linguistic forms, is associated with a focalising function, and more specifically, that of narrow focus.[27] However, it is noted that clefts fulfil varying functions across different languages, and the frequency and function that clefts fulfil in a given language may depend on other properties of that language. In this section, I discuss the place of the *sé*-cleft as one available focalisation strategy amongst others in Réunion Creole. In this regard, I show that Réunion Creole patterns differently from its lexifier French and make an attempt at beginning to understand the syntax of focus in Réunion Creole, which is currently poorly understood.

Cleft constructions are thought to occur more often in (spoken) French than in other languages. According to Van Valin's (1999) typology of the interplay between focus structure and syntax, French is a language with both rigid focus structure

---

[27] Though other focus structure articulations have been identified for *c'est*-clefts, *it*-clefts and comparable clefts in other languages (e.g. Prince 1978; Karssenberg and Lahousse 2018, and others).

and rigid word order. The cleft is a construction that allows several constraints in French to be satisfied (Lambrecht 2001; Van Valin 1999). Preverbal focus is highly restricted in French, thus, if a speaker wants to emphasise the subject of a sentence, they often resort to a cleft construction. Belletti (2005) argues that French even prefers a (reduced) cleft in response to subject-constituent WH-questions, illustrated in (39).

(39) A: *Qui est parti?*
 who be.3SG leave.PST.PTCP
 'Who left?'
 B: *C'est Jean (qui est parti)*
 it-be.3SG Jean who be.3SG leave.PST.PTCP
 It's Jean (who left).
 (Belletti 2005: 1)

The constraint against preverbal focus in French also means that the language does not generally permit focus fronting, a strategy which is reportedly found more often in other Romance languages such as Spanish, illustrated in (40).

(40) *A Esteban invitaron*[28] Spanish
 ACC Esteban invite.PST.3PL
 'It was Esteban that they invited.'
 (Cruschina and Remberger 2017: 503)

Focus fronting in these Romance languages is thought to be largely restricted to contrastive focus (Cruschina and Remberger 2017). Where other Romance languages exhibit focus fronting, French reportedly prefers clefting (Belletti 2005).[29] However, several authors have argued that focus fronting is indeed possible in French, but under stricter conditions (e.g. De Cat 2007; Cruschina and Remberger 2017).

---

[28] Julio Villa-García's comments highlight that the acceptability of this sentence may vary between varieties of Spanish. For him, this sentence is odd; a left dislocated structure would be preferred:

(v) *A Esteban, lo invitaron.*
 ACC Esteban 3SG invite.PST.PL
 'Esteban, we invited him.'

[29] According to some authors (e.g. É.Kiss 1998), contrastive focus (also known as corrective focus), is distinct from information focus. Both signal the presence of alternatives in a given context, but in the latter, that set of alternatives is an open set, while in the former, there is one single alternative (Cruschina and Remberger 2017). Note that other authors, such as Lambrecht, do not distinguish between these two types of focus.

In the remainder of this section, I show that preverbal focus is undoubtedly permitted in Réunion Creole and argue that the language therefore patterns more freely in regard to focus structure than its lexifier. Firstly, I found preverbal focus in the corpus, where a constituent in focus is followed by a focus particle *minm*, as illustrated by example (41).

(41) Episa néna la kour dérièr ek le boukan... atér
then have the court behind with the cabin ground
-la **minm** zot i resoi le moun
DEM FOC 3PL FIN recieve the people
'Then there's the courtyard behind with the cabin...THERE they receive guests.' (Magazine)

Focus fronting was also accepted in interviews: example (42a), in which the focal object appears in non-canonical position at the front of the clause, was accepted in the same context as the cleft construction in (42b). For two of the six speakers asked, the addition of the focus particle *minm* is obligatory, but for the remaining four, it is optional.

(42) a. Ali (minm) mwin la vi!
3SG.FOC FOC 2SG PRF see
'HIM I saw!'
b. Sé (a)li (ke) mwin la vi![30]
COP 3SG REL 1SG PRF see
'It's HIM that I saw!'

During an interview, an informant also offered example (43), exhibiting focus fronting with the focus particle *minm*.

(43) Kisa li té sa war yèr? Azot minm li sa invité
who 3SG IPFV go see yesterday 3PL FOC 3SG go invite
'Who was he going to see yesterday? THEM he's going to invite.'

These examples indicate that Réunion Creole has an alternative focalisation strategy available – focus fronting with (or without) a focus particle *minm* – alongside the *sé*-cleft construction.

---

30 Versions of this cleft sentence with the 3SG pronoun in its long form (*ali*) and short form (*li*) were both accepted. When the pronoun is fronted as in (42a), the long form is required.

Finally, Réunion Creole does not seem to require a (reduced) cleft in response to a subject-constituent WH-question. In interviews, in response to a subject-constituent WH-question like (44a), three of the seven informants produced a sentence with canonical word order like that in(44b), three produced a cleft like that in (44c), and one produced the response in (44d), which contains a reduced cleft followed by a sentence with canonical word order.[31]

(44) a. *Kisa i sava Boukan Kanot?*
    who FIN go Boucan Canot
    'Who is going to *Boucan Canot* beach?'
  b. *Noémi sava Boukan Kanot.*
    Noémie go Boucan Canot
    'Noémie is going to *Boucan Canot*.'
  c. *Sé Noémi i sava Boukan Kanot.*
    COP Noémie FIN go Boucan Canot
    'It's Noémie who is going to *Boucan Canot*.'
  d. *Sé Noémi, Noémi i sava Boukan Kanot.*
    COP Noémie Noémie FIN go Boucan Canot
    'It's Noémie, Noémie is going to Boucan Canot.'

The variety of responses exemplifies the variation that exists in Réunion Creole: preferences could be speaker-dependent (and those producing the cleft structure may be influenced by French) or reflect different varieties of Réunion Creole (cf. section 2). Overall though, the Réunion Creole examples presented in this section indicate that the language is less constrained regarding the possible positions of focus in the sentence than French is reported to be, and word order may be freer in Réunion Creole than it is in French, since the fronting of an object constituent for focalising was found in the corpus and accepted by all informants. Since focus fronting is reported to be highly constrained in French, yet still possible (cf. De Cat 2007; Cruschina and Remberger 2017 and references therein), a detailed comparison of the availability of this focalisation strategy in the two languages would be an interesting avenue for future research.

The combination of rigid word order and rigid focus structure in French is described as a factor contributing to the high occurrence of cleft constructions in that language, given that cleft constructions allow preverbal focus to be avoided.

---

[31] Between interviews, there were minor variations in the questions asked, i.e. a different name (e.g. 'Romain' rather than 'Noémie') or beach (e.g. 'Grande Anse' rather than 'Boucan Canot'), and hence slightly different responses, but with the structures exhibited in the examples in (44).

However, Dufter (2009) argues that the (un)availability of other focalisation strategies in French is sometimes overstated as an explanation for the high frequency of clefts in the language, as focus marking is not their only function. This point is also supported by corpus studies which have found that the typical narrow-focus structure articulation associated with *c'est*-clefts is not always found (see, for example, Karssenberg 2018; Karssenberg & Lahousse 2018). Indeed, despite the observation that Réunion Creole seems freer in regard to its focus structure and its word order, the *sé*-cleft appears to be a fairly common focalising strategy, judging from the corpus and the acceptability of cleft constructions. When accounting for different frequencies of clefts found in the Romance languages, De Cesare (2017: 546) reminds us of the importance of other factors such as language contact phenomena too. This is one very important consideration in the case of Réunion Island, where Réunion Creole is in extremely close contact with French, and indeed has French as a source language. On this note, De Cesare (2017: 561) signals the need for empirical research on French clefts outside of France. Indeed, we cannot assume that the patterns of cleft usage in Réunion French pattern in the same manner as that of European varieties of French (which they themselves may pattern differently).

In this section, I have argued that Réunion Creole is freer than French in regard to its word order and focus structure. In particular, Réunion Creole does clearly permit preverbal focus, and has an alternative strategy for exhibiting argument focus: a focus fronting strategy (with or without focus particle *minm*).

6 Conclusion

This article has provided the first detailed description of the structure of *sé*-cleft constructions in Réunion Creole. It has provided evidence that Réunion Creole has two copulas: *sé* and *lé*. While the latter is more frequently recognised in general descriptions of the language, this article has argued that *sé* is indeed a copula, rather than a focusing particle, since it carries temporal inflection. *Sé* occurs as the preferred copula in narrow focus cleft constructions but is also attested in other copular constructions in the language, notably in identifying and specifying copular constructions. Given that *sé* is analysed as a copula, I argued that *sé* focus constructions both with and without a relative marker are variants of the same narrow focus cleft construction. Taking a comparative approach, this article has highlighted where the *sé*-cleft differs from the comparable cleft construction of its lexifier, French, and of other creole languages with the same lexifier. The most striking difference, where Réunion Creole appears to be unique among the French creoles, is in preferably omitting a relative marker in its subject cleft relative clauses. While Réunion Creole prefers locative marker *ou(sa)* over *ke* in its locative restrictive relative clauses, the reverse is true of locative cleft relative clauses, highlighting that the two relative clause types exhibit morphosyntactic differences in this language.

In addition to providing a detailed investigation of the structure of the *sé*-cleft, this article has begun to address the syntax of focus in a broader perspective in Réunion Creole. I have claimed that Réunion Creole is more flexible than French regarding its word order and the possible positions of focus in the sentence: Réunion Creole permits preverbal focus more freely than French, and the canonical SVO word order of predicate focus may be altered as a result. In order to further this understanding of the interplay between focus structure and syntax in Réunion Creole, I suggest a detailed comparison of the distribution of competing focalisation strategies in the language for future research.

References

Albers, Ulrike. 2019. *Le syntagme nominal en créole réunionnais: forme et interprétation*. Marseilles: Université d'Aix-Marseille PhD dissertation.

Albers, Ulrike. 2020. A description of bare noun phrases in Reunion Creole. *Journal of Pidgin and Creole Languages* 35(1). 1–36.

Armand, Alain. 2014. *Dictionnaire kréol rénioné-français*. 2nd edn. Saint André: Epica Editions.

Baude, Olivier (compiler). 2010. *Corpus de la parole*. Edited by Délégation générale à la langue française et aux langues de France & Institut de linguistique Française & Typologie et universaux linguistiques. Retrieved from the platform COCOON, http://purl.org/poi/crdo.vjf.cnrs.fr/cocoon-fd48c512-26d0-3bd3-b02b-4ae995285d05. (accessed 19 December 2019).

Belletti, Adriana. 2005. Answering with a cleft. The role of the null subject parameter and the vP periphery. In Laura Brugé, Giuliana Giusti, Nicola Munaro, Walter Schweikert & Giuseppina Turano (eds.), *Proceedings of the XXX Incontro di Grammatica Generativa*, 63–82. Venice: Cafoscarina.

Bentley, Delia. 2017. Copular and existential constructions. In Andreas Dufter & Elisabeth Stark (eds.), *Manual of Romance morphosyntax and syntax*, 332–366. Berlin/Boston: De Gruyter Mouton.

Bollée, Annegret. 2013. Reunion Creole. In Susanne Maria Michaelis, Philippe Maurer, Martin Haspelmath & Magnus Huber (eds.), *Atlas of pidgin and creole language structures online*. Leipzig: Max Planck Institute for Evolutionary Anthropology. http://apics-online.info/contributions/54 (accessed 4 June 2020).

Büring, Daniel. 2010. Towards a typology of focus realization. In Malte Zimmerman, & Caroline Féry (eds.), *Information structure: Theoretical, typological, and experimental perspectives*, 177–205. Oxford: Oxford University Press.

Chaudenson, Robert. 1974. *Le lexique du parler créole de la Réunion*. Paris: Librairie Ancienne Honoré Champion.

Collins, Peter. 1991. *Cleft and pseudo-cleft constructions in English*. London: Routledge.

Corne, Chris. 1995. Nana k nana, nana k napa: The paratactic and hypotactic relative clauses of Reunion Creole. *Journal of Pidgin and Creole Languages* 10(1). 57–76.

Corne, Chris. 1999. *From French to Creole: The development of new vernaculars in the French colonial world*. London: University of Westminster Press.

Cougnon, Louise-Amélie. 2012. *L'écrit sms. Variations lexicale et syntaxique en francophonie*. Louvain-la-Neuve: Université Catholique de Louvain PhD dissertation.

Cozier, Franz K. 2006. The co-occurrence of predicate clefting and wh-questions in Trinidad dialectal English. *Natural Language & Linguistic Theory* 24(3). 655–688.

Cruschina, Silvio & Eva-Maria Remberger. 2017. Focus fronting. In Andreas Dufter & Elisabeth Stark (eds.), *Manual of Romance morphosyntax and syntax*, 502–535. Berlin/Boston: De Gruyter Mouton.

De Cat, Cécile. 2007. *French dislocation: Interpretation, syntax, acquisition*. Oxford: Oxford University Press.

De Cesare, Anna-Maria. 2017. Cleft constructions. In Andreas Dufter & Elisabeth Stark (eds.), *Manual of Romance morphosyntax and syntax*, 536–568. Berlin/Boston: de Gruyter Mouton.

de Rooij, Vincent. 1994. Variation. In Jacques Arends, Pieter Muysken & Norval Smith (eds.), *Pidgins and creoles: An introduction*, 53–64. Amsterdam/Philadelphia: John Benjamins Publishing Company.

Declerck, Renaat. 1988. *Studies on copular sentences, clefts, and pseudo-clefts*. Leuven: Leuven University Press.

DeGraff, Michel. 2004. Against creole exceptionalism. *Language* 80(4). 834–839.

DeGraff, Michel. 2007. Haitian Creole. In John Holm & Peter Patrick (eds.), *Comparative creole syntax: Parallel outlines of 18 creole grammars*, 101–126. London: Battlebridge Publications.

Dufter, Andreas. 2008. On explaining the rise of "*c'est*"-clefts in French. In Ulrich Detges & Richard Waltereit (eds.), *The paradox of grammatical change: Perspectives from Romance*, 31–56. Amsterdam/Philadelphia: John Benjamins.

Dufter, Andreas. 2009. Clefting and discourse organization: Comparing Germanic and Romance. In Andreas Dufter & Daniel Jacob (eds.), *Focus and background in Romance languages*, 83–121. Amsterdam/Philadelphia: John Benjamins.

Féry, Caroline & Shinichiro Ishihara. 2009. How focus and givenness shape prosody. In Malte Zimmermann & Caroline Féry (eds.), *Information structure: Theoretical, typological, and experimental perspectives*, 36–63. Oxford: Oxford University Press.

Gaze, Laetitia. 2019. *Le préverbe i en créole réunionnais: étude de syntaxe comparée*. La Réunion : Université de La Réunion PhD dissertation.

Gürer, Asli. 2020. Prosodic marking of focus. In Asli Gürer (ed.), *Information structure within interfaces: Consequences for the phrase structure*, 83139. Boston/Berlin: de Gruyter Mouton.

Hill, Virginia. 2017. Restrictive relative clauses in Acadian French. *Bucharest Working Papers in Linguistics* 20(2). 5–27.

Holm, John. 1988–89. *Pidgins and creoles*. 2 vols. Cambridge: Cambridge University Press.

Holm, John. 2004. *Languages in contact: The partial restructuring of vernaculars*. Cambridge: Cambridge University Press.

Huddleston, Rodney. 2002. The clause: Complements. In Rodney Huddleston & Jeffrey Pullum (eds.), *The Cambridge grammar of the English Language*, 213321. Cambridge: Cambridge University Press.

INSEE. 2021. La France et ses territoires. *INSEE Références*, Édition 2021. https://www.insee.fr/fr/statistiques/5040030 (accessed 23 August 2021).

Karssenberg, Lena. 2018. *Non-prototypical clefts in French: A corpus analysis of* il y a *clefts*. Berlin: de Gruyter Mouton.

Karssenberg, Lena & Karen Lahousse. 2018. The information structure of French *il y a* & *c'est* clefts: A corpus-based analysis. *Linguistics* 56(3). 513–548.

Kiss, Katalin É. 1998. Identificational focus versus informational focus. *Language* 74. 245–273.

Lahousse, Karen & Beatrice Lamiroy. 2012. Word order in French, Spanish and Italian: A grammaticalization account. *Folia Linguistica* 46. 1–29.

Lambrecht, Knud. 1994. *Information structure and sentence form: Topic, focus, and the mental representations of discourse referents*. Cambridge: Cambridge University Press.

Lambrecht, Knud. 2001. A framework for the analysis of cleft constructions. *Linguistics* 39. 463–516.

Ledegen, Gudrun. 2012. Prédicats « flottants » entre le créole acrolectal et le français à la Réunion: explorations d'une zone ambiguë. In Claudine Chamoreau & Laurence Goury (eds.), *Changement linguistique et langues en contact : approches plurielles du domaine prédicatif*, 251–270. Paris: CNRS Editions.

Lumsden, John S. & Claire Lefebvre. 1990. Predicate-cleft constructions and why they aren't what you might think. *Linguistics* 28. 761–782.

Maurer, Philippe & the APiCS Consortium. 2013. Focusing of the noun phrase. In Susanne Maria Michaelis, Philippe Maurer, Martin Haspelmath & Magnus Huber (eds.), *The atlas of pidgin and creole language structures*, 414–417. Oxford: Oxford University Press.

Michaelis, Susanne Maria, Martin Haspelmath & the APiCS Consortium. 2013. Subject relative clauses. In Susanne Maria Michaelis, Philippe Maurer, Martin Haspelmath & Magnus Huber (eds.), *The atlas of pidgin and creole language structures*, 366–369. Oxford: Oxford University Press.

McLellan, Alina. 2023. *Relative and cleft constructions in Kréol Rényoné*. Manchester: University of Manchester PhD dissertation.

Moseng Knutsen, Anne. 2009. Sociolinguistic variation in African French: The Ivorian relative clause. In Kate Beeching, Nigel Armstrong & Françoise Gadet (eds.), *Sociolinguistic variation in Contemporary French*, 159–175. Amsterdam/Philadelphia: John Benjamins Publishing Company.

Muysken, Pieter. 1977. Movement rules in Papiamentu. *Amsterdam Creole Studies 1*. 80–102.

Prince, Ellen F. 1978. A comparison of wh-clefts and *it*-clefts in discourse. *Language* 54(4). 883–906.

Quirk, Randolph, Sidney Greenbaum, Geoffrey Leech & Jan Svartik. 1985. *A Comprehensive grammar of the English language*. London: Longman.

Selkirk, Elisabeth. 1984. *Phonology and syntax: The relations between sound and structure*. Cambridge: MIT Press.

Selkirk, Elisabeth. 1995. Sentence prosody: Intonation, stress, and phrasing. In John Goldsmith (ed.), *Handbook of phonological theory*, 550–569. Oxford: Basil Blackwell.

Seuren, Pieter A.M. 1993. The question of predicate clefting in the Indian Ocean creoles. In Francis Byrne & Donald Winford (eds.), *Focus and grammatical relations in creole languages*, 53–64. Amsterdam/Philadelphia: John Benjamins.

Syea, Anand. 2017. *French creoles: A comprehensive and comparative grammar*. London/New York: Routledge.

Van Valin Jr., Robert D. 1999. A typology of the interactions of focus structure and syntax. In Ekaterina Raxilina & Jakov Testelec (eds.), *Typology and the theory of language: From description to explanation*, 511–524. Moscow: Languages of Russian Culture.

Van Valin Jr., Robert D. 2005. *Exploring the syntax-semantics interface*. Cambridge: Cambridge University Press.

Van Valin Jr., Robert D. 2008. *Investigations of the syntax-semantics-pragmatics interface*. Amsterdam & Philadelphia: John Benjamins.

Van Valin Jr., Robert D. & Randy J. LaPolla. 1997. *Syntax: Structure, meaning and function*. Cambridge: Cambridge University Press.

Watbled, Jean-Philippe. 2013. Le système verbal du créole réunionnais: principes syntaxiques et prosodiques. In Laurence Pourchez (ed.), *Créolité, créolisation : regards croisés*, 79–96. Paris : Archives contemporains.

Watbled, Jean-Phillippe. 2015. Les particularités morphosyntaxiques du créole réunionnais. *Etudes créoles*, 33 (2). https://hal.univ-reunion.fr/hal-01501112/document (accessed 20 June 2021).

Watbled, Jean-Philippe. 2018. Les langues créoles de l'océan Indien: propriétés spécifiques et propriétés universelles. Paper presented at *Définis-moi "l'Indianocéanie", Université de La Réunion, October 2018*. 153–169. https://hal.univ-reunion.fr/hal-03079505 (accessed 11 August 2021).

Wittmann, Henri & Robert Fournier. 1981. Bom sadek i bez li: la particule *i* en français. *Revue québécoise de linguistique théorique et appliquée*. 177–196.

Mara Marsella and Laura Tramutoli
8 (*It-*)clefts in Palenquero Creole and the specificational copula

Abstract: Palenquero Creole is a Caribbean Spanish-based creole spoken in San Basilio de Palenque (Colombia). It presents four overtly expressed copula forms: *ta* (lexically from Sp. *estar*) a locative copula; the forms *é (*or *era)* and *sendá*, which occur with both individual-level adjectival predicates and nominal predicates; and *jue* (lexically from Sp. < *fue*), which has the same functions as *é* and *sendá*, but works as a focus marker, too (section 2). This paper examines what distribution the copula forms of *é/era; jué; sendá* have within cleft-clauses. The authors approach this topic by analysing a corpus of primary data in addition to Friedemann and Patiño Rosselli (1983) and Maglia and Moñino's (2015) existing corpora (section 3). In particular, the authors show that the presence of the copula é or *sendá* can be attributed to sociolinguistic factors, namely the age of speakers. Lastly, the authors analyse peculiar *(it-)*cleft constructions in Palenquero. These allow a null subject in the main clause, exhibiting a high proximity to its pro-drop lexifier language (Spanish), while selecting the copula *jue* in the cleft clause (section 5). The last section of the paper (section 6) will highlight the writers' conclusions.

Keywords: Palenquero, *(it-)*clefts, copula system, specificational copula

1 Introduction

Despite the increasing documentation that Palenquero Creole (a Caribbean Spanish-based creole spoken in San Basilio de Palenque, Colombia (Figure 1)) has received over the past twenty years, many phenomena of the language have still not been thoroughly documented and analysed. This article aims to provide a better understanding of the copula system and the strategies for cleft-constructions by covering two central issues: the functions of copulas in relation to their compatibility and distribution within cleft clauses, and the role of *jue* as a marker of *(it-)*cleft constructions in Palenquero.

Mara Marsella, Università degli Studi "G. D'annunzio" Chieti-Pescara, e-mail: mara.marsella@unich.it, who is responsible for sections 3, 5 and 6.
Laura Tramutoli, University of Bologna, e-mail: laura.tramutoli@unibo.it, who is responsible for sections 1, 2 and 4.

https://doi.org/10.1515/9783110734140-009

This article is structured as follows: we provide some background information about copulas in Palenquero (section 2.1) and its focusing structures (section 2.2), and, after reporting about the collection and processing of primary data (section 3), we present the results for the distribution of copulas in pseudo-cleft sentences (section 4) and *it*-cleft sentences (section 5). We conclude (section 6) by arguing that the distribution of copula forms is determined by one main sociolinguistic parameter, i.e. the age of informants.

Figure 1: San Basilio de Palenque map.

2 Background

2.1 The copula system in Palenquero

Palenquero Creole has a complex system of copulas, constituted by all verbal elements, and all encoded by phonologically realised (overt) forms (Friedemann and Patiño Rosselli 1983, Schwegler and Green 2007, Maglia and Moñino 2015, Lipski 2020, Marsella (forthcoming)).[1]

---

[1] On zero-form copulas in Palenquero, cf. Schwegler and Green (2007: 288).

2.1.1 The copula é/era

The copula *é* lexically derives from the Spanish verb *ser* 'to be', and also retains some properties of the latter: it occurs with individual-level adjectival predicates (1a) and before nominal predicates (1b), as well as in locative sentences with a "second-order entity" subject.

(1) Palenquero; copula *é*
(1.a.) *Ese   é   kuento pa   hende   trarisioná ri   to   suto.*
       DEM   COP tale   for   people traditional of   all   1PL
       'This is a tale for all the traditional people, like us.'
(1.b) *Suto   é   jarocho   akí.*
       1PL   COP cheerful here
       'We are cheerful people here.'

É is used only in present-tense sentences, while its variant *era*, which derives from (and is phonologically identical to) the Spanish third-person singular imperfective past inflected form *era* occurs in imperfective past sentences in Palenquero.

Both *é* and *era* cannot be preceded by any TMA preverbal particle (Schwegler and Green 2007: 288; Lipski 2020: 74–75).

2.1.2 The copula *jue*

Jue derives from the Spanish third person singular preterite inflected form *fue* and is generally used in perfective past sentences (2a) with both nominal and individual-level adjectival predicates. Lewis (1970), Friedemann and Patiño Rosselli (1983: 130), Maglia and Moñino (2015: 88) and Lipski (2020: 75) argue that *jue* may also be used without a past meaning, namely as an equivalent morpheme to *é* (2b).

(2) Palenquero; copula *jue*
(2.a) *Pambelé   jue   un   trumpiaró   ri   boxeo.*
       Pambelé COP   a   fighter   of   box
       'Pamebelé was a boxer.'
(2.b) *Ñeke   jue   ron   má   sabroso   loke   ten.*
       Ñeke COP   rum   more   tasty   COMP   have
       'Ñeke is the best rum they have.'

This copula cannot be preceded by any TMA preverbal particle (Schwegler and Green 2007: 288), but instances of its occurrence with the imperfect marker *-ba* are common (Swearingen Davis 2001).

2.1.3 The copula *sendá*

Sendá derives from the Spanish verb *sentarse* 'to sit'. According to Escalante (1979) and Friedemann and Patiño Rosselli (1983: 131–132) it is the copula with the lowest frequency of occurrence in Palenquero. It is still not clear what functional difference distinguishes *sendá* from *é* (and *era* and *jue*), as both appear with nominal and adjectival predicates in equative sentences (Schwegler and Green 2007: 288–289; Lipski 2020: 76; Gutiérrez Maté 2017: 22) (3). Specifically, *sendá* occurs with referential and non-referential nominal complements, and with individual-level adjectival predicates. It occurs as a bare morpheme in present-tense sentences, it can be preceded by TMA particles and followed by the imperfective suffix *-ba*. *Sendá* can be combined with the preverbal perfective marker *a*, without necessarily conveying a past tense meaning (Moñino 1999; Schwegler and Green 2007).

(3) Palenquero; copula *sendá*
    Si e   (a)ke-ba eturiá, e   (a)ké sendá un rodtó.
    If 3SG IRR-ba study 3SG IRR   COP   a   doctor
    'If I had studied, today I would be a doctor.'
    (Friedemann and Patiño Rosselli 1983: 181)

2.2 Focusing constructions in Palenquero

Other than a handful of references to Palenquero's highlighter copulas in Friedemann and Patiño Rosselli (1983: 179) and Schwegler and Green (2007: 289–290), the first research entirely dedicated to focus constructions is Gutiérrez Maté (2017). Notably, the aim of his work is to describe all the possible focus constructions in Palenquero (including clefts, pseudo-clefts and inverse pseudo-clefts) where, according to the author, only the copula *jue* – and less frequently the form *é* – is selected as the exclusive focus particle. The author also provides a key hypothesis concerning the Kikongo influence on the formation of the focus marker *jue*.

As for the structural physiognomy of focalisation mechanisms in Palenquero, the author recognises three main types of sentence containing the highlighters *jue* and *é* (Gutiérrez Maté 2017: 14–15), distinguishing among clefts, pseudo-clefts and inverse pseudo-clefts.

Palenquero's clefts are introduced by the focus marker *jue* (or *é*) (FOC) and the focused element (FE), followed by a pseudo-relative clause (PSR) – introduced by the relativizer *loke*[2] – defined by Heine and Reh (1984) as "out-of-focus" (4).

---

2 As for the relativizer introducing the pseudo-relative clause, following the Spanish pattern, Palenquero's focusing constructions (i.e. clefts, pseudo-clefts and inverse pseudo-cleft) do not contain the generic relative pronoun *ke* (< Sp. *que*) (De Cesare 2014: 26), as these sentences resort to the complementizer *loke* (< Sp. *lo que*, also present in Spanish light-headed relative clauses in the sense of Citko (2004)). Examples of Standard Spanish clefts, pseudo-clefts and inverse pseudo-clefts are presented in *(i)*, *(ii)* and *(iii)*, respectively. As can be noted, the examples in *(i)*, *(ii)* and *(iii)* exhibit the same order of the three main units constituting the focalising constructions (i.e. FOC, FE and PSR) in Palenquero as in the corresponding sentences (4)–(6).

(i) Spanish cleft
Fueron	*las*	*llaves*	*lo que*	*perdió*	*Juan.*
COP.PAST.3PL	DET	keys	REL	loose.PAST.3SG	Juan
FOC	FE		PSR		

'It was the keys that Juan lost.' (Pinedo 2000: 130)

(ii) Spanish pseudo-cleft
Lo que	*perdió*	*Juan*	*fueron*	*las*	*llaves.*
REL	Loose.PAST.3SG	Juan	COP.PAST.3PL	DET	keys
PSR			FOC	FE	

'What Juan lost was the keys.' (Pinedo 2000: 131)

(iii) Spanish inverse pseudo-cleft
Eso	*fue*	*lo que*	*perdió*	*Juan.*
DET	COP.PAST.3SG	REL	loose.PAST.3SG	Juan
FE	FOC	PSR		

'That's what Juan lost.' (Pinedo 2000: 131)

It is worth noting that Standard Spanish differs from other languages – such as English, Italian or French – in the way it introduces the pseudo-relative in clefts; in fact, while English selects the relativizer *that* in the same way that Italian and French respectively employ the forms *che/que* 'that', in Spanish the pseudo-relative is introduced by a more complex item, *lo que*, made up of the neuter 3SG article *lo* 'the' and the relativizer *que* (De Cesare 2014: 25–26). On the other hand, while in Spanish *lo que* introduces the pseudo-relative also in pseudo-clefts and in inverse pseudo-cleft constructions, English, Italian and French select a WH-word – i.e. *what, which, who, where* (see Collins 1991).

(4) Cleft
    Jue   fiebre mala loke kaí mi.
    COP   fever   bad   REL   fall 1SG
    FOC   FE   PSR
    'It was a severe temperature that I had.'
    (Gutiérrez Maté 2017: 14; translation mine)

Pseudo-clefts in Palenquero are introduced by *loke* and a pseudo-relative clause, followed by the focus marker and the focused item (5).

(5) Pseudo-cleft
    Loke nu   a   traé   machete jue ma uto.
    REL   NEG PFV bring machete COP PL other
    PSR   FOC FE
    'The ones who did not bring a machete were the others.'
    (Gutiérrez Maté 2017: 14; translation mine)

Inverse pseudo-clefts, instead, are introduced by the focused element, followed by the focus marker, the relativizer *loke* and the pseudo-relative clause (6).

(6) Inverse pseudo-cleft
    E   jue   loke suto tené <de último>.
    3SG COP REL   1PL   have last
    FE   FOC PSR
    'He is the one (=*the son*) we had last.'
    (Gutiérrez Maté 2017: 14; translation mine)

These three sentential types parallel typical Standard Spanish focus sentences, exhibiting the same sentential collocation of the focus marker, of the focused element, and of the pseudo-relative clause (Gutiérrez-Bravo 2019). Furthermore, Gutiérrez Maté (2017) described two other types of focus constructions in Palenquero - see the examples in (7) and (8) -, with the same structure of sentences in (5) and (6) respectively, but showing the omission of the relativizer *loke*.

(7) Pseudo-cleft with the relative marker *loke* omitted
   Suto   ase   asé má   bien   é   losa.
   1PL   HAB   do   more good   COP   farming
   PSR (Ø REL)   FOC   FE
   '(What) we do best is farming.'
   (Gutiérrez Maté 2017: 15; translation mine)

(8) Inverse pseudo-cleft with the relative marker *loke* omitted
   Lengua   jue   i   ta   ablá.
   Palenquero COP   1SG   PROG   speak
   FE   FOC   PSR (Ø REL)
   'Palenquero is (what) I am speaking.'
   (Gutiérrez Maté 2017: 15; translation mine)

The main difference, again, is the absence of the relativizer *loke* not introducing the pseudo-relative; it is a typical syntactic feature of some non-standard Spanish varieties and dialects, including Colombian Spanish (Curnow and Travis 2004), (9).

(9) Pseudo-cleft with relative marker omitted in Colombian Spanish
   Ella   está   estudiando   es   derecho,   ¿no?
   3SG   AUX   studying   COP   law   not
   PSR (Ø REL)   FOC   FE
   'She's studying (is) law, isn't she?'
   (Curnow and Travis 2004)

The research by Gutiérrez Maté (2017), however, does not consider the occurrence of the innovative copula *sendá* in constructions with a similar informative-pragmatic organisation.

3 Data

In addition to the data reported in Friedemann and Patiño Rosselli (1983) and Maglia and Moñino (2015), the corpus used for the purposes of the present research was built through a semi-structured sociolinguistic inquiry.

A total of 36 speakers were interviewed in total, specifically: i) 12 young speakers aged between 12 and 20; ii) 12 adult speakers aged between 30 and 45; iii) 12 older traditional speakers aged 60 and above. More specifically, young members of the community are L1 Spanish speakers (the local variety of Colombian coastal Spanish) and L2 Palenquero speakers, as they learnt the Creole at school thanks to the revitalization programmes enhanced by the Colombian government to promote Palenque's language, culture and traditions. In this sense, they can be categorised as *heritage speakers* (Polinsky 2016: 325) as they recognize the school as the place where they learnt more about Palenquero. Adults, by contrast, are fully Spanish-Palenquero bilinguals, who preferred to speak Spanish at the expense of the Creole for much of their lives as a consequence of the strong stigmatisation they suffered during the '70s as Afro-descendants.[3] Older speakers are fully bilingual with a high competence of both Spanish and Palenquero, and for this reason considered as "traditional" Palenquero proficient.

The answers were collected and recorded *in loco* with the collaboration of a leader of the community during the summer of 2020.

Two questionnaires – qualitatively identical – were organised into two parts: a first section required the translation of 15 sentences (cleft, pseudo-clefts, and inverse pseudo-clefts) from Spanish into Palenquero.

A second assignment with an opposite goal (the translation of Palenquero sentences into Spanish) required the translation of 15 focus sentences where all the copular morphemes of the rich Palenquero paradigm (viz. *é, era, jue, sendá*) were selected.

Every translation task alternated with random clauses (to be translated from Spanish into Palenquero and vice versa) which did not show specific syntactic marked constructions with a dislocated thematic element or a Topic-Comment redistribution, as a mean to overcome unconscious priming effects.

---

3 As reported by Friedemann and Patiño (1983:189–190) after a fieldwork trip during the '70s, Palenqueros used to shun conversations in Creole, especially outside the village, as their speech was heavily stigmatised and subjected to scorn and derision. As their language was the reflection of their ancestry and African roots of which they were ashamed, the intergenerational transmission of the Creole was interrupted, and adult Palenqueros did not pass on the Creole to their children and younger residents. Reporting the sociolinguistic scenario of the village during the '90s, Schwegler (1996, v.1:42, 2001:412) pointed out that, whereas older residents of Palenque exhibited a full bilingualism Spanish/Palenquero, the youngest possessed a minimal knowledge of the Creole and a superficial understanding of the most typical expressions, displaying a monolingual competence. In this regard, identical considerations are found in Pfeiderer (1998) as well as in Moñino (2002).

Nevertheless, in the last twenty years the ethnic education programme promoted by the Colombian government encouraged children and young students of the village to learn Palenquero at school as a L2. Many teachers and other leaders of the community have been proactively involved in the language revitalization programme, with the aim of halting and reversing the extinction of Palenquero.

4 Results: The distribution of copulas in cleft-sentences

4.1 Pseudo-clefts

In regard to pseudo-clefts (ex.: [*what we are going to build here] is a football field*), the data collected show that the copula *é* (and its variants), the copula *jue*, and the copula *sendá* are both used in these constructions. In particular, the alternation of the first two copulas and the copula *sendá* finds an explanation in sociolinguistic variation, matching the difference between the age groups of the older and younger informants, as proposed in Marsella (forthcoming) for the general use of copulas in Palenquero.

Indeed, we can see a clear distinction in the copula form selected by the oldest group of informants and that preferred by adults and younger speakers. When asked to translate sentences containing pseudo-clefts from Spanish to Palenquero, the first group (traditional speakers) generally chose *é* and its variants (sometimes phonetically closer to the Spanish inflected forms of *ser*, but still referable to the paradigm of *é*). Another option for this group of informants is *jue*, which is the preferred choice when the past copula *fue* is present in Spanish sentences to which it is phonetically closer. All these copulas seem to have a free distribution in the speech of older traditional informants.

Table 1 summarises the results for selected copulas in four representative Spanish sentences[4] by five informants of the traditional old speakers' group.[5]

In the sentences where speakers produced a copula, the values for *é* and *jué* are almost equal in frequency, and not much can be said about the ratio of their distribution. In contrast, it can be indeed observed that old speakers do not use *sendá*, which is systematically present in sentences translated by adult or young speakers.

---

4 The sentences are representative of a diversely inflected copula *ser* in Spanish (at least for tense, aspect, person).
5 In the tables, *x* refers to elicited information other than a copula (i.e. elicited via other linguistic means other than a copula), while ? refers to non-performed task of elicitation by the speakers.

Table 1: Copulas in pseudo-clefts by traditional old speakers.

Pseudo-cleft sentence in Spanish	Copulas in Palenquero					
	Inf.[6]1	Inf.2	Inf.3	Inf.4	Inf.5	Inf.6
1. Lo que construiremos aquí será un campo de fútbol.	x	é	x	?	é	x
2. Todo lo que sabemos sobre la mohana son pocas leyendas.	x	é	son	é	é	x
3. Lo que las mujeres venden son enyukados, caballitos y alegrías.	x	x	x	jue	é	x
4. A quien premiaron fue Pambelé.	jue	jue	x	jue	jue	x

In fact, when the same sentences are presented to informants from the adults' and young speakers' groups, the copula is predominantly encoded by the *sendá* form. Tables 2 and 3 summarise the results for the same sentences presented in Table 1, respectively for these other age groups.

Table 2: Copulas in pseudo-clefts by adult speakers.

Pseudo-cleft sentence in Spanish	Copulas in Palenquero					
	Inf.1	Inf.2	Inf.3	Inf.4	Inf.5	Inf.6
1. Lo que construiremos aquí será un campo de fútbol.	a sendá	a sendá	a sendá	a sé-ba?	sendá	a sendá
2. Todo lo que sabemos sobre la mohana son pocas leyendas.	a sendá	a sendá	a sendá	a sendá	a sendá	a sendá
3. Lo que las mujeres venden son enyukados, caballitos y alegrías.	jue	a sendá	a sendá	a sendá	jue	a sendá
4. A quien premiaron fue Pambelé.	a sendá	a sendá	jue	jue	jue	a sendá

Differences occur between the use of the copulas found in the two age groups. Although adult speakers and younger speakers use *sendá*[7] on most occasions, with or without an additional TMA marker, *jue* is also used with no other marker when a past tense is required by the original sentence.

---

6 Inf. stands here for informant.
7 The *a sendá* form reported in the Tables 2, 3 and 5 is a past form, constituted by *a* (past/perfective marker) + *sendá*.

Table 3: Copulas in pseudo-clefts by young speakers.

Pseudo-cleft sentence in Spanish	Copulas in Palenquero					
	Inf.1	Inf.2	Inf.3	Inf.4	Inf.5	Inf.6
1. Lo que construiremos aquí será un campo de fútbol.	a sendá	a sendá	será	será	sendá	é
2. Todo lo que sabemos sobre la mohana son pocas leyendas.	a sendá	a sendá	a sendá	sendá	a sendá	son
3. Lo que las mujeres venden son enyukados, caballitos y alegrías.	a sendá	a sendá	a sendá	jue	a sendá	a sendá
4. A quien premiaron fue Pambelé.	a sendá	a sendá	jue	jue	jue	jue

Not only do these data confirm that *sendá* is mainly used in the speech of newer generations, they also demonstrate that, from a grammatical point of view, *sendá* fills the functions that in the traditional speakers' competence are realised by two different copula forms, namely *é* and *jue*, without producing a significant shift or reanalysis of meaning.

4.2 Inverse pseudo-clefts

The third type of clefts discussed in §3, e.g. inverse pseudo-clefts (such as in 6.; ex.: *[He/this/this one is] the son we had last*), show the same sociolinguistically motivated alternation that is featured in regular pseudo-clefts.

While old traditional speakers select *é* and *jue* as copula, adult speakers introduce *sendá* systematically and use it in the same contexts as the former. Tables 4 and 5 show the copula forms chosen in the translation of three sentences with inverse pseudo-cleft structures by speakers of the older traditional and adults groups, respectively.

Table 4: Copulas in inverse pseudo-clefts by old traditional speakers.

Inverse pseudo-clefts in Spanish	Inf.1	Inf.2	Inf.3	Inf.4	Inf.5	Inf.6
1. El que siempre llega tarde es Juan.	x	é	é	é	x	x
2. La que me gusta más es la carne a la Catalina Luango.	x	x	jue	é	x	x
3. El hombre representado por la estatua es Pambelé.	x	jue	é	é	x	x

Table 5: Copulas in inverse pseudo-clefts by adult speakers.

Inverse pseudo-clefts in Spanish	Inf.1	Inf.2	Inf.3	Inf.4	Inf.5	Inf.6
1. *El que siempre llega tarde es Juan.*	a sendá	a sendá	a sendá	a sendá	a sendá	x
2. *La que me gusta más es la carne a la Catalina Luango.*	a sendá	x	a sendá	a sendá	x	x
3. *El hombre representado por la estatua es Pambelé.*	a sendá	a sendá	a sendá	a sendá	a sendá	x

The copula "innovation" is visible in this case too. Unfortunately, no data about inverse pseudo-clefts for the young speakers' groups are available in our corpus. However, if we had to relate this feature to data on pseudo-clefts (previous section) and more generally on copulas, we predict that *sendá* in inverse pseudo-clefts is also the preferred choice for younger speakers.

5 (*It-*)cleft sentences pro-drop parameter

In addition to pseudo-clefts and inverse pseudo-clefts, another focus strategy in Palenquero are *(it-)*cleft clauses. These involve a marked biclausal structure, which places a specific element in a focus position following the template in Table 6.

Table 6: *(It-)*cleft structure.

(*It-*)cleft construction			
It	is	money	that he wants.
(cleft pronoun)	COP	NP	REL
FOC		FE	PSR
(focus)		(focused element)	(pseudo-relative clause)

In these sentences, the semantic role of the proleptic cleft pronoun[8] is controversial. Some linguists believe that it is provided with referential power (*extra positional approach*, Bolinger 1972; Gundel 1977, among others), while others treat it as a dummy and pleonastic expletive element semantically inert and void (*expletive approach*, Heggie 1988; Lambrecht 2001).

---

[8] Always overtly expressed in non-pro-drop languages such as English *it*, German *es*, Dutch *het*, French *ce*.

From a syntactic perspective, the presence or the omission of the cleft pronoun in such sentential constructions varies cross-linguistically. Unlike English, German, Dutch and French, pro-drop languages such as Italian, Spanish and Portuguese do not employ a cleft pronoun in similar focus constructions: the clause is introduced by the copula (FOC), followed by the focused item (FE) and the pseudo-relative clause (PSR),[9] and the matrix subject of the cleft coincides with an inflectional morpheme (Lambrecht 2001:464; De Cesare 2014:16–17), (10a).

(10) [+ pro-drop]
(10.a) Spanish
Es   este   coche el que compré.
COP.PRES.3SG DEM car   COMP   buy.PAST.1SG
'It is this car that I bought.' (Pinedo 2000: 131)

In creole languages, nine noun focalising strategies have been identified (see Maurer 2013 for a comprehensive outline). Notably, creoles featuring the construction displayed in Table 6 may be characterised by a cleft pronoun introducing the focus clause and preceding the copular item (11a). It is common in Kriol, Ghanaian Pidgin English, Singaporean English, and it was typical in Negerhollands too.

(11) [- pro-drop]
(11.a) Ghanaian Pidgin English
Ì   bì   dɛm   we   dè   kam   briŋ   dɛ   blaŋkɛs.
3SG COP 3PL   COMP 3PL come   bring DET blanket.PL
'It was them who brought the blankets.' (Huber 1999: 196)

In similar focus clauses, other creole languages do not select a cleft pronoun before the copula forming the focus. Most of them are Ibero-Romance creoles (see the cases of Papiamentu, Zamboanga Chabacano, Cape Verdean Creole). Some English-based contact languages – such as Bahamian Creole or Trinidad English Creole – do not select a cleft pronoun in the preliminary focus section of the construction (12).

---

9 Thus, the label *(it-)*cleft is not appropriate for pro-drop languages since these languages are not opened by any form of pronoun (De Cesare 2014:16).

(12) [+ pro-drop]
(12.a) Cape Verdean Creole (Santiago)
Ø Ê   nha   pai   ki   fase-l.
Ø COP POSS father REL do-3SG
'It was my father who did it.' (Baptista 2006)

(12.b) Trinidad English Creole
Ø Is   John to buy papers today.
Ø COP John to buy papers today
'It is John who is supposed to buy the papers today.' (Solomon 1993:77)

5.1 (It-)clefts in Palenquero

Among the several copular morphemes constituting the Palenquero copula system (§2), results of the investigation show that the form *jue* is the only copular morpheme selected in cleft constructions with a structure as the one presented in Table 6.

Specifically, Palenquero exhibits a [+ pro-drop] value – as the cleft-pronoun in the focus section of the clause is omitted (13) – coherently with the structure of *(it-)*cleft clauses in its lexifier (10).

(13) *Jue* in cleft sentences [+ pro-drop]
Ø   Jue   betia mi   animá   loke nguta   ma   Tatiana.
Ø   COP   horse POSS   animal REL   like   more Tatiana
FOC FE   PSR
'It was my horse Tatiana's favourite animal.'

Interestingly, as shown in §4, a sociolinguistic implication can be observed in the rendering of similar *(it-)*cleft focus constructions.

In fact, when asked to translate *(it-)*cleft clauses from Spanish to Palenquero, traditional older members of the community exhibited a strong tendency to omit the proleptic cleft pronoun (14).

(14) Traditional older speakers
SP.   >   PAL.
Era mi padre quien tenía los ojos > *Jue pae mi loke teneba ma ojo azú.*
azules.
'It was my father who had blue eyes.'

| SP. | > | PAL. |

Fue el mes pasado que decidí volver a la escuela. > *Jue mé pasao lok' i desidí bae andi ekuela.*

'It was last month when I decided to come back to school.'

Young members of the community – learners of Palenquero as an L2 – exhibited a different trend, as the translation of similar marked syntactic expressions from Spanish into Palenquero underwent significant changes in structural terms.

As in (15), the marked word order of the focalization strategy expressed through a canonical *(it-)*cleft is neutralised in Palenquero by L2 Palenquero speakers, who render the cleft as a non-marked clause with SVO word order, and – apparently – without resorting to any prosodic realisation which might evoke a focus marking.

Moreover, besides the neutralisation of the focalisation strategy, the copula selected is always the form *sendá*. In other words, the sociolinguistically-motivated alternation of the copular morphemes *é* (and its variants) and *sendá* is consistent with the trend shown in Tables 1–5, dedicated to pseudo-clefts and inverse pseudo-clefts.

(15) Young speakers

| SP. | > | PAL. |

Fue él quien hizo una buena acción. > *Ele a asé un kusa bueno.*

'It is him who did a good deed.'

| SP. | > | PAL. |

Fue mi tía la primera maestra de Palenquero aquí. > *Cha mi sendaba primó piacha ri Palenke.*

'It was my auntie the first Palenquero language teacher here.'

6 Conclusions

As marked syntactic constructions, cleft sentences express a pragmatic presupposition and have the function of structurally separating a discourse prominent constituent from the rest of the clause. Specifically, creole languages exhibit several focalisation strategies with a heterogeneous positioning of the syntactic constituents (e.g. FOC, FE, and PSR). The focus marker (FOC) can be formed by a copula or a focus particle, some creoles show bare clefts without a copular morpheme, others resort to *in situ* focusing mechanisms with an unmarked syntactic order. Moreover, the copula or the focus particle constituting the FOC is tendentially a single precise item in creole languages (see Holm and Patrick 2007 for a crosslinguistic comprehensive overview).

According to Schwegler and Green (2007: 289) and Gutiérrez Maté (2017) in Palenquero creole, the copula *jue* is always selected in clefts, pseudo-clefts, and inverse pseudo-clefts as a highlighter. However, through a sociolinguistic approach, the present study offers an innovative overview of the distribution of the copulas in Palenquero infocus position. In fact, as shown in §4, the alternation of the copulas *jue* and *sendá* in pseudo-clefts and inverse pseudo-clefts is bound to a demographic factor (viz. speaker age) more than to a grammatical constraint or morphosyntactic environment.

Furthermore, the rendering of cleft clauses by young speakers of Palenquero as an L2 both provides interesting insights into the intralinguistic variation related to the two copular morphemes (*jue* vs *sendá*) and the role of extra-linguistic factors, and enables the observation of two other intriguing syntactical issues. First, the data suggest that the formation of cleft clauses in Palenquero involves cleft pronoun dropping, exhibiting clear proximity to the lexifier language. Second, young members of the community do not resort to cleft constructions introduced by a copular morpheme, preferring a non-marked syntactic organisation following a basic SVO word order with *sendá* as a copula.

References

Baptista, Marlyse. 2006. When substrates meet superstate: The case of Cape Verdean Creole. In Jürgen Lang & John Holm, Jean-Louis Rougé &Maria Joao Soares (eds.), *Cabo Verde: Origens da sua sociedade e do seu crioulo*, 91–116. Tübingen: Narr.
Bolinger, Dwight. 1972. A look at equations and cleft sentences. In Evelyn S. Firchow (ed.), *Studies for Einar Haugen*, 96–114. The Hague: Mouton.
Citko, Barbara. 2004. On headed, headless, and light-headed relatives. *Natural Language & Linguistic Theory* 22(1). 95–126.
Collins, C. Peter. 1991. Pseudocleft and cleft constructions: A thematic and informational interpretation. *Linguistics* 29(3). 481–519.
Curnow, Timothy J. & Catherine E. Travis. 2004. The emphatic es construction of Colombian Spanish. In Christo Moskovsky (ed.), *Proceedings of the 2003 Conference of the Australian Linguistic Society*. http://www.als.asn.au
De Cesare, Anna Maria. 2014. Cleft constructions in a contrastive perspective. Towards an operational taxonomy. In Anna Maria De Cesare (ed.), *Frequency, forms and functions of cleft constructions in Romance and Germanic: Contrastive, corpus-based studies*, 9–48. Berlin/Boston: De Gruyter Mouton.

Escalante, Aquiles. 1979 [1954]. *El Palenque de San Basilio*. Barranquilla: Editorial Mejoras.
de Friedemann Nina. S. & Carlos Patiño Rosselli. 1983. *Lengua y sociedad en el palenque de San Basilio.* Bogotá: Publicaciones del Instituto Caro y Cuervo.
Gundel, Jeanette K. 1977. Where do cleft sentences come from? *Language* 53. 53–59.
Gutiérrez-Bravo, Rodrigo. 2019. Las oraciones pseudohendidas en español: Sintaxis y propiedades informativas. In Manuel Leonetti & María Victoria Escandell Vidal (eds.), *La estructura informativa*, 359–392. Madrid: Visor.
Gutiérrez Maté, Miguel. 2017. La partícula focal jue (< español fue) en el criollo palenquero ¿gramaticalización y/o sustrato? *Revista Internacional de Lingüística Iberoamericana* 15(2). 7–46.
Heggie, Lorie. A. 1988. *The syntax of copular structures*. Los Angeles: University of Southern California PhD dissertation.
Heine, Bernd & Mechthild Reh. 1984. *Grammaticalization and reanalysis in African languages.* Helmut Buske Verlag: Hamburg.
Holm, John A. & Peter L. Patrick. 2007. *Comparative creole syntax. Parallel outlines of 18 creole grammars.* (Westminster Creolistics series 7). London: Battlebridge.
Huber, Magnus. 1999. *Ghanaian pidgin English in its West African context. (Varieties of English Around the World).* Amsterdam/Philadelphia: John Benjamins.
Lambrecht, Knud. 2001. A framework for the analysis of cleft constructions. *Linguistics* 39. 463–561.
Lewis, Anthony R. 1970. *A descriptive analysis of the Palenquero dialect (a Spanish-based creole of northern Colombia, South America)*. Mona, Jamaica: University of the West Indies MA thesis.
Lipski, John M. 2020. *Palenquero and Spanish in contact. Exploring the interface.* (Contact Language Library 56). Amsterdam: John Benjamins.
Maglia, Graciela & Yves Moñino. 2015. *Kondalo pa bibí mejó. Contarlo para vivir mejor. Oratura y oralitura de San Basilio de Palenque (Colombia).* Bogotá: Editorial Pontificia Universidad Javeriana.
Marsella, Mara. [forthcoming]. The copula *sendá* in the revitalization process of Palenquero Creole. New pieces of evidence. *Journal of Pidgin and Creole Languages*.
Maurer, Philippe & the APiCS Consortium. 2013. Focusing on the noun phrase. In Susanne Michaelis, Philippe Maurer, Martin Haspelmath & Magnus Huber (eds.), *The atlas of pidgin and creole language structures*, 414–417. Oxford: Oxford University Press.
Moñino, Yves. 1999. El sistema modo-aspectual del verbo en palenquero: Una semántica gramatical africana. In *Lenguas abórigenes de Colombia. Memorias 6: Congreso de lingüística amerindia y criolla*, 147–160. Bogotá: CCELA-Universidad de los Andes.
Moñino, Yves. 2002. Las construcciones de genitivo en palenquero: ¿Una semantaxis africana? In Moñino Yves & Armin Schwegler (eds.), *Palenque, Cartagena y Afro-Caribe: Historia y lengua*, 227–248. Tübingen: Niemeyer.
Pfeiderer, Bettina. 1998. *Sprachtod und Revitalisierung der spanisch basierten Kreolsprache Palenquero (Kolumbien)* (Romanistische Linguistik). Berlin: Freie Universität Berlin.
Pinedo, Alicia. 2000. English clefts as discourse-pragmatic equivalents of Spanish postverbal subjects. *Estudios Ingleses de la Universidad Complutense* 8. 127–151.
Polinsky, Maria. 2016. Looking ahead. In Pascual y Cabo Diego (ed.), *Advances in Spanish as a heritage language*, 325–346. (Studies in Bilingualism 49). Amsterdam/Philadelphia: John Benjamins.
Schwegler, Armin. 1996. *"Chi ma nkongo": Lengua y rito ancestrales en el Palenque de San Basilio (Colombia)*, 2 Vols. Madrid/Frankfurt: Iberoamericana/Vervuert.

Schwegler, Armin & Kate Green 2007. Palenquero (Creole Spanish). In John Holm & Peter Patrick (eds.), *Comparative creole syntax. Parallel outlines of 18 creole grammars*, 273–306. London: Battlebridge.

Solomon, Denis. 1993. *The Speech of Trinidad. A reference grammar*. St. Augustine: UWI, The School of Continuing Studies.

Swearingen Davies, Martha. 2001. The past imperfect in Palenquero. *Studies in Language* 24(3). 568–581.

Wenli Tang
9 A cartographic approach to Chinese V *de* O clefts

Abstract: This paper investigates so-called V *de* O clefts in Chinese, a specific type of "clefts" where the *de* particle appears between the verb and the object, and proposes a cartographic approach to their syntactic and semantic properties. While some common generalizations about this pattern are shown to hold upon closer examination (i.e., exhaustive focus, obligatory past reading, ban on TMA markers), some do not (i.e., strict adjacency effect, term focus restriction). Two key projections are argued to exist in the relevant functional hierarchy, each linked to one crucial element in the pattern: (i) a FocP selected by the copula *shi*; (ii) an Asp*P headed by the verbal particle *de*. The former explains the focus effects with syntactic encoding and the latter accounts for the temporal/aspectual peculiarities with the marking of perfective aspect (related predictions about predicate restrictions are also presented). The derivation of V *de* O clefts involves overt focus movement of an extended "eventive" projection, which minimally contains an Asp*P. This movement is triggered by a focus feature either on the whole constituent (VP/S+VP) or on a smaller constituent within it (verb/object/subject/adjunct), the latter case demonstrating a pied-piping movement.

Keywords: Chinese V *de* O clefts, cartography, copula, Focus projection, perfective aspect

1 V *de* O clefts in (northern) Mandarin Chinese

So-called V *de* O clefts as in (1) are widely agreed to be one of the Chinese equivalents of English *it*-clefts:

Note: The original idea for this article dates back to the preparation of my master's thesis in 2017, although significant changes have since taken place, both empirically and theoretically. Various versions were presented at the 2nd International Workshop on Syntactic Cartography in Beijing, the 35ᵉ *Journée de linguistique d'Asie orientale* in Paris and the 4th CreteLing poster session; I thank the audiences for their feedback. My gratitude also goes to Gioia Cacchioli, Genoveva Puskas, Giuseppe Samo, Ur Shlonsky, Yangyu Sun, and Peiwen Zhou for helpful discussions as well as to the anonymous reviewer for their detailed comments. I am mostly indebted to Caterina Bonan, one of the co-editors of this volume, for her generous encouragement and patience. Naturally, all remaining errors are my own.

Wenli Tang, University of Geneva, e-mail: wenli.tang@unige.ch

(1) V *de* O pattern
 Shi wo dapo de na-ge huaping.[1]
 be 1SG break DE that-CL vase
 'It was I who broke that vase.'

Similar to their English counterparts, V *de* O clefts are also believed to show a focus-presupposition bipartition (Paul and Whitman 2008; Hole 2011 among others), with the focused element immediately following the copula *shi*:[2]

(2) Focus-presupposition bipartition
 Shi [*wo*]$_{focus}$ [*dapo de na-ge huaping*]$_{presupposition}$.
 be 1SG break DE that-CL vase
 'It was [I]$_{focus}$ [who broke that vase]$_{presupposition}$.'

In addition to the verb-adjacent position, the functional element *de* can also occur in a sentence-final position, resulting in another cleft pattern:[3]

(3) V O *de* pattern
 Shi wo dapo na-ge huaping de.
 be 1SG break that-CL vase DE
 'It was I who broke that vase.'

Despite the apparent free alternation,[4] the above two patterns do show differences in terms of distribution and interpretation (see Paul and Whitman 2008 for an overview; also cf. Section 5). One distinctive property of V *de* O clefts concerns tense/time: a past time reading of the sentence is obligatory, which can be obtained

---

1 The following abbreviations are used in the glosses: 1/2/3—first/second/third person; SG—singular; CL—classifier; NEG—negation; PFV—perfective aspect; SFP—sentence-final particle.
2 For ease of reference, *shi* will be referred to as "the copula" throughout descriptive discussions here, despite different analyses in existing literature for the syntactic status of this element (cf. Section 2.2).
3 In addition to the patterns shown here, bare *shi*/*de* sentences with similar meanings have been considered further subtypes of Chinese clefts (often under the same cover term *shi. . .de construction*). However, the bare patterns will not be discussed in this paper: bare-*shi* seems to involve a different structure, while bare-*de* cases can mostly be seen as variants of the non-bare version with the copula dropped (indeed, all examples presented here can retain their acceptability/interpretation with *shi* removed).
4 Descriptive studies often depict the variation as the sentence-final particle *de* optionally preceding the object (e.g., Li, Thompson, and Zhang 1998: 95–96; Yuan 2003: 6).

without any tense/aspect marker, as in (1). In fact, the markers are even forbidden there, as opposed to V O *de* clefts where they are allowed:

(4) a. Tense/aspect marker in V *de* O
   Shi wo dapo (*le) de na-ge huaping.[5]
   be 1SG break PFV DE that-CL vase
   'It was I who broke that vase.'
  b. Tense/aspect marker in V O *de*
   Shi wo dapo (le) na-ge huaping de.
   be 1SG break PFV that-CL vase DE
   'It was I who broke that vase.'

Focusing on the V *de* O pattern in (northern) Mandarin Chinese,[6] this paper aims to answer the following questions: Is it a real equivalent to English *it*-clefts? In what respects are they similar/different? More specifically, is there really an overt focus-presupposition bipartition as often stated? If not, how is focus encoded? Perhaps even more importantly, how do we account for the peculiarities of V *de* O clefts as seen above?

Starting with common generalizations about this pattern, I show that not all of them hold when subjected to closer scrutiny: some do (e.g., exhaustive focus, obligatory past time reading), while others do not (e.g., strict adjacency effect, term focus restriction). Although an overt focus-presupposition bipartition is shown to be absent, I agree with previous scholars in attributing the focus interpretation to *shi*: specifically, it selects a FocP as its complement (cf. Belletti's 2009, 2015 analysis for English/French-type clefts). The peculiarities of the V *de* O pattern, on the other hand, can be explained if we take the functional element *de* to head an Asp*P encoding perfective aspect, which existentially closes off an event (Ramchand and Svenonius 2014). V *de* O clefts are derived when an extended "eventive" projection minimally containing Asp*P is focus-moved to SpecFocP (often in a pied-piped way).

---

5 Note that this should be distinguished from the right dislocation case, which does allow the perfective marker *le*: right dislocation comes with a distinct prosodic pattern, with a potential pause preceding the right-dislocated object. In that case, the pattern involved would be V O *de* instead of V *de* O.
6 As is well noted, the V *de* O order is mainly restricted to northern Mandarin dialects, V O *de* being the predominant order in southern China (Simpson and Wu 2002: 169; Paul and Whitman 2008: 427–428). This paper focuses on the former in northern Mandarin, where both patterns are extensively present, while making comparisons where relevant.

The paper is organized as follows. In Section 2, I introduce the common generalizations about V *de* O clefts before turning to the proposals built on them. Section 3 discusses the challenging data for previous accounts. Section 4 presents the new analysis, which not only accounts for the updated data range but also makes the right prediction on predicate restrictions (as shown in Section 5). Section 6 concludes with further issues/implications for future research.

2 Previous discussions

This section introduces previous observations and proposals about V *de* O clefts, focusing on three most influential analyses from the last two decades (Simpson and Wu 2002; Paul and Whitman 2008; Hole 2011).

2.1 Generalizations

The following properties are claimed to be characteristic of Chinese V *de* O clefts (Paul and Whitman 2008: 429–433; Hole 2011: 1710–1714):
i.   The sentence has to be interpreted with an exhaustive focus;
ii. The focused element must be adjacent to the copula;
iii. A past time reading of the presupposition is obligatory;
iv. Markers of tense/modality/aspect (TMA) cannot occur in the presupposition part;
v.   Only arguments/adjuncts can bear the focus, i.e., term focus only.

Exhaustive focus is illustrated below, where the V *de* O sentence cannot be followed by an utterance with an additive effect:

(5) Exhaustive focus
Shi wo mai de mianbao. (#Lusi ye mai le.)
be 1SG buy DE bread Lusi also buy PFV
'It was I who bought the bread. (#Lusi also bought some.)'

Indeed, one cannot felicitously suggest another bread-buyer after identifying *wo* "I" as the only buyer. Such behavior resonates with the standard claim about English *it*-clefts (e.g., Chomsky 1977; Kiss 1998), confirming the reasonable association between them.

Another argument for matching these cross-linguistic clefts is the adjacency between the focused constituent and the copula. This is shown straightforwardly in all the examples so far (see also the discussion below related to the term focus restriction).

Properties (iii–v), on the other hand, distinguish V *de* O clefts from their English counterparts.[7] As already partly shown, the presupposition has to be interpreted as a past event (6) and no TMA marker can appear within it (7):

(6) Future-oriented temporal adverb (+ future-marking modal)
  * *Shi wo mingtian (hui) mai de mianbao.*[8]
    be 1SG tomorrow will buy DE bread
    Intended: 'It is I who will buy the bread tomorrow.'

(7) TMA markers
  * *Shi wo {hui/ keyi} mai {le} de mianbao.*
    be 1SG will can buy PFV DE bread
    Intended: 'It is I who {will/can/has buy/bought} the bread.'

These restrictions are clearly not inherent to clefts in general, as evidenced by the well-formed English translations.

In terms of focusable categories, it is often claimed that only term focus (i.e., focus on arguments/adjuncts) is available in the V *de* O pattern. In addition to the subject clefts we have seen so far, adjunct clefts as below are also commonly noted:

(8) Adjunct focus
  Wo shi zai zheli mai de mianbao.
  1SG be at here buy DE bread
  'It was here that I bought the bread.'

Much less discussed is another type of term clefts, where the object is focused (therefore stressed, indicated by underline[9]):

---

[7] In fact, properties (iii–v) also distinguish V *de* O clefts from the similar looking V O *de* pattern, but a comprehensive investigation into all patterns of Chinese clefts will have to wait for future research.
[8] Note that this sentence can sound right with a different interpretation: "(It) is the (kind of) bread that Zhangsan will buy tomorrow." That would become a case of simple predication, with a dropped *pro* as subject and a noun phrase modified by a relative clause as predicate.
[9] Focused elements are stressed by default, being phonologically more prominent than the non-focus parts in the sentence; it is explicitly marked here because the same sequence can yield different focus interpretations, each of them associated with a specific prosodic pattern (see Section 3.2).

(9) Object focus
Wo shi mai de <u>mianbao</u>.
1SG be buy DE bread
'It was bread that I bought.'

Cases like this have been mostly ignored by previous studies on Chinese clefts: they clearly violate the adjacency restriction. Unlike what we have seen so far with the canonical (i.e, subject/adjunct) clefts, an object can be focused in a non-copula-adjacent position. Indeed, the object simply cannot be fronted to the copula-adjacent position (10a), even though object fronting does exist elsewhere in Chinese (10b/c).

(10) a. Object fronting in V *de* O clefts
  * Wo shi mianbao mai de.
    1SG be bread buy DE
    Intended: 'It was bread that I bought.'
  b. Object fronting in non-clefts I
    Wo mianbao mai le (, niunai mei mai).
    1SG bread buy PFV milk NEG.past buy
    'I bought bread (, but not milk).'
  c. Object fronting in non-clefts II
    Mianbao wo mai le (, niunai wo mei mai).
    bread 1SG buy PFV milk 1SG NEG.past buy
    'Bread I bought (, milk I didn't).'

In spite of their distributional deviance, V *de* O sentences with object focus still count as clefts, since they do otherwise behave on a par with the more typical types (Paul and Whitman 2008: 428–429, footnote 15). The contradiction between adjacency and object focus thus poses a challenge to any analysis aiming at descriptive adequacy; in the next subsection, we will see how previous research approach it.

2.2 Proposals

Despite the consensus on treating V *de* O sentences as a cleft construction, previous opinions vary considerably concerning their internal structure. The focus interpretation is mostly associated with *shi*: some straightforwardly label it as a focus marker (e.g., Yuan 2003), while most still see it as a copula or functional verbal/auxiliary element (e.g., Simpson and Wu 2002; Paul and Whitman 2008).

For many, an overt focus-presupposition bipartition also exists in Chinese clefts, accounting for their similarity to English *it*-clefts (Paul and Whitman 2008; Hole 2011). The distinctive properties, on the other hand, are mostly attributed to *de*. Previous descriptivists have treated it as a nominalizer (Zhu 1978; Paris 1979), a tense/aspect marker (Song 1981; Shi 1984), or a preposed sentence-final particle (Li, Thompson, and Zhang 1998; Yuan 2003), while more recent generative studies have analyzed it as T^0 (Simpson and Wu 2002), Asp^0 (Paul and Whitman 2008), or C^0 (Hole 2011).

Let us take a closer look at the last three analyses to see how they address (or not) the empirical generalizations observed:

Simpson and Wu (2002) are among the first to bring the V *de* O pattern into theoretical discussions. They observe the important distinction between different patterns of Chinese clefts in terms of possible time readings and suggest distinct treatments for past-only and non-past clefts. More specifically, they claim that *de* in V *de* O clefts is a past tense morpheme heading a TP, which is selected by *shi*, a higher verbal/auxiliary element. The past time restriction is thus explained, along the same lines as Stowell's (1996) double-tense analysis for the English present perfect. What they fail to mention is how the focus effects come about in their theory.

Paul and Whitman (2008) do take focus into account. They associate the exhaustive focus with adjacency and assume the presence of an overt focus-presupposition partition in Chinese clefts. As with English *it*-clefts, this bipartition is also allegedly selected by the copula; however, in the Chinese case, it is headed by an Asp^0, which is lexicalized by the verb-adjacent *de*. The complement of the copula being smaller than TP naturally explains the ban on TMA markers, and a [past] tense feature on *de* is assumed to account for the obligatory past reading. Object clefts are left untreated due to the violation of adjacency, the latter playing a central role in their analysis: they take object focus to involve a different mechanism (Paul and Whitman 2008: 431, footnote 18).

Contrary to Paul and Whitman (2008), Hole (2011) calls for a unified treatment of all *shi...de* clefts, including those with sentence-final *de*. Adopting the bipartition view, he attempts to resolve the contradiction between adjacency and object clefts with a highly modular proposal: object clefts are claimed to be the only exception where the partitioning only takes place at LF. *De* is treated as a C head carrying an [exhaustive] feature, which attracts the fronted focus and leads to the bipartition. As for the temporal restriction and TMA ban, Hole (2011: 1714) assumes that the presupposition of V *de* O clefts does contain TMA information, with their default values being [+anterior, -irrealis, +terminative]; explicit TMA material is forbidden due to PF-level constraints. Finally, *shi* is seen as a predicational copula, which simply mediates between topics/subjects and comments/predicates.

3 Challenging evidence

In this section, I present some evidence challenging two of the generalizations introduced in the last section: the adjacency restriction and the term focus restriction.

3.1 Focus shifting via stress placement

Contrary to the adjacency claim, the copula is not always immediately followed by the focus. In addition to clear cases with object focus as seen earlier, V *de* O clefts with a shiftable focus also demonstrate the lack of adjacency:

(11) Focus shifting via stress placement
 Wo shi zuotian qi che qu de Faguo.
 1SG be yesterday ride bike go DE France
 i. 'It was yesterday that I went to France by bike.'
 ii. ?'It was by bike that I went to France yesterday.'
 iii. ?'It was France that I went to by bike yesterday.'
 iv. 'I went to France BY BIKE YESTERDAY.'
 v. *'It is that I went to France by bike yesterday.'

According to the strict adjacency/bipartition view, (i) should be the only possible reading we can get, with the copula-adjacent adjunct *zuotian* "yesterday" in focus and thus stressed. However, if we move the narrow stress to other constituents or simply remove it, the same sentence can be interpreted differently, as shown by the readings above: (ii/iii) can be obtained with stress assigned to the respective constituent in focus and (iv) is the reading we get if the sentence is uttered with a relatively neutral prosodic pattern (the last reading, however, is never possible; see the discussion below).

As can be observed, (ii) and (iii) are obtained with somewhat degraded naturalness.[10] It seems to result from some pragmatic factor: there simply exists another

---

10 This is sometimes argued to save the validity of the adjacency restriction. Hole (2011: 1712), for instance, takes it to mean that only certain contexts can license the prosodically-marked focus, which differs from, and affects the prosodic behavior of, the copula-adjacent "cleft focus". More specifically, he claims that readings like (ii) are only available in corrective situations like below, where "the cleft focus is downgraded prosodically due to its second-occurrence status":

a. Non-adjacent focus in corrective context
 A: Tingshuo ni shi zuotian zuo huoche qu de Faguo.
  hear.say 2SG be yesterday sit train go DE France
 A: 'I heard that it was yesterday that you went to France by train.'

preferred way to express the same meaning, namely putting "yesterday" before the copula, since non-focused information is usually given and thus tends to occur in a topical position.

The careful reader may have noticed the distinction in the translations for (i–iii) and for (iv). Indeed, for a non-contrastive/neutral context where reading (iv) is most readily available, the in-situ focusing strategy seems preferred to clefting in English:

(12) Neutral context for reading (iv)
    A: *Tingshuo ni qu Faguo le.*
       hear.say 2SG go France SFP
    A: 'I heard that you went to France.'
    B: *Dui, wo shi zuotian qi che qu de (Faguo).*
       right 1SG be yesterday ride bike go DE France
    B: 'Yes, I went {there/to France} BY BIKE YESTERDAY.'

In such situations, the V *de* O sentence just serves to add new information about the presupposed event ("speaker B going to France" in this case), without contrasting with or correcting anything in the previous discourse, or the common ground.

However, the proposition focus reading (v) is never possible, even uttered with a neutral prosodic pattern in an appropriate context. Imagine that speaker B lives in a Swiss city bordering France and that crossing the border by bike is possible, though much more tiring than taking public transport. (11) still cannot be a felicitous answer to a *how-come* question like below:

(13) Neutral context for intended reading (v)
    A: *Ni zenme kanqilai zheme lei?*
       2SG how.come look so tired
    A: 'How come you look so tired?'

    B: *Bu, wo shi zuotian qi che qu de Faguo.*
       no 1SG be yesterday ride bike go DE France
    B: 'No, it was yesterday that I went to France BY BIKE.'
       (adapted from Hole 2011: (14'))

This line of reasoning, however, still fails to explain readings like (iv), where "by bike yesterday" cannot be treated as one clefted constituent (cf. Cheng 2008: 250 for discussion on the similar behavior of V O *de* pattern).

B: # Wo   shi zuotian   qi   che   qu   de   Faguo.[11]
       1SG   be   yesterday   ride   bike   go   DE   France
B: '(It is that) I went to France by bike yesterday.' (intended)

The availability of (iv) and unavailability of (v) shows an interesting contrast: it seems to suggest that the event in question has to be *existentially presupposed*, considering that its existence cannot be conveyed as new information.

3.2 More focusable categories

As mentioned earlier, focus in V *de* O clefts is often claimed to fall on arguments/adjuncts only. A closer examination proves otherwise: with the right predicate, prosody and context, V *de* O clefts can also express non-term focus, as shown in (d–f) below (term focus examples repeated in (a–c); focus indicated by underline).

(14) a. Subject focus
        Shi wo   mai   de   mianbao.
        be   1SG buy   DE   bread
        'It was I who bought the bread.'
     b. Adjunct focus
        Wo   shi   zai   zheli   mai   de   mianbao.
        1SG   be   at   here   buy   DE   bread
        'It was here that I bought the bread.'
     c. Object focus
        Wo   shi   mai   de   mianbao.
        1SG   be   buy   DE   bread
        'It was bread that I bought.'

---

11 Dropping the copula *shi* appears to rescue the felicity of the answer, but the focal stress would then necessarily fall on *qi che* "by bike", forcing the rest of the sentence to be presupposed and yielding a narrow focus interpretation: "It was by bike that I went to France yesterday."

The proper way to express wide propositional focus in this case would be to use a non-cleft sentence with a sentence-final particle *le* (see Soh 2009 and references therein for detailed discussions on this particle):

a. *Wo   zuotian   qi   che   qu   Faguo   le.*
    1SG   yesterday   ride   bike   go   France   SFP
    '(It is that) I went to France by bike yesterday.'

d. Verb focus
   Wo shi <u>mai</u> de mianbao.
   1SG be buy DE bread
   'I BOUGHT the bread. (I didn't BAKE it myself.)'
e. VP focus
   Wo shi <u>mai</u> de <u>mianbao</u>. (Lusi shi <u>shua</u> de <u>wan</u>.)
   1SG be buy DE bread   Lusi be brush DE bowl
   'I bought the bread. (Lusi did the dishes.)'
   [as an answer to "What did you and Lusi do for the family dinner?"]
f. Proposition focus
   Shi <u>wo</u> <u>jiao</u> <u>zhu</u> de <u>ta</u>.[12]
   be 1SG call stop DE 3SG
   '(It is that) I stopped her/him from leaving (by calling).'
   [as an answer to "Why is (s)he still here?"]
   (Li, Thompson, and Zhang 1998, (4'))

As can be observed, all examples above show the temporal restriction: none of them allow a non-past reading. The ban on TMA markers also seems universal: their appearance would render (d–f) ungrammatical, just as it would do in (a–c) (cf. (7) from Section 2.1). In terms of exhaustivity, the translations of (d–f) may not serve as transparent indications (unlike those of (a–c)), but this does not mean that non-term focus in V *de* O clefts can be non-exhaustive. In fact, the effect can be better detected once we consider another way of translating (d–f):

(14) d'. Verb focus
     'I BOUGHT the bread. (I didn't BAKE it myself.)' OR:
     'It is buying that I did to get the bread (, not baking).'
  e'. VP focus
     'I bought the bread.' OR:
     'It was buying the bread that I did (for the family dinner).'
  f'. Proposition focus
     '(It is that) I stopped her/him from leaving (by calling).' OR:
     'It was my stopping her/him from leaving (that led to her/him still being here).'

By rephrasing the translations in the form of *it*-clefts, we can now capture the exhaustive effect with non-term focus as well as with term focus.

---

12 This sentence can of course have a narrow focus reading, too, with the subject alone in focus.

Another crucial observation can be made on the basis of these rephrased translations: compared to term focus, the expression of non-term focus with V *de* O clefts appears more selective in terms of context and predicate type. For instance, the translation in (14d') shows that to get a verb focus cleft, the result state entailed by the verb has to be existentially presupposed (i.e., "I already have/own the bread" here) and there should be alternative ways to achieve this state. (14e') also demonstrates the importance of an appropriate context.

The proposition focus in (14f), compared with the impossible case in (13) above (repeated below with context omitted), reveals further restrictions:

(15) a. Proposition focus (= 14f)
   Shi <u>wo</u> <u>jiao</u> <u>zhu</u> de <u>ta</u>.
   be   1SG   call   stop   DE   3SG
   '(It is that) I stopped her/him from leaving (by calling).'
 b. Intended proposition focus in (13)
 * <u>Wo</u> shi <u>zuotian</u> <u>qi</u> <u>che</u> <u>qu</u> de <u>Faguo.</u>
   1SG be   yesterday   ride bike go   DE   France
   Intended: '(It is that) I went to France by bike yesterday.'

A noticeable difference between the above two cases lies in the position of the subject: it follows the copula in (15a) but precedes the copula in (15b). However, the latter is not ruled out simply for distributional reasons, as the wide propositional focus reading remains inaccessible with a post-copula subject:

(16)   Intended proposition focus with post-copula subject
 * Shi <u>wo</u> <u>zuotian</u> <u>qi</u> <u>che</u> <u>qu</u> de <u>Faguo.</u>
   be   1SG   yesterday   ride bike go   DE   France
   Intended: '(It is that) I went to France by bike yesterday.'

Here again, the translations may give us a clue. If we try to rephrase the translation for (13/15b) in the same way as we did for (14f/15a), we have the following pair:

(15) a'. Proposition focus
   '(It is that) I stopped her/him from leaving (by calling).' OR:
   'It was my stopping her/him from leaving (that led to her/him still being here).'
 b'. Intended proposition focus
   Intended: '(It is that) I went to France by bike yesterday.' OR:
   Intended: 'It was my going to France by bike yesterday *(that led to me looking tired).'

The noticeable difference here concerns the (im)possibility of dropping the presupposed result state in the translation. While (15a′) allows the result state to be dropped as a presupposed entailment, (15b′) does not. What really rules out (15b/16) thus seems to be related to predicate type: "Stopping her/him from leaving" naturally entails "her/him still being here" as the result state, which can be dropped if presupposed, whereas "going to France by bike" does not necessarily lead to "looking tired" the following day,[13] hence the impossibility to drop the presupposition. In other words, a causal relation *per se* does not warrant the availability of proposition focus with V *de* O clefts; it has to be weaved into the denotation of the predicate.

In view of this point, the earlier conjecture needs to be revised as follows: The *whole event* is not necessarily existentially presupposed; the *result state* entailed by it is (which of course means, or presupposes, that the event must have an inherent result state).

To the best of my knowledge, most of the new data discussed here remain untouched, thus unpredicted, by previous generative work on V *de* O clefts (see Yang and He 2021 for a recent constructionist view, though). In the following, I will propose a new analysis which not only takes into account all the data available, but also makes the right prediction.

4 A cartographic analysis

With a more complete empirical picture in mind, we can now attempt to answer the questions raised at the beginning of this paper:
– Is the Chinese V *de* O pattern a real equivalent to English *it*-clefts? In what respects are they similar/different?
  Answer: In a way yes, since all Chinese V *de* O clefts can be paired with an English translation in the form of *it*-clefts (albeit less natural in some cases), as we have seen in the last section. This parallel demonstrates their common association with exhaustive focus.
  But the former is remarkably more restricted. As pointed out by previous work, no TMA markers are allowed in the presupposition part and a past reading is obligatory in V *de* O clefts, whereas there are no such constraints for *it*-clefts. In addition, V *de* O clefts show higher selectivity in terms of context, predicate type, etc.

---

[13] Depending on how far your starting point is from the border, how good a cyclist you are and/or how well you have slept afterwards.

- Is there an overt focus-presupposition bipartition?
  Answer: No. The sentence cannot be bipartitioned when the focus is not adjacent to the copula, e.g., on the object or the second adjunct.
- How is focus encoded?
- How do we account for the peculiarities of V *de* O clefts?
  Answers: I follow most existing literature in attributing the focus interpretation to *shi* and the peculiarities of V *de* O clefts to *de*. More specifically, I believe that each of these two elements is associated with a key functional projection: *shi* with FocP and *de* with Asp*P (related in different ways). Below I discuss how exactly focus is encoded in the functional hierarchy involving *shi* (Section 4.1) and how the syntactic status of *de* helps to account for the particular behaviours observed of this pattern (Section 4.2).

4.1 Copula *shi* and FocP

Following Paul and Whitman (2008) and Hole (2011), I consider *shi* in Chinese V *de* O clefts to be a copular verb, instead of a focus marker. This can be easily captured by examples like below:

(17) Negation + *shi*
   Wo   bu   shi   zai   zheli   mai   de   mianbao.
   1SG   NEG   be   at   here   buy   DE   bread
   'It was not here that I bought the bread.'

Given that it can be negated with the sentential negation marker *bu*, *shi* must be a verbal/predicative element, instead of a fully grammaticalized focus marker (as with English *it*-clefts). But it is arguably not far from focus markers if we adopt a cartographic approach (Rizzi 1997; Cinque and Rizzi 2010; Rizzi and Cinque 2016).

Rizzi (1997) proposes to decompose the CP layer (i.e., the left periphery) into a sequence of hierarchically organized functional heads:

(18) ForceP > TopP* > FocP > TopP* > FinP > IP (Rizzi 1997: 279)[14]

Among these projections, FocP is claimed to host focus information in its specifier, including fronted *wh*-phrases in languages with *wh*-movement. Crucially, the head

---

14 The asterisk indicates that Italian topics can be reiterated.

of FocP can be lexicalized by focus markers in languages which have them (see, e.g., Aboh 2004 for Gungbe; cf. Durrleman and Shlonsky 2015 for Jamaican Creole).

Now if we return to clefts, recent cartographic studies (Belletti 2009, 2015; Haegeman, Meinunger, and Vercauteren 2015) have claimed a close relationship between the copula and the FocP (its head being null) for English-type clefts.[15] More specifically, a left peripheral FocP is selected by the copula as its complement. This "embedded" analysis is shown to fare better than the "matrix" accounts (Meinunger 1998; Frascarelli and Ramaglia 2013) in terms of predictions (see Haegeman, Meinunger, and Vercauteren 2015 for more detailed arguments).

To capture the crosslinguistic parallel, I assume that a similar functional hierarchy also exists in Chinese V *de* O clefts: *shi* does not lexicalize Foc^0 but stays a copular verb which selects FocP[16] (with a null head) as its complement.

But what about the differences? Questions naturally arise when we consider the distinctive properties of the V *de* O pattern, notably the lack of an overt focus-background bipartition (which is at the origin of the name *clefts*). I argue that focus is indeed syntactically encoded there with a FocP and that there is also overt focus movement; but crucially, what is moved to SpecFocP differs from English-type clefts, accounting for the remarkable distinctions.

---

15 Belletti (2009, 2015) observes a subject-object asymmetry in relation to different types of cleft focus: subject clefts can express either new information or corrective/contrastive focus, while object/non-subject clefts can only express the latter. Two Focus projections are employed to account for this: a left peripheral FocP dedicated to contrastive/corrective focus and a vP peripheral FocP (Belletti 2004) for new information focus.

16 Chinese V *de* O clefts do not seem to show the same asymmetry as mentioned in the last footnote. For instance, all examples in Section 3.2 with different constituents in focus can be used as felicitous answers to *wh*-questions, thus expressing new information focus (as shown by the explicit contexts in Section 3 and exemplified below by an object cleft).

a. A: *Ni   mai   {le/   de}   shenme?*   B: *(Wo)   (shi)   mai   de   mianbao.*
      1SG   buy   PFV   DE   what   1SG   be   buy   DE   bread
      'What did you buy?'   'I bought BREAD.'

It appears that at least in the Chinese pattern investigated here, the type of focus involved is invariably identificational/exhaustive (Kiss 1998; Cruschina 2021 among others), with further subtypes (new information vs contrastive/corrective) derivable in appropriate contexts. I thus leave open which FocP is involved here while keeping the core insight of the embedded analysis: the copula in clefts necessarily selects a FocP as its complement (with possible crosslinguistic variation in the specific type of focus hosted). I thank the anonymous reviewer who asked for clarification on this point.

4.2 Nature of *de*: Asp*

So, what exactly is focus-moved in Chinese V *de* O clefts? A simple and intuitive answer is the whole sequence "V *de* O": The FocP hypothesis can be maintained as long as we assume this. A more revealing answer relies on the syntactic status of *de*. Earlier discussions around the rephrasable translations already reveal the essence of the proposal: FocP could host in its specifier some "eventive" projection, containing minimally the verb and the object. The functional element in between thus most likely belongs to the extended verbal domain.

Here I propose that *de* heads some sort of Asp*P, an aspectual projection that specifically encodes perfective aspect and existentially closes off an event (Ramchand and Svenonius 2014). Assuming the existential closure of the event has many merits. To begin with, it immediately explains away the necessary past-time/anterior reading, which comes about as soon as the perfective aspect is combined with the speech time. TMA markers are banned simply because their denotations contradict what is already encoded by Asp*P: an existentially closed event cannot be further quantified/split/closed again. Another advantage is that it corresponds nicely to the observation that only events entailing an inherent result state can be clefted with a proposition focus reading (cf. Section 3.2), as the perfective aspect intrinsically requires a result state too. Syntactically speaking, a projection smaller than Asp*P does not qualify to be focus-moved to SpecFocP.

Now that we have the key ingredients outlined, the movement to derive V *de* O clefts can be schematized as below:

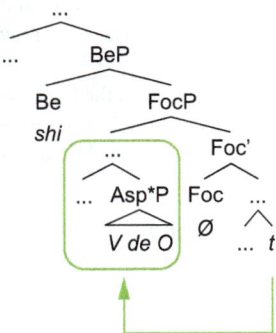

Figure 1: Overt focus movement in Chinese V *de* O clefts.

In brief, V *de* O clefts are derived when an extended "eventive" projection containing Asp*P is focus-moved to SpecFocP. Crucially, the focus feature triggering the movement can be carried by different elements within the moved projection, accounting for the various focusable categories. In a minimal case where only Asp*P is moved, either the verb or the object, or both together, are focused semantically as (part of) the event description. When the subject/adjunct bears the focus, it pied-pipes its containing projection (larger than Asp*P) as an event modifier. Finally, as a maximal case, an event as a whole can be focused, with its entailed result state presupposed.

5 Prediction: Predicate restrictions

Once we have a plausible analysis that can account for all the available data, it should also be able to make testable predictions. One of such predictions made by the new analysis concerns predicate types.

As mentioned earlier, the cleft patterns V *de* O and V O *de* have been assumed as equivalents by some, due to their apparent interchangeability in certain contexts. However, if we take the verb-adjacent *de* to be a perfectivity-encoding aspectual head, distinct from the clause-final *de*, the two patterns must behave quite differently in terms of the compatibility with predicates of different lexical aspect, or *Aktionsart*.

Starting with the V *de* O pattern, it is expected to show intolerance only to stative predicates, given their difficulty to combine with the perfective aspect (regardless of which element is focused). This seems to be the case indeed:

(19) V *de* O + different predicate types
 Wo shi {*xihuan/ mai/ dapo} de na-ge huaping.
 1SG be like buy break DE that-CL vase
 'It is/was that vase that I {*like/bought/broke}.'

As for the V O *de* pattern, the situation turns out to be more complicated, showing variation according to the focused constituent. For example, only telic verbs are allowed with subject focus:

(20) Subject focus + different predicate types
 Shi wo {*xihuan/ *mai/ dapo} na-ge huaping de.
 be 1SG like buy break that-CL vase DE
 'It is/was I who {*likes/*bought/broke} that vase.'

Adjunct focus allows both telic verbs and statives:

(21) a. Adjunct focus + stative predicate
Wo shi <u>yinwei</u> zhe-ge <u>yuanyin</u> xihuan na-ge huaping de.
1SG be because.of this-CL reason like that-CL vase DE
'It is for this reason that I like that vase.'
b. Adjunct focus + eventive predicates
Wo shi <u>zai</u> <u>zheli</u> {?*mai/ dapo} na-ge huaping de.
1SG be at here buy break that-CL vase DE
'It was here that I {bought/broke} that vase.'

Object focus demonstrates yet another pattern: only statives (marginally) allowed.

(22) a. Object focus + stative predicate
? Wo shi xihuan <u>na-ge</u> <u>huaping</u> de.
1SG be like that-CL vase DE
'It is that vase that I like.'
b. Object focus + eventive predicates
Wo shi {*mai/ *dapo} <u>na-ge</u> <u>huaping</u> de.
1SG be buy break that-CL vase DE
'It was that vase that I {bought/broke}.'

The varied interaction between different patterns, focus types and predicate types can be summarized as below:

Table 1: Varied predicate restrictions in Chinese *shi...de* clefts.

Pattern & focus type		Stative (e.g., *like*)	Eventive	
			Atelic (e.g., *buy*)	Telic (e.g., *break*)
V *de* O (all types)		*	OK	OK
V O *de*	Subject focus	*	*	OK
	Adjunct focus	OK	*	OK
	Object focus	?OK	*	*

Interestingly, every two adjacent rows in the table overlap without being identical. This puzzle, if not entirely a coincidence, deserves some principled explanation. A desirable theory of Chinese *shi...de* clefts should be able to capture both the distinctions and the similarities reported. For our purpose here, it suffices to observe the distinctive results for the two patterns as predicted.

6 Conclusion

In this paper I have investigated the syntax and semantics of Chinese V *de* O clefts. I have shown that while some of the common generalizations hold upon closer examination (e.g., exhaustive focus, obligatory past time reading), some do not (e.g., strict adjacency effect, term focus restriction). I have argued for the existence of two key functional projections, each linked to one crucial element in the pattern: (i) a FocP selected by the copula *shi*; (ii) an Asp*P headed by *de*. The former explains the focus effects with syntactic encoding, while the latter accounts for the temporal/aspectual peculiarities by marking perfective aspect (related predictions on predicate restrictions also presented). The derivation of V *de* O clefts involves overt focus movement of an extended "eventive" projection, which minimally contains Asp*P. This movement is triggered by a focus feature either on the whole constituent or on a smaller constituent within it (the latter involving pied-piping).

If this approach proves to be on the right track, many more interesting questions arise. Below are some of the topics/implications to be explored in future research:

What are the omitted derivational steps to complement the creation of V *de* O clefts? If *de* is a perfective marker, what distinguishes it from the verbal *le* (the widely accepted perfective marker in canonical sentences)?

How do V O *de* clefts differ from and relate to V *de* O? Is there any common nature between the verbal *de* and the sentence-final *de*? Is a unified analysis possible for all Chinese cleft patterns, bare or non-bare (cf. Cheng 2008)?

Assuming the similar function of the copula, what then underlies the different "clefting" strategies in Chinese and English? What parallels can be drawn between *de* and *-en*, the respective Asp* heads in the two languages (cf. Simpson and Wu 2002)?

References

Aboh, Enoch Oladé. 2004. *The morphosyntax of complement-head sequences: Clause structure and word order patterns in Kwa.* New York: Oxford University Press.

Belletti, Adriana. 2004. Aspects of the low IP Area. In Luigi Rizzi (ed.), *The structure of CP and IP.* Volume 2: *The cartography of syntactic structures*, 16–51. New York: Oxford University Press.

Belletti, Adriana. 2009. Answering strategies: New information subjects and the nature of clefts. In Adriana Belletti, *Structures and strategies*, 242–265. New York: Routledge.

Belletti, Adriana. 2015. The focus map of clefts: Extraposition and predication. In Ur Shlonsky (ed.), *Beyond functional sequence.* Volume 10: *The cartography of syntactic structures*, 42–60. New York: Oxford University Press.

Cheng, Lisa Lai-Shen. 2008. Deconstructing the *Shì . . . de* Construction. *The Linguistic Review* 25(3–4). https://doi.org/10.1515/TLIR.2008.007.

Chomsky, Noam. 1977. On wh-movement. In Peter Culicover, Thomas Wasow & Adrian Akmajian (eds.), *Formal Syntax*, 71–132. Academic Press, New York.
Cinque, Guglielmo & Luigi Rizzi. 2010. The cartography of syntactic structures. In Bernard Heine & Heiko Narrog (eds.), *The Oxford handbook of linguistic analysis*, 51–65. Oxford: Oxford University Press.
Cruschina, Silvio. 2021. The greater the contrast, the greater the potential: On the effects of focus in syntax. *Glossa: A Journal of General Linguistics* 6(1). doi.org/10.5334/gjgl.1100.
Durrleman, Stephanie & Ur Shlonsky. 2015. Focus and *Wh* in Jamaican creole: Movement and exhaustiveness. In Ur Shlonsky (ed.), *Beyond functional sequence*. Volume 10: *The cartography of syntactic structures*, 91–106. New York: Oxford University Press.
Frascarelli, Mara & Francesca Ramaglia. 2013. (Pseudo)clefts at the syntax-prosody-discourse interface. In Tonjes Veenstra & Katharina Hartmann (eds.), *Cleft structures*, 97–138. Amsterdam: John Benjamins.
Haegeman, Liliane, André Meinunger & Aleksandra Vercauteren. 2015. The syntax of it-clefts and the left periphery of the clause. In Ur Shlonsky (ed.), *Beyond functional sequence*. Volume 10: *The cartography of syntactic structures*, 73–90. New York: Oxford University Press.
Hole, Daniel. 2011. The deconstruction of Chinese *Shì. . .de* clefts revisited. *Lingua* (Focus Marking Strategies and Focus Interpretation) 121(11). 1707–1733. https://doi.org/10.1016/j.lingua.2011.07.004.
Kiss, Katalin É. 1998. Identificational focus versus information focus. *Language* 74(2). 245–273.
Li, Charles N., Sandra A. Thompson & Bojiang Zhang. 1998. Cong Huayu Jiaodu Lunzheng Yuqici '*de*' [A Discourse Approach to the Particle De]. *Zhongguo Yuwen [Studies of the Chinese Language]* 263(2). 93–102.
Meinunger, André. 1998. A monoclausal structure for (pseudo-)cleft Sentences. *Proceedings of NELS (North East Linguistic Society)* 28. 283–298.
Paris, Marie-Claude. 1979. *Nominalization in Mandarin Chinese*. Paris: Université Paris VII, Département de Recherches Linguistiques.
Paul, Waltraud & Whitman John. 2008. *Shi . . . de* focus clefts in Mandarin Chinese. *The Linguistic Review* 25(3–4). https://doi.org/10.1515/TLIR.2008.012.
Ramchand, Gillian & Peter Svenonius. 2014. Deriving the functional hierarchy. *Language Sciences* 46. 152–74. https://doi.org/10.1016/j.langsci.2014.06.013.
Rizzi, Luigi. 1997. The fine structure of the left periphery. In Liliane Haegeman (ed.), *Elements of grammar*, 281–337. Dordrecht: Springer.
Rizzi, Luigi & Guglielmo Cinque. 2016. Functional categories and syntactic theory. *Annual Review of Linguistics* 2(1). 139–63. https://doi.org/10.1146/annurev-linguistics-011415-040827.
Shi, Youwei. 1984. Biao yiran yi de 'de_b' buyi [Supplementary notes on the realis-marking 'de_b']. *Yuyan Yanjiu* [Language Studies] 4. 249–255.
Simpson, Andrew & Zoe Wu. 2002. From D to T – determiner incorporation and the creation of tense. *Journal of East Asian Linguistics* 11(2). 169–209. https://doi.org/10.1023/A:1014934915836.
Soh, Hooi Ling. 2009. Speaker presupposition and Mandarin Chinese sentence-final -*le*: A unified analysis of the "change of state" and the "contrary to expectation" reading. *Natural Language & Linguistic Theory* 27(3). 623–57. https://doi.org/10.1007/s11049-009-9074-4.
Song, Yuzhu. 1981. Guanyu shijian zhuci 'de' he 'laizhe' [On tense markers de and laizhe]. *Zhongguo Yuwen* [Chinese Language] 4. 271–276.
Yang, Kun & Qingshun He. 2021. The development of VdeO clefts in Chinese: A diachronic constructionist approach. *Lingua*. 103214. https://doi.org/10.1016/j.lingua.2021.103214.

Yuan, Yulin. 2003. Cong jiaodian lilun kan juwei '*de*' de jufa yuyi gongneng [On the syntactic and semantic function of *de* in the sentence final position: From a viewpoint of the modern focus theory]." *Zhongguo Yuwen [Chinese Language]* 1. 3–16.

Zhu, Dexi. 1978. 'De'zi jiegou he panduan ju [De-marked structure and copular sentences]. *Zhongguo Yuwen* [Chinese Language] 1.23–27; 2.104–109.

Index

Aboh 249
Accessibility Hierarchy 44–45, 47, 73
Ackermann 164, 172
Adani 45, 162–163
agentivity 66–67
Agugliaro 48, 51, 54
Akmajian 38, 106
Albers 185, 187–188, 192, 197
André 138
Antinucci 11, 15, 20, 28
Aravind 137, 148, 158
Ariel 163
Armand 189
Armenian 63
Arosio 45
Arsenijevic 44
Arsiero 48, 50, 53
asymmetry
– subject vs non-subject 6, 45, 47, 58, 64–65, 68, 72, 74, 91, 97, 249
Avesani 25, 31–32, 39–40

Bahamian Creole 229
Ball 69
Bantu 43
Baptista 230
Baroni 159, 163
Baude 188
Bayer 64
Belletti 4–5, 11, 13–14, 21–22, 26, 32, 39, 41–42, 45, 58–59, 73, 81–85, 87, 89–91, 100, 135–137, 146–147, 152–153, 157–159, 161–162, 164, 209, 237, 249
Bellunese 46
Benincà 146
Bennati 81
Bentea 137, 161
Bentley 181, 195–196
Bernardy 164
Bertollo 3–4, 43, 60, 62
Bever 158, 161
Bianchi 23, 25, 62, 83
biclausality 5–7, 11–33, 38, 40–41, 63, 95, 181–182, 192, 205, 28

Birner 147
Bocci 5, 21–23, 25, 31–32, 62, 82–83
Boersma 115
Bolinger 2, 107, 109–110, 228
Bollée 182–183, 185, 190, 198
Bonan 3, 13, 46, 82, 235
Borremans 135, 149
Bostoen 43
Bourgoin 5, 107, 123
Branchini 45
Brandt 162–163
Brandtler 70
Brilmayer 66
Büring 201
Burzio 48

Cacchioli, Gioia 235
Calabrese 25
Caloi 84
Canal 45, 158, 161, 164
Canut 136, 138, 151
Cape Verdean Creole 229–230
Cardinaletti 4, 11, 15, 19–20, 25, 28, 30, 136, 163
Casalicchio 141
Cesiomaggiore 54
Chafe 149
Chaudenson 185
Chaves 159, 164
Cheng 243, 253
Chesi 45, 158, 161, 164
Chinese
– Mandarin 2, 6
  – northern 235–253
Chomsky 2, 38, 42, 87, 106, 238
Chowdhury 159, 164
Cinque 11, 15, 20, 28, 158, 248
Citadella 37, 55
Citko 221
Clark 116
cleft
– declarative 2, 4, 7, 11, 13, 20, 27, 100
– interrogative/question 2, 4, 7, 11–13, 15, 19, 24, 41, 66, 120, 150

- inverse 3, 7, 40–41, 54, 73, 220–224, 226–228, 231–232
- object 27, 41–42, 65, 68, 81, 84–88, 91, 96, 99, 100–101, 136, 158–159, 163–165, 171, 173, 204, 241, 249
- pseudo- 39, 113, 218, 220–228, 231–232
- reduced/truncated 105, 115–116, 119–120, 125, 127, 131, 135–136, 140–141, 143–146, 149, 152, 209, 211
- subject 5, 14, 17–18, 41, 45, 53, 58–59, 65, 67–68, 73, 81–82, 85–86, 88–91, 100–101, 136–137, 158–159, 162, 171, 173, 182, 204, 206, 212, 239, 249,

Cognitive Grammar 109
Cohn 151
Collins 55, 115, 118, 126, 182, 221
Comrie 44–45, 66
Construction Grammar 109
contact 212
copula 2–4, 6–7, 14–15, 17, 24, 27, 41, 54, 82, 183, 186–187, 190, 192, 195–197, 229
- specificational 38–39, 106–107, 113, 194, 218–220, 225–228, 248–249
Corne 182–183, 185–186, 188, 198, 202–203, 205
Cornips 47
Cougnon 188
Cozier 199–200
Craparo 51
Croatian 84
Cruschina 7, 13, 23, 25, 32, 44, 60–62, 73, 83, 209, 211, 249
Crystal 115
Curnow 223

Dal Pozzo 84
Davidse 5, 106–107, 113–115
De Cat 136, 146, 209, 211
De Cesare 114, 128, 157, 212, 221, 229
de Rooij 185
declarative 2, 4, 7, 12, 19, 27, 37
Declerk 38, 113–115, 117, 123, 126, 194
DeGraff 182, 199–200
Del Puppo 45, 59, 136
Demuth 138
den Dikken 38, 40–41, 82
Destruel 135
Devlin 168

Dick 158
Diessel 146, 152
D(iscourse) linking 163
Doetjes 135, 157
Donnellan 113
Dowty 67
Duden 59
Dufter 149, 157, 159, 183, 194, 212
Durrell 3, 35, 37, 59–60, 65, 68, 73
Durrleman 137, 161, 249
Dutch 228–229

Eisenbeiss 138
English 2, 5, 36–37, 40, 42–43, 55, 74, 84, 106, 109, 137, 146, 158, 164, 182–183, 194, 200, 221, 228–229, 237–239, 241
- Early Modern 69
- Middle 68–69
- Old 44, 69
- Singaporean 229
- spoken 125
EPP (see also subject) 83, 88
Erteschik-Shir 149
Escalante 220
Esser 118
exhaustiveness (implicature / presupposition) 5, 13, 56, 114–115, 126, 245
existential 55, 114

Féry 201
Fin(P) 13–14, 82
Finnish 84
Firbaas 124
Fischer 3, 35, 37
Flecken 151
focus (FocP) / focalization 2, 4–5, 7, 12–14, 20–23, 27, 31–32, 36–37, 39, 41, 43, 46, 57–58, 67, 81–82, 87, 92, 109–112, 118–126, 146, 190, 198, 205, 208–211, 220–223, 237, 248–249
- contrastive 41, 62, 81, 111–112, 146
- corrective 14, 41, 60, 81, 84–86, 93–94, 100–101
- exhaustive 237–238, 241
- fronting 7, 31, 38–40, 61–62, 73, 183, 209–210
- identificational 112

- (new) information 7, 14, 41–43, 62, 81, 83–88, 94, 96, 98, 100, 111–112
- narrow 21–22, 27, 112, 146, 208, 212
- particle / marker 128, 183, 210, 240
- presentational 112
- selective 5, 126–130
- wide 112
Force(P) 17
Fournier 186
Franck 5, 161, 167
Frascarelli 5, 13–14, 32, 39–40, 146, 157, 161, 249
Freezing 14
French 2, 5, 7, 12–14, 42–43, 55, 61, 82–94, 97–98, 100, 135–153, 157–174, 183–185, 194, 197 203–204, 208, 211–212, 221, 228, 237
- formal 6
- Old 98
- spoken 2–4, 6
Fricke 65–67
Friedemann 218–220, 223–224
Friedman 45, 58–59, 87, 137, 153, 158, 161–162, 164
Futrell 159, 164

Garassino 114, 128, 157
Gaze 185–186, 192
German 59–68, 73–74, 84, 228–229
- colloquial 44, 60
- Standard 37, 44, 72
- written 65
Germanic 2–3, 39, 61, 63
Ghanaian Pidgin English 229
Gibson 162–163
Giorgi 63
Giusti 163
Givón 117
Gordon 162
grammaticalicalization 6, 98
Grammis 60, 73
Greaves 11
Green 218–220, 232
Grillo 158a
Ground(P) 24, 58
Guadeloupean 203
Guasti 45, 59, 83
Guesser 84
Gulordava 159, 164, 169

Gundel 35, 38, 44, 69, 228
Gungbe 249
Gürer 201
Gutiérrez-Bravo 222
Gutiérrez Maté 220–223, 232
Guyanese 203

Hackl 45, 137, 148
Haegeman 5–6, 13–14, 32, 39–40, 135, 146–147, 152, 157, 249
Haider 63
Haitian 199–200, 203
Hale 51, 58, 165
Halliday 105, 107–109, 111–112, 114–115, 118, 122, 125, 127, 129–131
Hamann 140
Hartmann 43
Hauge 70
Haviland 116
Hedberg 44, 56, 106, 114–115
Heggie 228
Hewbrew 164
Heycock 38
Higgins 113
Hinterhölzl 63
Hjelmslev 108
Hole 236, 238, 241–243, 248
Holm 182, 188, 199–200, 232
Holmberg 63
Horn 114
Huddleston 106, 113–115, 147, 196
Hupet 136

Ibero-Romance Creoles 229
Illasi 55
Indian Ocean Creoles 204–205
information structure 5–6, 44, 62, 69, 105–106, 109–112, 148–152
interrogative (see also cleft : interogative/question) 2–4, 7, 27, 46–47, 54–58, 70, 92, 97–98, 118, 120, 150, 160
- mood 107
- Wh-questions 2, 4, 11–33, 43, 59, 71, 209, 211
  - D-linked 24–25
intervention effects 40, 45, 58, 86–88, 137, 157–174
IntP 23–24, 33

Ishihara 201
Italian 2, 4–5, 13, 21, 25, 28, 40–42, 46, 55, 84,
　　89–90, 158, 164, 183, 221, 229
– central regional 25
– colloquial 17
– informal 11
– northern regional substandard 47, 55
– Standard 43, 48, 61

Jackendoff 66
Jamaican Creole 249
Japanese 82–83
Jespersen 1, 36, 68, 126
Jourdain 5, 135–137, 151

Karipuna 203
Karssenberg 5, 55, 135, 139, 149, 157, 208, 212
Kasper 47
Kato 3
Kayne 38, 44
Keenan 44–45
Keyser 51, 58
Khan 168
Kikongo 220
Kimps 113
Kirundi 43
Kiss 106, 112, 131, 146, 157, 209, 238, 249
Krapova 158
Kratzer 44
Kretzschmar 66
Kriol 229
Kroch 38
Kwa languages 200

Labelle 136, 146
Laenzlinger 137
Lafkioui 43
Lahousse 5, 135, 137, 147, 149, 151, 157, 183,
　　208, 212
Lakretz 173
Lambrecht 1, 5, 7, 36, 44, 61, 106, 109, 112,
　　114–116, 121, 135, 148, 153, 182–184, 209,
　　228–229
Lamiroy 183
Langacker 107, 109
Lapolla 201
Lappin 164

Le 168
Ledegen 188
Ledgeway 7
Lefebvre 199–200
Lehmann 130
Leonard 159, 164
Leonini 83–84, 89–91
Levelt 148, 153
Levin 48, 58, 162
Levy 165
Lewis 45, 163, 219
Li 236, 241, 245
Lie 38–62, 70–71
Linzen 159, 163–164, 169
Lipski 218–220
Lobo 3, 136–137, 140–141, 152, 158
locality 40, 42, 47, 52, 59, 72, 86–88, 157–158,
　　160–164, 169, 171–174
Lohndal 35, 38, 70–71
Los 35, 44, 68, 74
Louisiana Creole 203
Lumsden 199–200
Luo 45

MacWhinney 138
Maglia 217–219, 223
Manzini 44, 46
marginalization / marginalized constituent 15,
　　20–21, 25–26, 28, 30–32
Marotta 25
Marsella 6, 218, 225
Martini 158, 161–163
Martinican 203
Marvin 164
Maurer 183, 229
Mauritius Creole 203
McCoy 164
McGregor 109, 130
McLellan 6, 201, 205–206
Meinunger 5–6, 13–14, 32, 38–40, 146–147,
　　157, 249
Merlo 5, 45, 158–159, 164, 166, 171–172, 174
Meulleman 142
Minimal Link Condition 42
Minimal search 87
Mioto 3
Moñino 217–219, 223–224

monoclausality 5, 39-40, 95, 115, 146, 182, 205
Monselice 55-56
Moro 38, 82
Moseng Knutsen 202
Motta di Livenza 56-57
movement 40, 42, 87, 162, 164, 201, 250
- A-bar 15, 45, 72, 157, 167
- focus 147, 235, 249-250, 253
- I-to-C 15
- pitch 110
- remnant 40
- tone 118, 120-121
- verb 73
- V-to-C 63, 68-88
- Wh- 18, 57, 95, 147, 152, 248
Moulton 44
Munaro 46
Muysken 199

Neapolitan 43
Nelson 123
Nguni 43
Nigero-Congo 43
Njende 113, 115
Nordgård 70
North-Eastern Italian dialects 43
northern Italian dialects 7, 13, 46
Norwegian 37, 69-71, 74, 83
- dialects 38, 74
  - Hedalen 71
  - Valdres 71
Nshemezimana 43
null subject (parameter) *see* pro-drop parameter

O'Grady 107, 110, 117

Paczynski 151
Palanquero 2, 6-7, 217-232
Palasis, Katerina 135, 138
Papiamentu 229
Paris 241
Patiño Rosselli 217-220, 223-224
Patrick 232
Patten 117, 124
Paul 236-238, 240-241, 248
Percus 38
Perlmutter 48, 51

Pesetsky 163
Pfeiderer 224
Pinedo 221, 229
Pinelli 39-40
Pitner 60
Pivi 136
Poletto 3, 35-36, 39-40, 46-47, 55, 63
Polinsky 224
Portuguese 3, 141, 152, 229
- Brazilian 84
Pozzan 21
Pramaggiore 56
Prince 106, 117, 122, 124, 157, 208
pro-drop parameter 7, 28, 40, 42, 48, 54, 58, 161, 187, 217, 228-230
pronoun
- expletive 38-39, 53, 55, 71, 83, 88, 182, 197-198, 228
- null *see* pro-drop parameter
- quasi-argumental 2-4
prosody 5, 25-28, 32, 61, 65, 83, 85, 106-108, 110, 115-116, 118, 141, 231, 242-244
Pullum 106, 113-115
Puskas, Genoveva 235

Quirk 200

raddoppiamento sintattico 25, 27
Ramaglia 5, 13-14, 39-40, 146, 157, 249
Ramchand 237, 250
Rappaport 48, 58
Rebuschi 135
Reeve 38-39, 44, 146-147, 157
Reinhart 149
relative (clause) / relativization 5, 44-45, 58, 60, 106, 113-114, 151, 167, 194, 198, 201-205, 221
- free 40
- headless 44
- restrictive 111, 113, 116, 139, 202-204, 206-208, 213
Relativized Minimality 5, 42, 59, 87-88, 101, 153, 160-162
relativizer 2, 6, 44, 182
Remberger 209, 211
Renaud 167-168
Réunion Creole 2, 6, 181-213

Rialland 135
Ribeiro 3
Rizzi 5, 14, 19, 22–23, 25, 42, 45, 58–59, 62, 82, 87–88, 137, 146–147, 153, 158, 160, 162, 169, 174, 248
Rochemont 112
Rodrigues 203
Roggia 157
Role and Reference Grammar 201
Romance 7, 43–44, 59, 61–62, 64, 67, 70–71, 73, 209
– medieval 7
Romanian 7
Roussou 44
Russian 164

Sabel 43
Saito 23
Samo 5, 45, 159, 164, 166, 171–172, 174, 235
Samoan 51
Santos 136–137, 141, 152
Sauppe 151
Savoia 46
Schachter 44
Schreiber 65–67
Schultze-Berndt, Eva 181
Schwegler 218–220, 224, 232
Schwenter 114, 129
scrambling 63, 68
Seki 115
Selkirk 201
Semiotic Grammar 109
Seuren 200
Seychelles Creole 203
Shi 241
Shlonsky 12–13, 87–88, 235, 249
Sicilian 44, 73
Simpson 238, 240–241, 253
Sleeman 146
small clause 14, 40, 82
Snow 138
Soare 137
Soares-Jesel 136–137, 140–141, 152
Søfteland 69
Soh 244
Solomon 230
Song 241

Sorace 81
southern Italian dialects (*see also* Neapolitan; Sicilian) 7
Spanish 183, 209, 219, 221–222, 224–225, 220, 230–231
– Colombian 223–224
Speyer 69
St. Lucian 203
Stark 157
Starke 87, 158, 160
Stowell 241
subject (*see also* EPP; pronoun : expletive) 4, 7, 27, 32, 48, 151, 188
– clitic 14, 46, 56–58
– DP 15, 19–21
– inversion 53–54
– position 40, 88
– post-verbal 21–24, 26, 32
– preverbal 19, 21, 87, 101
– SubjP 87
subjectification 109
subjunctive 15–19
Sulger 43
Sun, Yangyu 235
Svartvik 115
Svenonius 237, 250
Swearingen Davis 220
Swedish 69–70, 74
Syea 182, 185, 203–205

Tailleur 98
Tang 6
Tayo Creole 203
Thompson 236, 241, 245
Thornton 161
Tilmant 136
TMA marker 185–186, 192, 219–220, 226, 235, 238–239, 241, 245, 247, 250
Tollan 51, 67
Tomaselli 63
Tomasello 146, 152
Tönnis 65–67, 73
topic(alization) (Top(ic)P) 21–22, 39–40, 106, 149, 151, 174, 197, 224, 241, 243, 248
– aboutness 149
– familiar (FamTop(P)) 14, 16, 21, 28
– stage 149

topicality 63
Torrence 43
Tramutoli 6
transitive verb 50, 55–56, 67, 72
Traugott 68, 109
Travis 223
Tremblay 138
Trevisan 3, 13, 46
Trinidad English Creole 229–230
Trotzke 64
Tuller 140

unaccusatives / unaccusativity 49, 51, 54–56
unergative 50, 57, 67, 72
uniqueness (presupposition) 13

Van den Eynde 114
Van Dyke 45
Van Praet 118
Van Valin 201, 208–209
Vanelli 3, 35–36, 46–47, 55
Vangsnes 35, 38, 70–71
Vasishth 45, 162–163
Vaswani 169
Veenstra 43
Velleman 126, 128
Venetan 3–4, 36–38, 46–59, 62, 64, 66–67, 70, 72–73
Verb second (V2) 7, 37–39, 42, 44, 63–64, 67–71, 73–74
Vercauteren 5–6, 13–14, 32, 39–40, 146–147, 249
Verhoeven 67
Verstraete 112
Villa-García, Julio 181, 209

Villata 5, 161, 163
Voice(P) 51–52, 58
Vorderwülbecke 60

Walkden 63
Waltereit 114, 129
Wang 66–67
Ward 147
Warren 163
Warstadt 159, 164
Watbled 185–186
Westergaard 35, 38, 70–71
Wexler 45, 137, 148
Whitman 236–238, 240–241, 248
Wilcox 159, 164–165, 169
Willems 142
Wiltschko 67
Wittmann 186
Wolfe 63
Wolof 43
Woods 63
word order 63, 69–70, 73–74, 81–83, 100, 109, 184, 196, 201, 209, 211–213, 231
Wu 238, 240–241, 253

Yuan 236, 240

Zafiu 7
Zamboanga Chabacano 229
Zamparelli 159, 164
Zeller 43
Zhang 236, 241, 245
Zhou, Peiwen 235
Zhu 241
Zulu 43

www.ingramcontent.com/pod-product-compliance
Lightning Source LLC
Chambersburg PA
CBHW060351190426
43201CB00044B/2024